A
HANDBOOK
OF THE
CHRISTIAN
FAITH

A
HANDBOOK

OF THE

CHRISTIAN
FAITH

JOHN SCHWARZ

First published in Great Britain in 2005 by
Society for Promoting Christian Knowledge
36 Causton Street
London SW1P 4ST

Originally published in the United States of America under the title *Word Alive!* by Tabgha
Foundation, and under the titles *The Compact Guide to the Christian Faith* and *A Handbook of
the Christian Faith* by
Bethany House Publishers
11400 Hampshire Avenue South
Bloomington, Minnesota 55438

British Library Calaloguing-in-Publication Data
A catalogue record for this book is available from the British Library.

ISBN 0-281-05729-X

10 9 8 7 6 5 4 3 2 1

Printed in Great Britain

PREFACE

Some people write several books. I write the same book several times. In 1980 I wrote a Bible study called *A Year With the Bible,* which I taught in several churches in Minneapolis. In the mid–1980s my wife and I went to Kenya as missionaries, where I taught a slimmed down version of the study in 1985 and 1986. In 1992 I began producing Christian education videos and developed a video-assisted Bible study course called *Word Alive!: An Introduction to the Christian Faith* and wrote a study manual for the course. In 1998 Bethany House Publishers asked if they could publish the study manual, which I revised and they published as *The Compact Guide to the Christian Faith.* I revised the book again in 2004, which is the book you are holding, now titled *A Handbook of the Christian Faith.*

When I started my Christian walk in 1976, I didn't know anything about the Bible, the church or what it meant to be a Christian. I decided that someday I would write the kind of book that I wished someone had given me when I became a Christian, a book that answered questions like the following:

- Who wrote the Bible? What does the Old Testament have to do with the New? Why are there four gospels rather than one? Why are there so many different translations?
- Why did the first-century church divide into Roman Catholic, Eastern Orthodox and Protestant? How are they different from one another? Why are there so many different Protestant denominations?
- What are the bottom-line Christian beliefs regarding God and Jesus, sin and salvation, grace and faith, and the end of the age and the life to come?
- How does Christianity differ from Judaism, Hinduism, Islam and other world religions, and from Mormonism, the New Age and other non-Christian belief systems?
- What does it mean to live as a Christian in the twenty-first century?

Is there a Christian worldview? What is the role of prayer? What about evangelism?

This book attempts to answer these and other questions. The first five chapters have to do with the Bible, the Old Testament, the life and ministry of Jesus, the four gospels and the Pauline Epistles and other writings in the New Testament. The second five chapters have to do with the history of Christianity, Christian doctrines and beliefs, other religions and beliefs, growing in and sharing Christ and some guidelines for Christian living.

The source materials for the book come from Bible study curriculum programs that I have studied; readings and classroom notes from Regent College, a graduate school of theology in Vancouver, British Columbia, where I received a Master's in Christian Studies in 1990; and from reading Bible dictionaries and commentaries and studying books on the Bible, the history of Christianity, world religions and how to live Christianly in the modern world. The book was reviewed and edited by Dr. Roy A. Harrisville Jr., professor emeritus, Luther Seminary, St. Paul, Minnesota; Rev. Norman H. Dodman, founder and principal lecturer, Nairobi (Kenya) Bible Training Institute; and Dr. Alfred A. Glenn, adjunct professor, Fuller Seminary Southwest, Phoenix, Arizona. I want to thank Julie Smith, Bethany House Publishers' managing editor for nonfiction, for her vision, editing, encouragement and help in making this book a reality.

The book that you are holding in your hands reflects an orthodox view of Scripture; the version of the Bible I used in quoting from Scripture is the *New Revised Standard Version*. I have tried to reflect different ways that scholars and Bible commentators have understood the biblical text, but throughout I emphasize the historic teachings and positions of the apostolic church. Where there were differences—for instance, in quotations, the spelling and/ or capitalization of words, the dating of events, matters of geography, the translation of Greek and Latin words and other particulars—I used a "majority rule" approach. Finally, in an effort to make the book easy to read, I have amplified material parenthetically rather than in footnotes and have used clear headers, quotation marks, italics, even in quoting from the Bible, and italics to highlight important words, phrases and thoughts.

John Schwarz

CONTENTS

············ CHAPTER 1 ············

THE BIBLE

The Bible is God's Word to us. It is the traveler's map, the pilgrim's staff, the pilot's compass, the soldier's sword and the Christian's charter. It should fill the memory, rule the heart and guide the feet. It should be read slowly, frequently and prayerfully.

SOURCE UNKNOWN

THE STORY AND MESSAGE OF THE BIBLE

The starting place for the study of the Christian faith is the Bible, the written witness to God's words and acts on the plane of history. In this chapter we will survey the Old and New Testaments, and also the Apocrypha, the intertestamental ("between the testaments") books that Martin Luther and the Reformers eliminated when they translated the Scriptures from Hebrew and Greek into the languages of the common people. Then we will look at the Bible's various translations—from Greek to Latin to English—and the ongoing revision of the Bible (in the last century alone there were more than one hundred new translations). And then we will look at three concepts that relate to the Bible: God's *revelations* to Israel and his self-revelation in Jesus of Nazareth, the *inspiration* of the authors of Scripture, and the *authority* of the Bible in matters of faith and practice. Last, we will look at some general principles to follow in reading and interpreting the Bible, five popular translations of the Bible and some resources to use in studying the Bible.

THE TWO COVENANTS OR TESTAMENTS

Although the Bible has many books, it is really one book—one continuous story—with two distinct parts or "testaments," from the Latin *testamentum,* meaning "oath" or "covenant." The *Old Testament* contains the covenant God made with the people of Israel at Mount Sinai: "Now therefore, if you obey my voice and keep my *covenant,* you shall be my treasured possession out of all the peoples" (Ex. 19:5). The *New Testament* contains the new covenant, which was foretold by the prophet Jeremiah: "The days are surely coming [said the Lord] when I will make a *new covenant . . .*" (Jer. 31:31). This covenant was instituted by Jesus at the Last Supper, when he said to his disciples: "This cup that is poured out for you is the *new covenant* in my blood" (Luke 22:20).

THE BIBLE: FORMATION, STRUCTURE AND BOOKS

The English word *Bible* comes from the Greek word *biblia,* meaning "books." So the Bible is a collection of books, though technically not all are "books." In the Old Testament the books of Psalms and Proverbs are collections of poems and sayings, and in the New Testament the majority of the books are letters.

The books themselves were written over a period spanning at least twelve hundred years—from 1100 B.C. to A.D. 100 ("B.C." stands for "before Christ;" "A.D." comes from the Latin *Anno Domini,* meaning "in the year of our Lord"). The books were written by many different authors, some of whom are known and many of whom are not, especially in the Old Testament, and they were written in many different places, including Palestine, Babylon, Corinth, Ephesus, Rome, Antioch and the Isle of Patmos. The Bible has been translated into some two thousand languages, and more than 80 percent of the world's population has access to the Bible or some portion of it in their own language.

THE OLD TESTAMENT

The Old Testament has thirty-nine books in Protestant Bibles, forty-six books in Catholic Bibles and fifty books in Orthodox Bibles (see next section), divided into four broad sections, as follows:

- The *Torah* or *Pentateuch* are five "foundation" books—Genesis, Exodus, Leviticus, Numbers and Deuteronomy—in which God calls (elects) Israel to be his people, frees Israel from its bondage in Egypt and enters into a covenant with Israel at Mount Sinai.
- The *Historical Books* are Joshua, Judges, Ruth, 1 and 2 Samuel, 1 and 2 Kings, 1 and 2 Chronicles, Ezra, Nehemiah and Esther. The Historical Books trace the history of Israel over a period of some eight hundred years: The entry of the Israelites into the Promised Land (Canaan) under Joshua in 1250 B.C.; the settlement of the land during the two-hundred-year period of the judges; the monarchies of Saul, David (c. 1000 B.C.) and Solomon as kings over Israel; the split and division of the land into the kingdoms of Israel and Judah and their defeat by the Assyrians (in

721 B.C.) and the Babylonians (in 586 B.C.); the Exile in Babylon and the return of the exiles to Israel (in 538 B.C.); and the resettlement of Jerusalem and Judea under the leadership of Ezra and Nehemiah (mid–400s B.C.).

- The *Prophets* are the collected writings of the four "major" prophets—Isaiah, Jeremiah, Ezekiel and Daniel—and the twelve "minor" prophets—Hosea, Joel, Amos, Obadiah, Jonah, Micah, Nahum, Habakkuk, Zephaniah, Haggai, Zechariah and Malachi. The prophetic writings also include the book of Lamentations, Jeremiah's laments over the Babylonian destruction of Jerusalem in 586 B.C.
- The *Writings,* also called the devotional and wisdom literature, comprise the books of Job, Psalms, Proverbs, Ecclesiastes and the Song of Solomon or Song of Songs.

THE NEW TESTAMENT

The New Testament has twenty-seven books, also divided into four sections:

- The *Gospels* of Matthew, Mark, Luke and John are the written testimonies to the life, death and resurrection of Jesus.
- The *Acts of the Apostles* are the historical account of the early days of the Jerusalem church and the three missionary journeys of Paul, covering the period A.D. 30 to the early 60s.
- The *Letters* or *Epistles* comprise thirteen letters written by or attributed to Paul—letters written to church communities in Rome, Corinth, Galatia, Ephesus, Philippi, Colossae and Thessalonica, and personal letters written to Timothy, Titus and Philemon; the letter to the Hebrews; and the seven "general" letters of James, Peter, John and Jude.
- The *Revelation* to John consists of apocalyptic visions about the sovereignty of God and his coming victory and triumph over the forces of evil.

THE HEBREW SCRIPTURES

The *Hebrew* Scriptures—meaning the Old Testament, because the New Testament was written in *Greek*—is a record of God's words to and dealings with the people of Israel, whom he called to be "a light to the nations" (Isa. 42:6). The stories of God's words and acts were passed down in oral form from one generation to the next. Beginning with the kings of Israel (1020 B.C.), the stories and traditions were written down and collected and then, during and following the Exile (500s B.C.), were blended and combined into books. It is believed that the Torah was completed around 400 B.C., the Historical Books and the Prophets around 200 B.C. and the Writings around 100 B.C. Scholars used to believe that the Hebrew *canon*—the books that were accepted by the rabbis as sacred or inspired Scripture—was agreed-upon and closed by a council of elders at Jamnia, the present city of Jabneh, around the end of the first century A.D. This view has since fallen out of favor.

THE JEWISH AND CHRISTIAN OLD TESTAMENT CANONS

Jews, Protestants, Catholics and Orthodox have different canons, that is, different numbers of books.

- The Jewish canon contains twenty-four books, because many books in the Hebrew Scriptures are not divided. For instance, Kings, Samuel and Chronicles are each one book, Ezra and Nehemiah are one book, and the twelve minor prophets are one book (the Book of the Twelve).
- The Protestant Old Testament contains thirty-nine books, and they are arranged differently than the books in the Jewish canon (see The Order of Books).
- The Catholic Old Testament contains forty-six books; the seven additional books come from the Septuagint (see The Apocrypha).
- The Orthodox Old Testament contains fifty books: The Catholic Old Testament books plus 1 Esdras, 3 Maccabees, the Prayer of Manasseh and Psalm 151.

Also, the Hebrew Scriptures have a threefold rather than a fourfold order. What the Christian Old Testament calls the Historical Books, the Hebrew Scriptures call the Former Prophets—the books of Joshua, Judges, Samuel and Kings—which in the Hebrew canon are prophetic or "religious history" rather than "history history." The Hebrew or Jewish

Bible is sometimes called the *Tanak* or *Tanakh,* a word based on the first letters of the Hebrew names for its three sections—*T* for *Torah* (the Pentateuch), *N* for *Niviim* (the Prophets) and *K* for *Kethuvim* (the Writings), with vowels added for pronunciation.

THE SEPTUAGINT

The Bible of the early Greek-speaking church was the Septuagint. When Alexander the Great conquered the ancient world in the fourth century B.C., Greek became the *lingua franca* or common language of the world. (The life dates of most people mentioned in this book, such as Alexander, are in the index.) Over time, Jews living outside of Palestine began to speak Greek rather than Hebrew and there was need for a Greek translation of the Scriptures. Around the year 250 B.C., a group of Jewish elders and scribes in Alexandria, Egypt, which had the largest Jewish community in the ancient world, translated the Scriptures into Greek. According to Jewish legend, there were seventy-two translators—six from each of the twelve tribes—who translated independently of one another, and when they finished there was not a single discrepancy among them! The name *Septuagint* comes from the Latin *septuaginta,* which means "seventy," the nearest round number for the seventy-two translators. The Septuagint is sometimes abbreviated LXX, the Roman numeral for 70. The Septuagint became the Bible for Greek-speaking Jews living outside of Palestine, and also for the early Christians.

THE ORDER OF BOOKS

The order of books in the Christian Old Testament is based on the Septuagint, which differs from the Hebrew Scriptures. Also, in the Hebrew Scriptures, the last section comprises the Writings rather than the Prophets, and the Writings include five books that the Christian Old Testament includes among the Historical Books (Ruth, Chronicles, Ezra, Nehemiah and Esther) and two books that it includes among the Prophets (Daniel and Lamentations).

THE APOCRYPHA

The Septuagint contains fifteen books that are not in the Hebrew Scriptures, books such as Tobit, Judith, 1 and 2 Maccabees and Baruch. When

Jerome translated the Old Testament into Latin around the year 400, he included several Septuagintal books, with a caution that they were not to be considered on the same level as the books in the Hebrew canon. Over time, however, these *deuterocanonical* (meaning "second canon") books were given equal status with the canonical books in the Hebrew Scriptures, and some gave birth to Catholic doctrines, such as purgatory, which comes from 2 Maccabees 12:43–45.

When Martin Luther and others translated the Bible into the common language of the day (in the early to mid–1500s), they either put the deuterocanonical books in a separate section between the Old and New Testaments—between Malachi and Matthew—called the *Apocrypha,* from a Greek word meaning "secret" or "hidden," referring to their questionable authorship and authenticity, or eliminated them altogether. The reason the Reformers rejected the deuterocanonical books is that they had not been received by the Jewish elders into the Hebrew canon. To counter the Reformers' rejection of the deuterocanonical books—and to authenticate its teachings based on these books—the Catholic Church accorded twelve of the apocryphal books full canonical status at the Council of Trent in 1546.

Despite their noncanonical status, the deuterocanonical books are important documents. Books such as 1 and 2 Maccabees provide a history of God's chosen people during the period between the Old and New Testaments. Other books, such as the Wisdom of Solomon, reflect changes that began to occur in Jewish religious thinking prior to the coming of Jesus, such as a growing belief in an afterlife, which is only briefly alluded to in the Old Testament. Today some Protestant Bibles, such as the *New Revised Standard Version,* have editions that include the Apocrypha.

Because the books of the Apocrypha have long been excluded from Protestant Bibles, most Protestants know very little about them. The following is a list of these books as they appear in Catholic Bibles.

HISTORICAL BOOKS

Tobit is the story of a pious, law-abiding Jew (Tobit) whose blindness is healed by the magic formulas of an angel (Raphael). *Judith* is a simple, readable story about a beautiful widow who, like Esther, saves her people. *Additions to Esther* are additions to give the book of Esther a more "religious" feel (the name of God is not mentioned in the canonical book of Esther). The books of *1* and *2 Maccabees* tell of the repressive reign of the Seleucid (Syrian) ruler Antiochus Epiphanes and the revolt and cleansing of the temple under the leadership of Judas Maccabeus and his brothers.

PROPHETIC BOOKS

Baruch is a book attributed to the secretary of Jeremiah, to which has been added *The Letter of Jeremiah,* written to those about to be taken into captivity by the Babylonians. The canonical book of Daniel was enlarged to include three deuterocanonical writings: *The Prayer of Azariah* and *The Song of the Three Young Men,* the words of Daniel and his three companions in the fiery furnace (Dan. 3:24–90); *Susanna,* a story of two wicked elders who desire the beautiful Susanna, who is saved by Daniel (Dan. 13); and *Bel and the Dragon,* a tale set in the time of Daniel contrasting the true worship of God with the false worship of the Babylonian gods (Dan. 14).

WISDOM BOOKS

The *Wisdom of Solomon,* obviously not written by Solomon, defines the origin, nature and function of wisdom and the fate of those who do good and those who do evil. *Ecclesiasticus* or *Sirach* (the author of the book, which is also known as *The Wisdom of Jesus ben-Sirach*) is a collection of sayings and advice similar to the book of Proverbs.

THE NEW TESTAMENT

In the Old Testament, the Pentateuch and the Historical Books appear more or less in chronological order, and the four major and twelve minor prophets, with a few exceptions, appear in the order in which they were written. In the New Testament, the books do not appear in chronological order. For instance,

- Paul, who died in the mid–60s, wrote his letters prior to the writing of the Gospels, the first of which (Mark) is dated around the year 70, and prior to the Acts of the Apostles, which describes his travels.
- The letters of Paul are ordered according to recipient and roughly in

order of length rather than chronologically. The nine church letters are first, followed by four personal letters. Romans is the first church letter because it is the longest letter, not because it was Paul's first letter (actually, it was one of his later church letters). And Philemon is last among Paul's personal letters because it is the shortest such letter, though it was probably first in point of time.

- The Gospels, as we will see in chapter 4, begin with Matthew, but the majority of New Testament scholars believe that Mark, not Matthew, was the first or earliest gospel to be written.

The books that make up the New Testament are written testimonies to the good news of Jesus and letters to Christian faith communities. In the mid-second century, the writings were gathered together to form the written witness to the new covenant or testament between God and humankind. The final recognition and acceptance of the books into the New Testament canon cannot be dated precisely, as with the Old Testament, but it appears that as early as the middle of the second century there was already general agreement on twenty of the twenty-seven books—all except Hebrews, James, 2 Peter, 2 and 3 John, Jude and Revelation.

The basis for books being accepted into the New Testament canon was threefold. First, the authors had to have had apostolic credentials or have enjoyed a close association with an apostle, such as Mark with Peter and Luke with Paul. Second, the writings had to be consistent with the church's teachings about Jesus. Third, the writings had to have had church-wide acceptance and usage.

Christians have good reason to be confident of the reliability and authenticity of the New Testament. More than five thousand Greek manuscripts have been found and cataloged, including complete New Testament manuscripts, such as the *Codex Sinaiticus,* discovered at Saint Catherine's Monastery at the foot of Mount Sinai in 1844 (now in the British Museum in London), and the almost complete *Codex Vaticanus* (now in the Vatican Library in Rome), both of which are dated to the middle 300s. By way of contrast, the earliest extant (existing) manuscripts of Julius Caesar are dated 1,000 years after his death, those of Plato 1,200 years after his death and those of Aristotle 1,400 years after his death, and scholars universally accept the authenticity of these manuscripts.

Another reason for confidence in the New Testament writings, in addition to the abundance of extant manuscripts, is that the writings were written within one or two generations of Jesus' death. The earliest letters of Paul are dated 50 or 51, just twenty years after Jesus' death; Mark's gospel is dated around the year 70, forty years after Jesus' death; and almost all of the books can be firmly dated before the close of the first century. According to the British scholar John A. T. Robinson, "The wealth of manuscripts, and, above all, the narrow interval of time between the writing and the earliest extant copies, make [the New Testament] by far the best-attested text of any writing in the ancient world" (*Can We Trust the New Testament?*).

THE BOOKS OF THE BIBLE

THE PROTESTANT OLD TESTAMENT CANON

- The *Pentateuch:* Genesis, Exodus, Leviticus, Numbers and Deuteronomy
- The *Historical Books:* Joshua, Judges, Ruth, 1 and 2 Samuel, 1 and 2 Kings, 1 and 2 Chronicles, Ezra, Nehemiah and Esther
- The *Writings:* Job, Psalms, Proverbs, Ecclesiastes and the Song of Solomon
- The *Major Prophets:* Isaiah, Jeremiah (and his Lamentations), Ezekiel and Daniel
- The *Minor Prophets:* Hosea, Joel, Amos, Obadiah, Jonah, Micah, Nahum, Habakkuk, Zephaniah, Haggai, Zechariah and Malachi

THE NEW TESTAMENT CANON

- The *Gospels:* Matthew, Mark, Luke and John
- The *Acts of the Apostles*
- The *Pauline Letters:* Romans, 1 and 2 Corinthians, Galatians, Ephesians, Philippians, Colossians, 1 and 2 Thessalonians, 1 and 2 Timothy, Titus and Philemon
- The *General Letters:* Hebrews, James, 1 and 2 Peter, 1, 2 and 3 John and Jude
- The *Revelation* to John

THE THEME AND MESSAGE OF THE BIBLE

Many students of the Bible claim that it has a unifying theme running from Genesis to Revelation. Some say the theme is that of *covenant*—the covenant that God made with Israel, and through Jesus with all humankind. Others say the theme is *salvation history*—the successive, progressive revelations of God so that all might come to the knowledge of the truth and be saved (1 Tim. 2:4).

A variation on the covenant and salvation history themes is *promise* and *fulfillment*—God's promises of a Messiah from the House of David (2 Sam. 7:12–16) and a new covenant (Jer. 31:31); and the fulfillment of these promises in Jesus of Nazareth (Luke 1:31–33), who established a new covenant at the Last Supper (Luke 22:20).

As for the message of the Bible, the first place to look is in the Bible itself. C. H. Dodd, in his classic book *The Apostolic Preaching*, says the message of the Bible can be derived from the speeches of Peter and others in the book of Acts and from the letters of Paul. The following is an example of the apostles' preaching from Peter's speech to the household of Cornelius in Acts 10:34–43: God sent a message to the people of Israel that Jesus, the one about whom "all the prophets testify," was "Lord of all. [He was] put to death . . . on a tree; but God raised him on the third day and allowed him to appear, not to all people but to us who were chosen by God as witnesses . . . who ate and drank with him after he rose from the dead. . . . He is the one ordained by God as judge of the living and the dead. . . . Everyone who believes in him receives forgiveness of sins through his name." The message of the Bible is that Jesus Christ is the one sent by God—the one prophesied by the prophets and witnessed by the apostles; the one sent to die for our sins—to forgive us and to save us; the one sent to reconcile us with God the Father—and also with each other.

THE BIBLICAL STORY

The Bible is a story, and like any good story it has a beginning—the first eleven chapters of Genesis (the period *before* history); a long middle section—God's progressive revelations to the patriarchs and prophets of

Israel in the Old Testament and to the apostles and followers of Jesus in the New Testament; and an ending—the book of Revelation (the period *after* history).

GOD'S FIRST COVENANTS

The prologue to the biblical story (Gen. 1–11) tells how God created the heavens and the earth, and life in all of its wonderful variety, and man and woman in his image and likeness, and how men and women rebelled against God and became estranged from God. The "salvation history" story starts with the call of Abraham, whose descendants were to be and bring God's blessing to all the nations. To show his love and purposes for Israel, God led the Israelites out of bondage in Egypt—the "salvation event" of the Old Testament—and entered into a covenant with them at Mount Sinai. Later, God promised that a descendant of King David would rule over a kingdom that would have no end. Israel waited for the *Messiah*—the Anointed One—from the House of David (the offspring of David). Malachi said that Elijah would return to announce the Messiah (Mal. 3:1; 4:5); Isaiah said that he would take upon himself the sins of the world (Isa. 53); the psalmist said that he would be mocked and abandoned but God would rescue and vindicate him for the sake of the world (Ps. 22).

GOD'S FURTHER COVENANT

The Old Testament is a story in search of an ending, which comes in the New Testament—the New Covenant—in which the promises of God to Israel are fulfilled. In "the fullness of time," God's Holy Spirit came upon Mary, who gave birth to Jesus in Bethlehem, the city of David. Jesus was baptized by John the Baptist, the Elijah-figure who announced that Jesus was the long-awaited Messiah. At the Last Supper, Jesus inaugurated a new, more inclusive covenant. In the year 30, Jesus was put to death by the authorities in Jerusalem, but God raised him from the dead to confirm his promise of eternal life to all who believed in him (John 6:40). When Jesus was arrested, his disciples, fearing for their lives, went into hiding. But the resurrected Jesus appeared to them, teaching them and telling them to be his witnesses "to the ends of the earth." Today, with 2 billion adherents,

Christianity is the largest religion in the world.

The central truth claims of Christianity are that Jesus was God incarnate, that he died a substitutionary death for us, that he was raised from the dead, and that all who believe in him will not perish but have eternal life (John 3:16). Is there any evidence that Jesus rose from the dead? The surest evidence is the witness of those who were martyred for their faith. To paraphrase the late Paul Little, "People will die for what they *believe* is true . . . but no one willingly dies, as did many of Jesus' followers, for something they *know* is false" (*Know What You Believe*).

THE TRANSMISSION AND TRANSLATIONS OF THE BIBLE

The earliest manuscripts were scrolls, such as the one from which Jesus read in the synagogue at Nazareth (Luke 4:17–20). They were written on papyrus (made from reeds), later on parchment (the skins of sheep, goats and other animals) and finally on paper. Early in the second century (c. 130), manuscripts began to be produced in book or leaf form, called *codices,* with pages that could be turned.

Like other books in the ancient world, Bibles were written in capital letters. Upper and lower cases were introduced in the ninth century and spacing two centuries later. There were no chapter or verse divisions until Stephen Langton, a lecturer at the University of Paris and later Archbishop of Canterbury, divided the Bible into chapters in 1226, and Robert Estienne, a French printer in Geneva, divided the chapters into verses in 1551. The *Geneva Bible,* published in Geneva in 1560, was the first Bible in which the text was divided into verses. Originally, copies of Bibles were made by hand, usually by scribes in scriptoriums, and were few in number and very expensive (it is estimated that the *Codex Sinaiticus* required the skins of 360 goats and sheep). In the year 1456, Johann Gutenberg of Mainz, Germany, invented the printing press, and the production of Bibles moved from handwriting to movable type.

EARLY TRANSLATIONS

The earliest Bibles were written in Greek, but as early as the second century A.D. the Bible began to be translated into other languages. When the church grew in the West and became Latin-speaking, there was need for a uniform, authoritative Latin Bible. Pope Damascus asked Jerome, the most accomplished scholar and linguist of his day, to translate the Hebrew and Greek Scriptures into Latin. Jerome completed his translation in 405, which came to be called the *Vulgate,* from the Latin *vulgatus,* a word meaning "common" or "ordinary" (language). The *Vulgate* became the Bible of the Western church until the Reformation, and it was the basis for all Roman Catholic translations until 1943. The *Vulgate* was the first Bible to be printed with movable type (the Gutenberg Bible).

TRANSLATIONS INTO ENGLISH

In the Bibles we study and read from in church, Jesus speaks modern-day English, and so does Abraham, though neither spoke the same language, and certainly not English. The first translation of the Bible into English was begun by John Wycliffe, who translated the Latin *Vulgate* into English in 1382 so that it could be read by the people in their own language. The first English Bible to be *printed* was a New Testament translation by William Tyndale, the "father" of the English Bible, who translated the Scriptures into English from the original languages (Hebrew and Greek). Tyndale's New Testament translation was printed in 1526. He was betrayed, arrested and burned at the stake in 1536 before completing his translation of the Old Testament. (Church leaders were afraid that giving people the Bible in their own language would weaken the leaders' hold on the interpretation of Scripture.)

After England split with the Roman Catholic Church in 1534, many English translations began to appear—so many, in fact, that King James I of England (reign: 1603 to 1625) commissioned a committee of fifty-four scholars to produce an "authorized" version, known today as the *King James Version* of 1611. The *KJV* became "the" Protestant Bible of the English-speaking world until well into the twentieth century, and its popularity continues even today with the *New King James Version* (*NKJV,* 1982), and with revised translations based on the *KJV,* such as the *New American Standard Bible* (*NASB,* 1971), which has a strong following among conservative Christians, and the *New Revised Standard Version* (*NRSV,* 1989).

RECENT TRANSLATIONS

The twentieth century witnessed more than one hundred new translations. There are three reasons for this. First, more ancient and accurate manuscripts have been discovered, such as the *Codex Sinaiticus* (dated to c. 350), which is several hundred years older than the Erasmus Greek New Testament of 1516 used by the King James translators. Second, important archaeological finds, such as the Dead Sea Scrolls at Qumran in 1947, the most important manuscript find in the twentieth century (some eight hundred manuscripts), and the Nag Hammadi Library in Upper Egypt in 1945, which contained twelve papyrus codices written in Coptic, an ancient Egyptian language, the most important being the apocryphal gospel of Thomas. These discoveries have given biblical scholars a far deeper understanding of the intertestamental world and of early Judaism, and also of early Christianity. Third, the desire to update antiquated biblical words, such as *thee* and *thou,* and to translate biblical words and texts in a less gender-oriented way, using, for example, *person* and *humankind* rather than *man* and *mankind.*

REVELATION, INSPIRATION AND AUTHORITY

We call the Bible the "Word of God," which is a metaphor or figure of speech, because God did not *dictate* the Bible, as Muslims believe he did the Koran. God *communicated* with those entrusted with the task of putting pen to paper through visions and dreams (see Num. 12:6) and through encounters with prophets and apostles whom he called to speak his Word to us and for us—"the Word of God in the words of men."

Three concepts that relate to the Bible are revelation, inspiration and authority. These concepts are interrelated, because the Bible's *authority* comes from its being the *inspired* witness to the *revelations* of God.

GENERAL AND SPECIAL REVELATION

It is said that religion is humankind's attempt to reach God, and that Christianity is God's attempt to reach humankind. God "reaches" humankind in and through revelation, both *general* and *special.* General Revelation refers to the testimony of the heavens and the earth, and of life on earth, which cannot be accounted for in terms of itself—a testimony to all people that there is a Creator, whom we call God. Special Revelation refers to specific revelations and disclosures, such as God revealing his name (see chapter 2), calling Abraham to be the "father" of his people, freeing the Israelites from their bondage in Egypt, giving the Ten Commandments to Moses on Mount Sinai, speaking through the prophets, coming to earth in the person of Jesus of Nazareth, sending his Spirit on Pentecost and calling Paul on the road to Damascus. The Bible is the written witness to the revelations God made to the Israelites and to the followers of Jesus.

THE INSPIRATION OF THE BIBLE

The Bible is the vehicle or medium through which God's Word comes to us. The divine selection of those who wrote the Scriptures, and the guidance to assure the faithful writing and transmission of their testimony, is called *inspiration* (see 2 Tim. 3:16), which comes from a Latin word that means "to breathe into." The authors, though, were human, and wrote for different audiences and had different sources, both oral and written (see Luke 1:1–4), which accounts for occasional differences in their stories. Some believe that every word in the Bible is inspired, which is called *verbal* or *plenary* inspiration. Others believe that the Bible *contains* the word of God (with regard to salvation), which allows for differences in the text and for some latitude in interpreting the text.

Fundamentalist Christians believe that the Bible is *inerrant*—that is, without error in all regards, even as to such matters as history, science and geography. Those holding this position believe that admitting to the possibility of errors in the Bible is the first step down the slippery slope to unbelief. A softer view of inerrancy, sometimes called "limited inerrancy," believes that the Bible is without error in all that it *teaches,* but not everything in the Bible is meant to be understood as "teaching." Evangelicals prefer the word *infallible,* meaning that the Bible is reliable and trustworthy, especially as to the self-revelation of God in Jesus Christ. Liberal Christians tend not to read the Bible as God's revealed, inspired Word but as writings dealing with humankind's religious quest.

Many understand the term "inspiration" to refer, secondarily, to more than just the manuscripts. Some apply the term to the Holy Spirit's inspiration of those who decided which books were and were not to be included in the canon (thus God's choice); to the inspiration of those who did and still do translate the Scriptures into English, Spanish, Chinese, Hindi, Swahili, Russian and other languages to assure the faithful transmission of God's Word to all people everywhere; and to the Spirit's inner illumination of believers who "hear the word and accept it [and are blessed] a hundredfold" (Mark 4:20).

THE AUTHORITY OF THE BIBLE

Because the Bible is the inspired witness to God's revelations, it is authoritative in matters of *orthodoxy* (Christian beliefs) and *orthopraxis* (Christian practice). Many outside the Christian faith do not accept the authority of the Bible because, among other things, their worldviews do not allow for the possibility of supernatural revelation. Those within the faith have a different problem—not with the authority of the Bible per se but how to interpret and apply its teachings to church governance, the sacraments, liturgy, missions, social justice and other matters.

An issue related to the authority of the Bible is the authorship of the individual books. Some conservative scholars believe that authority is related to authorship and take great pains to defend, for instance, Moses' authorship of the Pentateuch, the single authorship of the book of Isaiah and Paul's authorship of all thirteen of his letters. It would be nice to know who wrote all of the books of the Bible, but this is not possible. Further, *authorship* is not the same as *authority*, that is, the books in the Bible are not "authoritative" because we know for certain who wrote them. We don't know, for instance, who wrote all the Psalms and Proverbs, or the narratives of the kings in Samuel, Kings and Chronicles, or the books of Job or Hebrews. These books are authoritative because they are in the canon.

READING THE BIBLE

The story is told of a famous actor who was being honored at a banquet. After dinner an old clergyman asked him to recite the Twenty-third Psalm.

The actor said that he would be glad to do so, on condition that the clergyman do the same. Impressively, the actor recited the psalm, holding his audience spellbound. When he had finished, the clergyman did the same, and there was not a dry eye in the room. After a moment of silence, the actor said, "I reached your ears, but this man reached your hearts. I know the psalm, but he knows the Shepherd" (Millie Stamm, *Be Still and Know*). Many people, like the actor, read the Bible as wonderful literature; others, like the clergyman, read the Bible as the revealed, inspired Word of God.

GENERAL APPROACHES

The following should be kept in mind when reading the Bible:

- First, the Bible should be read with the view and expectation of "hearing" God speak through his Word. It is said that the Bible is God's "telephone line" to us.
- Second, the biblical story of salvation is one continuous story from Genesis to Revelation, not two separate, disconnected stories. The reader's focus should be on understanding the theme or message of the story (of salvation) rather than microscopically analyzing and dissecting the substories that make up the grand story.
- Third, don't be discouraged or put off by texts in the Bible that are difficult or hard to understand. Someone once asked William Booth, the founder of the Salvation Army, what he did when he came across something in the Bible he did not understand. Booth said, "I do the same thing I do when eating a fish: I put the bones on the side of the plate and get on with the good meat."

PRINCIPLES OF INTERPRETATION

The following are some basic principles to keep in mind in interpreting the Bible.

- First, the Bible should be read in its *plain* or *natural* sense. Some mistakenly overemphasize the Bible's divine nature and veer off into extreme literalism. Others overemphasize its human authorship and read it as a collection of religious stories, poems and legends.

- Second, the Bible has different literary *forms*. Some are statements of faith ("In the beginning when God created . . ."), others are history ("In the year of . . ."), some are prophetic ("Thus says the Lord . . ."), others are letters ("I, Paul, an apostle . . .") and so forth. These forms should be interpreted according to standards appropriate thereto. For instance, metaphors and anthropomorphisms such as trees clapping "their hands" (Isa. 55:12) and hyperbole like "the plank in your eye" (Matt. 7:4) are meant to be understood figuratively. Also, one needs to be conscious of the context of words, and even the words themselves, because words can have more than one meaning.

- Finally, the Bible is its own best commentary. This means that the New Testament interprets the Old Testament. For instance, when Jesus "declared all foods clean" (Mark 7:19), he overruled the codes regarding clean and unclean food (Lev. 11). Also, obscure, unclear passages should be interpreted in light of those that *are* clear, and passages that are partial and incomplete should be interpreted in light of those that are *more* complete. Further, conflicts between passages should be decided on the basis of *majority rule*. If a verse is contradicted by two or three others, the majority view should prevail, as, for example, with Paul's teachings on the role of women, which are clearly more positive than negative.

BIBLE TRANSLATIONS, BIBLE DICTIONARIES AND BIBLE COMMENTARIES

Five popular Bible translations and two resources that would be helpful to any student in his or her study of the Bible are set out below.

BIBLE TRANSLATIONS

The following are recent translations of popular, widely used Protestant Bibles. In purchasing them, an effort should be made to obtain "study" editions.

New Revised Standard Version (*NRSV,* 1989). The *NRSV* is a revision of the *Revised Standard Version* (*RSV*), which in turn was a revision of the

King James Version (the *RSV* translation was completed in 1952). The *NRSV* is considered by some scholars to be the most *faithful* rendering of the Greek text. The *NRSV*'s predecessor, the *RSV,* was the most ecumenical English Bible—accepted by Catholics, Protestants and Orthodox—and there is every reason to believe that the *NRSV* will one day be similarly received. Following the dictates of the National Council of Churches, which sponsored the revision, the *NRSV* attempts to be "as literal as possible, as free as necessary." One important change from the *RSV* is that, as much as possible, the *NRSV* avoids using masculine-oriented language when referring to people in general. The *NRSV* has many good study editions, with helpful introductions to each of the biblical books and footnote comments on important passages.

New International Version (*NIV,* 1978). The *NIV* is a completely new translation rather than a revision, sponsored by the International Bible Society, and the most popular version of the Bible in North America (40 percent of the Bible market, according to the Christian Booksellers Association). It is *intentionally conservative* in scholarship and translation and widely used by evangelicals. The *NIV Study Bible* is an excellent edition, with introductions to the individual books, extensive footnotes, helpful diagrams and drawings, several maps, an index and a concordance, which is an alphabetical listing of words with references to the books and verses in which they occur. There is also a New International Version (*NIrV*) for children (third-grade reading level).

Good News Bible (*TEV,* 1976). *Today's English Version,* or *Good News Bible,* as it is more popularly known, was prepared by the American Bible Society. It is a *thought-for-thought* rather than a word-for-word translation. The *TEV* has a sixth-grade reading level vocabulary, uses contemporary language, avoids technical religious terms, and some editions have line drawings that reinforce the text.

New Living Translation (*NLT,* 1996). The *New Living Translation* is a revision of Kenneth Taylor's *Living Bible,* published in 1971 by Tyndale House Publishers. The *NLT* is another *thought-for-thought* translation. It is very readable (sixth-grade reading level), translates words and terms into modern English (weights, measures, times, metaphors), uses consistent spelling (some biblical names have different spellings), avoids technical theological terms like justification, regeneration and sanctification, and uses "gender-inclusive" language.

The Message (*The Message*, 2002). *The Message* is a new popular, easy-to-read, contemporary language *paraphrase,* translated by Eugene H. Peterson. The reading level is fifth grade. *The Message*'s uniqueness is its use of modern-day American words and terms.

BIBLE STUDY RESOURCES

Two Bible study aids that have proven helpful to both beginners and advanced students of the Bible are Bible dictionaries and Bible commentaries. (The InterVarsity Press dictionary and commentary mentioned below are more conservative than Harper's and HarperCollins.)

Bible Dictionaries. Bible dictionaries contain brief overviews of the books of the Bible and information on biblical people, places, customs, words and the like. Two good dictionaries are *HarperCollins Bible Dictionary* (1996) and the *New Bible Dictionary* (InterVarsity Press, 1996).

Bible Commentaries. Bible commentaries contain introductions to each book of the Bible (author, date, message, outline of book and so forth), along with interpretative comments on the text and general articles on geography, history and other subjects. Two good one-volume commentaries are *Harper's Bible Commentary* (1988) and the *New Bible Commentary* (InterVarsity Press, 1994).

CHAPTER 2

THE OLD TESTAMENT

Emperor Frederick the Great once asked his personal physician, Dr. Zimmermann, "Can you name me a single proof of the existence of God?" Zimmermann replied, "Your Majesty, the Jews!" By that he meant that if one wanted to ask for a proof of God, for something visible and tangible, that no one could contest, which is unfolded before the eyes of all men, then we should have to turn to the Jews. Quite simply, there they are to the present day. Hundreds of little nations in the Near East ... have dissolved and disappeared in the huge sea of nations; [only] this one tiny nation has maintained itself.... If the question of a proof of God is raised, one need merely point to this simple historical fact. For in the person of the Jew there stands before our eyes the witness of God's covenant with Abraham, Isaac and Jacob, and in that way with us all. Even one who does not understand Holy Scripture can see this reminder.

KARL BARTH
Dogmatics in Outline

THE OLD TESTAMENT: THE ROOTS OF OUR FAITH

God entered into a covenant with Israel at Mount Sinai. Because Christians believe that God made a *new* covenant, based on the person and work of Jesus, they have traditionally referred to the covenant that God made with Israel as the *old* covenant. If God made a new covenant, some ask, why bother with the old covenant? Because it is impossible to understand the ministry and message of Jesus apart from the Old Testament. God's plan of salvation did not begin with the birth of Jesus; it began with the call of Abraham some two thousand years earlier.

In this chapter we will look at the prologue to the biblical story—the creation accounts, Adam and Eve and the downward fall. Then we will look at God's call of Abraham, the Exodus from Egypt and the Mosaic covenant, and the rise and fall of Israel. And then we will look at the sayings and writings of the prophets and Israel's wisdom and devotional literature. Last, we will look at Judaism today in the twenty-first century.

THE PENTATEUCH: CREATION, FALL, ELECTION, SALVATION AND COVENANT

The story of Israel becoming a nation is contained in the first five books in the Bible, which in the Jewish Bible are called the *Torah,* from the Hebrew word *tora,* meaning "instruction." They are also called the Five Books of Moses, the principal figure in four of the five books. In the Christian Bible, the first five books are called the *Pentateuch,* meaning "five scrolls," from the Greek words *penta,* meaning "five," and *teukhos,* meaning "scrolls." The Torah is the most important part of the Hebrew Bible, much like the Gospels in the New Testament, and is central to Jewish worship, with the five books being read aloud in their entirety each liturgical year.

The Pentateuch contains Israel's most important and sacred writings, those in which God *spoke* to Israel's ancestors and leaders—to Abraham, Isaac, Jacob and Moses; chose or *elected* Israel—the covenant with Abraham;

rescued or *saved* Israel from its bondage in Egypt—the Exodus; and entered into a *covenant* with Israel at Mount Sinai. The five books of the Pentateuch are as follows:

Genesis: The creation of the universe, planet Earth, living creatures and the human race; the "fall" of Adam and Eve; the stories of Cain and Abel, Noah and the Flood and the Tower of Babel; the call of Abraham to go to a new land; and the stories of Abraham, Isaac, Jacob and Joseph.

Exodus: Israel's enslavement in Egypt; the call of Moses at the burning bush; the Exodus ("going out") from Egypt; God's special covenant with Israel at Mount Sinai; and the Ten Commandments.

Leviticus: Priestly (Levitical) instructions pertaining to worship, sacrifices and offerings; rules regarding clean (*kosher*) and unclean food; codes of behavior pertaining to diseases, sexual relations and cleanliness; and *Yom Kippur,* Israel's Day of Atonement.

Numbers: The census (numbering) and organization of the twelve tribes of Israel into a community or nation; God's call to take possession of Canaan, the land promised to Abraham's descendants; challenges to Moses' leadership; and Israel's forty years of wandering in the wilderness.

Deuteronomy: The second (*deutero*) telling or retelling of Israel's story; the *Shema,* Israel's great confession of faith; Moses' farewell instructions to the twelve tribes before their invasion of Canaan under the leadership of Joshua; and Moses' death.

THE PROLOGUE TO THE BIBLICAL STORY

Genesis 1–11 is the prologue to the biblical story and the answer to Israel's question: Why did God call Abraham? God called Abraham as the first step in his plan to rescue the human race from its sinful disobedience and alienation. The working out of this plan is recorded in the biblical narrative that begins in Genesis 12 and continues through the Pentateuch, historical narratives and prophetic books in the Old Testament, and the Gospels, letters and writings in the New Testament.

THE TWO CREATION ACCOUNTS
(GENESIS 1–2)

There are two Creation accounts in Genesis. The first (1:1–2:4a) is a careful, orderly, systematic statement about the creation of the heavens and the earth, the vegetation and living creatures, and man and woman. The second (2:4b–25) is the story of how God formed man, breathed life into him and from one of his ribs made woman. One way to look at the two accounts is to recall the opening scene in the movie *The Sound of Music*. The camera comes in over the Alps and then zooms in on Maria as the focal point of the story. Genesis 1 opens with the universe and then, in Genesis 2, zooms in on Adam and Eve as the focal point of the story.

In the Beginning God Created. Genesis opens with the announcement that "In the beginning . . . God created the heavens and the earth." The universe began with God, who created out of nothing rather than forming what already existed. The Creation stories, though, are less about the *how* of Creation than the *who* of Creation—the one behind Creation, the one who brought everything into being.

Man and Woman: The Crown of God's Creation. The story of the creation of man and woman is different from God's creation of the stars and the earth and "living creatures of every kind." God is intimately involved in the creation of humankind. In the first story God says, "Let us *make* humankind in our image, according to our likeness" (Gen. 1:26). In the second story he *"formed* man from the dust of the ground, and breathed into his nostrils the breath of life; and the man became a living being" (Gen. 2:7). Then, from man's rib, God made woman. Later in the Creation story, man is called *Adam,* a Hebrew word meaning "humankind" (expressing the *unity* of humankind), and woman is called *Eve,* a word meaning "life" (the *mother* of all living beings).

Many see Adam and Eve in symbolic or figurative terms. Their names may be symbolic, but Scripture intends us to understand them as the progenitors of the human race. Some scientists are beginning to believe in a common ancestor of the human race, such as University of California-Berkeley molecular geneticists Vincent Sarich and Allan Wilson, whose research and writings suggest that *Mitochondrial* (a Greek word for cells containing genetic materials and enzymes necessary for life) *Eve* may be the "common mother" from whom the human race descended.

When God breathed life into man, he imparted something of himself—a soul, if you wish—which makes humans different from all other creatures. To be made in the image of God means in the *spiritual* image and likeness of God, because God is spirit (John 4:24), which makes it possible for humanity to have a spiritual relationship with God.

(Note: Throughout this book, I often refer to God as *he, him* and *his,* but God has no gender: both sexes were created in his image and likeness. I use this language because I am following the biblical text, which most often uses male pronouns when referring to God.)

THE FALL IN THE GARDEN (GENESIS 2—3)

We usually read Genesis 1 and 2 as a unit: the creation of the universe (Gen. 1) and the creation of humankind (Gen. 2). However, Genesis 2 can also be read with Genesis 3 and the subsequent chapters as the downward fall of the human race. God put Adam in the Garden of Eden to till and keep it, and told him that he could eat of every tree, "but of the tree of the knowledge of good and evil you shall not eat." The serpent seduced Eve into eating fruit from the forbidden tree, which Adam also ate. The story of forbidden fruit is the Bible's way of explaining how sin came into the world—the sin of disobeying God, of acting independently of God, of trying to be God. When Adam and Eve ate from the tree, they fell out of harmony with God (from whom they hid), with each other (their shame of nakedness) and with the world (their expulsion from the Garden).

THE DOWNWARD FALL: BROTHERS, FLOOD AND TOWER (GENESIS 4—11)

The story of the Fall in the Garden continues with the sins of the descendants of Adam and Eve.

Cain and Abel. Cain and Abel were the sons of Adam and Eve. Cain was a farmer and offered God a sacrifice of "the fruit of the ground." Abel was a shepherd and offered God "the firstlings of his flock." God "had regard for Abel and his offering" but for Cain's offering "he had no regard." Why did God look with favor upon Abel's offering but not upon Cain's?

We are not told. Many believe that Abel's offering was accepted because he gave God his best (the "firstlings"), whereas Cain did not (see Heb. 11:4). Cain became jealous and killed Abel, the first murder in the Bible.

Noah and the Flood. Humankind continued its downward slide. Its sin became so great that God "was sorry that he had made humankind on earth" and decided to blot out everything he had made. But before doing so he called Noah, "a righteous man, blameless in his generation" (6:9). God flooded the earth, but saved Noah and his family as a *remnant* to perpetuate his purposes. After the Flood, God entered into an everlasting covenant with Noah and all living creatures, the sign of which, God said, would be his "bow in the clouds" (9:8–17).

The Tower of Babel. Noah found favor with God, but his descendants, like those of Adam and Eve, fell out of favor, as told in the final story of the prologue—the Tower of Babel. Humankind's continued self-centeredness led them to build a *ziggurat,* a Mesopotamian temple-tower, to their glory, rather than to God's. God "came down" and confused their tongues—made them *babble*—so they could no longer conspire to do evil, and then scattered them far and wide.

The Fall stories tell us about the origin of sin, the universality of sin and God's judgment of sin. But they also tell us of God's love for humankind: God made *clothes* for Adam and Eve before sending them out of the Garden; God gave Cain a *mark of protection* before sending him out as a wanderer upon the earth; God told Noah to build an *ark* for himself and his family before sending the Flood; and God called *Abraham* to be the father of a community that would lead the peoples of the earth into fellowship with him and with one another.

THE ANCESTRAL HISTORY OF ISRAEL

The first eleven chapters of Genesis provide a preamble for the biblical story—God's special love for humankind, the interconnectedness of the human race and the universality of human sin. The remainder of the Bible, starting in Genesis 12, is a response to the events in these chapters: God working out his plan of salvation by calling Abraham; entering into covenants with Abraham, Moses and David; settling Israel in the land of Canaan; calling prophets to exhort Israel to return to the covenant he made with them at Mount Sinai; and coming to earth in the person of Jesus of Nazareth.

"CALLS" IN THE BIBLE

In the biblical story, God *calls* people to be agents in his plan of salvation. According to the German Old Testament scholar Claus Westermann, God's calls have several common ingredients:

- The purpose of God's call was to send the one called on a *mission:* Abraham to Canaan, Moses back to Egypt, Samuel to Saul and then to David, Paul to the Gentiles.
- The one called was *not looking* to be called: Abraham was with his family in Haran, Moses was tending Jethro's flock in Midian, Samuel was with Eli, Isaiah did not consider himself worthy, Jeremiah thought he was too young, Paul was pursuing Christians in Damascus.
- The call came from *beyond:* in a voice to Abraham, in a burning bush to Moses, in dreams and visions to the prophets, in a dazzling light to Paul.
- The call changed the *destinies* of large numbers of people: the Exodus out of Egypt (Moses), the invasion and settlement of Canaan (Joshua), the Davidic kingship of Israel (Samuel), the evangelization of the Gentiles (Paul).
- The one called did not respond for his *own* glory but for the glory of the one who called him, namely, God.

Though those called often try to resist, most often the response is "Here I am," as in Abraham's call to sacrifice Isaac (Gen. 22:1), Moses at the burning bush (Ex. 3:4), Samuel in his apprenticeship with Eli (1 Sam. 3:4, 6, 8), David's enthronement (Ps. 40:7), Isaiah's response to God's query, "Whom shall I send?" (Isa. 6:8) and Ananias in Damascus (Acts 9:10).

ABRAHAM: THE FOUNDING PATRIARCH (GENESIS 12–25)

The biblical story of redemption does not begin with the birth of Jesus in Bethlehem. It begins with the call of Abraham—the founding father of

God's people—who was born in Ur in Mesopotamia, north of the Persian Gulf in modern-day Iraq. Ur was a Sumerian city whose people were literate, manufactured copper and glass, had wheeled vehicles, and practiced astronomy, medicine and mathematics.

The Call of Abraham. The call of Abraham inaugurates the *election* of Israel to be God's chosen people. From all of the nations of the world, God chose one man, Abraham, to be the founding father of a community that would be God's light to the nations and bring God's blessing to all peoples. Why did God call *Abraham*? We are not told. According to later rabbinic writings, God called many, but only Abraham responded.

God's Promises to Abraham. In Genesis 12, God spoke to Abraham in his seventy-fifth year, in Haran, where he was living with his father, Terah, and his family. God said, "Go from your country and your kindred and your father's house to the land that I will show you," a difficult command, because in ancient times the family unit remained intact until the patriarch died. God made three promises to Abraham. First, he would be the father of a "great nation" (God changed Abram's name to *Abraham,* which means "father of many"). Second, through him "all the families of the earth" would receive God's blessing (God's divine favor). Third, Abraham's offspring would be allowed to live in "this land," the land of Canaan, the *Promised* Land.

Grace and Faith. The story of Abraham is the story of *grace* and *faith,* a story that is played out from Genesis to Revelation. Rather than abandoning the fallen, sinful world of Genesis 1–11, God called Abraham to be the father of a community whose mission was to bring God's love, forgiveness and salvation to all nations ("peoples"). Abraham believed God's promises "and the Lord reckoned it to him as righteousness" (Gen. 15:6), an important Pauline theme. Thus the biblical story begins with God's *grace*—the calling of Abraham. This grace, to be "saving grace," must be accepted in *faith,* and as the biblical story unfolds, this comes to mean faith in Jesus Christ.

The Abrahamic Covenant. The Hebrew concept of *covenant* includes both promises and obligations. Three important covenants that God made with Israel were the covenant of election with *Abraham,* the "sign" of which was circumcision (for most Christians, the *sign* of belonging to God is baptism); the formal covenant with *Moses* at Mount Sinai, set forth, in part, in the Ten Commandments; and the covenant with *David*, promising that a descendant of his would rule over a kingdom that would have no end.

ISAAC: THE PROMISED SON (GENESIS 24—28)

Abraham was to be the father of a great nation, but his wife, Sarah, was *barren*, a theme that occurs throughout the Old Testament, and also in the New Testament with Elizabeth, the mother of John the Baptist. (In the biblical story, God's grace overcomes the barrenness of Sarah and others to continue on his plan of salvation.) Abraham and Sarah were very advanced in age, but God provided them with a son, Isaac, as he had promised.

When Isaac was a young boy, God commanded Abraham to take him to Mount Moriah (thought by some scholars to be the site on which Solomon's temple was later built in Jerusalem) and offer him as a burnt offering or *holocaust*. Abraham obeyed, but at the last minute God provided a ram for the sacrifice. Some have wondered why God put Abraham through this ordeal if he intended to supply a ram at the last minute. The Jewish writer Elie Wiesel, in his book *Messengers of God*, says that God knew about the ram, just as we do as readers, but Abraham did not. This was Abraham's final *test*. He proved faithful and obedient, someone God could depend on to put into action his plan of salvation. In his letters to the Galatians and Romans, Paul lifts up Abraham as one who, *by faith*, obeyed God and was "justified" (made right with God).

JACOB AND JOSEPH (GENESIS 27—50)

The second patriarch was Isaac, the "promised son," whom God blesses upon Abraham's death. There are not many stories about Isaac; he is more of a connecting link between Abraham and Jacob. The story of Israel's patriarchal history ends with Jacob, whose sons became the "tribes" of Israel, and with Joseph, who brought Jacob and his family to Egypt.

Jacob. Isaac married Rebekah, and they had twin sons, Esau and Jacob. Jacob, the younger, deceived his father and received the "birthright" (privileges accorded to the firstborn). Jacob fled to Aram (east of Canaan) to escape Esau, married the two daughters of Laban (Leah and Rachel), and through them and their two maidservants had twelve sons. Later in life, at Peniel (a Hebrew word meaning the "face of God"), Jacob wrestled with an angel of God, who changed his name from Jacob to *Israel*—"one who strives with God" to obtain his blessing (Gen. 32:28). At Bethel, Jacob received God's blessing (Gen. 35:9).

The twelve sons of Jacob—actually ten sons of Jacob and two sons of Joseph, Manasseh and Ephraim (see Gen. 48:1–5)—became the fathers of the twelve tribes of Israel. The descendants of Jacob's fourth son, Judah, became the remnant tribe—the tribe entrusted with the mission of being God's "light to the nations"—from which Joseph and Mary, Jesus' parents, were descended.

Joseph. The final story in Genesis is that of Joseph, the eleventh and favored son of Jacob, who was sold into slavery by his jealous brothers. Joseph was taken to Egypt and eventually became the viceroy, the second-ranking government official. His brothers went to Egypt to purchase grain because there was a famine in Canaan. They were reunited and reconciled with Joseph, and together with Jacob they settled in Goshen in northern Egypt. Joseph said to his brothers: "You intended to do harm to me, [but] God intended it for good" (Gen. 50:20) to carry on the promises that he made to Abraham, Isaac and Jacob.

EXODUS: THE "CENTER" OF THE OLD TESTAMENT

The Exodus—Israel's miraculous deliverance from bondage in Egypt—is the single most important event in Israel's history. The story of the Exodus is told every year at Passover. It is the story of the angel of death, who struck down "all the firstborn in the land of Egypt [but] *passed over* the houses of the Israelites" (Ex. 11–12, emphasis added), after which Moses led the Israelites out of Egypt.

It is said that the New Testament was written after the followers of Jesus had experienced the risen Christ—that is, from the other side of the Cross. The same might be said of the Old Testament: it was written after the Israelites had "experienced" the God of Abraham, Isaac and Jacob—that is, from the other side of the Red Sea.

MOSES: DELIVERER AND LAWGIVER
(EXODUS 2–4)

In the book of Exodus, an unnamed *pharaoh*—the Egyptian word for the king of Egypt—"arose over Egypt, who did not know Joseph," that is, did not acknowledge the privileges that had been accorded to his family. This pharaoh (probably Seti I or Rameses II) feared the Israelites because they were becoming "more numerous and more powerful" than the Egyptians. He laid heavy burdens on the Israelites, but they continued to multiply, so he ordered every male child born to an Israelite to be thrown into the Nile. Moses escaped the pharaoh's order when his mother set him adrift in the Nile in a watertight reed basket, which was lifted out of the water by the pharaoh's daughter, who set about to care for and raise Moses. The name *Moses* is derived either from a Hebrew verb meaning "to draw out" (Ex. 2:10) or, because he was named by the pharaoh's daughter, from an Egyptian word meaning "son of," as in Thut*mose,* "son of Thut."

Moses' birth parents were Levites (Levi was Jacob's third son). When Moses was forty years old—Acts 7 divides Moses' life into three forty-year periods—he killed an Egyptian who had beaten an Israelite, after which he fled to Midian, east of Egypt in present-day Saudi Arabia. Moses married Zipporah, the daughter of Jethro, had two sons and settled down as a shepherd. God heard the "groaning" of Israel and "remembered his covenant with Abraham, Isaac and Jacob" (Ex. 2:24). He called to Moses out of a "burning bush"—a bush that burned but was not consumed—to bring the Israelites out of Egypt.

Moses asked God, "If I come to the Israelites and say to them, 'The God of your ancestors has sent me to you,' and they ask me, 'What is his name?' what shall I say to them?" God said to Moses, "I AM WHO I AM" (Ex. 3:13–14). These words refer to God's nature and character. They tell us that God is a living, active being. I AM WHO I AM is expressed in the Old Testament by the four consonants YHWH (the origin and meaning of which has been much debated), to which, in the tenth century A.D., two vowels were added for pronunciation—*A* for Adonai ("Lord") and *E* for Elohim ("God")—to make *Yahweh.* (Jehovah is a popular translation of Yahweh, but there is no evidence that the Israelites ever used this name when referring to God.) The *NRSV* and other English-language Bibles, in their translation of the Hebrew letters YHWH, use the word LORD.

THE EXODUS AND THE SINAITIC COVENANT (EXODUS 12–24)

God carefully prepared Moses for his "calling." First, his early years with his mother, who conveniently was hired by pharaoh's daughter to "nurse" her own child (Ex. 2:8–10), made him aware of his heritage and prepared him for his mission. Second, his education in the pharaoh's household (Acts 7:20–22) prepared him to later confront the pharaoh. Third, his years in the Midian desert prepared him to lead the Israelites into and through the Sinai Peninsula where they received God's commandments. The two great events in Moses' life were the Exodus from Egypt and the covenant at Mount Sinai.

The Exodus From Egypt. The Exodus (the "going out") took place after "the Israelites had lived in Egypt four hundred thirty years" (Ex. 12:40). Although the Exodus is the most important event in Israel's history, we do not know where it took place. It was not the Red Sea at the southern end of the Sinai Peninsula (see map on p. 299), but more likely an inland lake or the "Sea of Reeds" (the words *yam suf* in the Hebrew Scriptures). Nor do we know the actual date, with opinion divided between 1446 B.C., based on 1 Kings 6:1, and 1290 B.C., based on archaeology (the majority view). Nor are we certain how many people were involved or how the "deliverance" through the waters was accomplished.

In the Exodus, the Israelites encountered the God of their forefathers, who saved them from certain death. It was and became the defining moment in Israel's history, which Jews celebrate with a ceremonial feast (Seder) on the first two nights of Passover, much like Christians celebrate Jesus' saving death and resurrection on Good Friday and Easter.

The Sinaitic Covenant. After escaping the pharaoh's soldiers, who were drowned in "the sea" (Ex. 14:28), Moses led the Israelites through the Sinai Peninsula. At Mount Sinai, God told Moses to tell the people of Israel that *if* [they] "obey my voice and keep my covenant" they would be his "treas-ured possession out of all the peoples" (Ex. 19:5). God then entered into a covenant with Israel, which Moses sealed with the blood of oxen (Ex. 24:5–8). (In the New Testament, Jesus sealed the new covenant with his *own* blood.) The ensuing history of Israel in the Promised Land—from its entry under Joshua in 1250 B.C. to the fall of Jerusalem in 586 B.C.—revolves around its fidelity, and far more often its infidelity, to the Sinaitic covenant.

The heart of the Sinaitic covenant is contained in the Ten Commandments (Ex. 20:3–17), which became the religious and moral law of Israel. (The term *Ten Commandments* comes from Exodus 34:28.) Of the Commandments, the first four—or three among Catholics and Lutherans, because they number the Commandments differently—are the most important because they set Israel apart from its neighbors. And of these four, the first is the most important of all: Israel was to have no other gods above or before "the Lord your God, who brought you out of the land of Egypt, out of the house of slavery" (Ex. 20:2). Chapter 10 contains brief comments on each of the Ten Commandments.

LEVITICUS, NUMBERS AND DEUTERONOMY

The last three books of the Pentateuch instruct the Israelites how to worship and serve God in the world.

LEVITICUS

Leviticus is the book of the Levites, the priestly descendants of Levi, one of the twelve sons of Jacob. It contains guidelines for sacrificial offerings, instructions regarding the ordination of priests, rules having to do with ritual purity (including clean and unclean food), instructions for the celebration of holy days, and various holiness codes. Chapter 16 contains instructions for observing *Yom* (day) *Kippur* (atonement), the most solemn day of the Jewish calendar—the Jewish equivalent of Good Friday—which comes ten days after Rosh Hashanah, the Jewish New Year, in September or October. *Yom Kippur* is the day when Israel confesses its sins, both "seen and unseen," so that it might be reconciled with God. Leviticus contains God's command to "love your neighbor as yourself" (Lev. 19:18), which Jesus said was the second greatest commandment (Mark 12:31).

NUMBERS

Numbers is about the organization ("numbering") of the twelve tribes and the forty-day information-gathering mission by the twelve spies who ventured into the Promised Land. The Israelites feared the Canaanites and refused to invade the land God had promised to Abraham's descendants, which brought God's judgment upon them: forty years of "wandering" in the wilderness, one year for each day the spies were in the land of Canaan. Numbers contains the familiar Aaronic blessing: "The Lord bless you and keep you . . . make his face shine upon you, and be gracious to you . . . lift up his countenance upon you, and give you peace" (Num. 6:24–26).

DEUTERONOMY

Deuteronomy (the "second law" or "repeated law") is a retelling of Israel's covenant relationship with God, because most of the elders had died during the long years in the wilderness. Chapter 6 contains the *Shema* (a Hebrew word meaning "hear" or "listen"), which is Israel's monotheistic creed or confession: "Hear, O Israel: The Lord is our God, the Lord alone. You shall love the Lord your God with all your heart, and with all your soul, and with all your might" (Deut. 6:4–5). Jesus said this was the greatest of all the commandments (Mark 12:28–30). Deuteronomy is the basis for Jesus' responses to Satan when he was tested in the wilderness: we do not live by bread alone (8:3); we are to worship only God (6:13); we are not to test the Lord our God (6:16).

THE HISTORICAL BOOKS: THE RISE AND FALL OF ISRAEL

The next section of the Old Testament contains the story of Israel in the land of Canaan, the land God promised to Abraham. The dates referred to in this section are taken from *A History of Israel* by John Bright, a recognized authority on the history of Israel.

THE INVASION AND CONQUEST OF CANAAN (JOSHUA AND JUDGES)

The book of Joshua is the story of the invasion of Canaan in 1250 B.C., forty years after the assumed date of the Exodus in 1290 B.C. After the initial invasion at Jericho, and the securing of footholds in the central hill country, a long period of conquest was required to subdue the land. The book of Judges is the story of twelve tribal leaders who led groups of Israelites during the occupation of the Promised Land from the death of Joshua to the rise of the monarchy. It is the story of charismatic leaders like Deborah, Gideon, and Samson, whom God called and raised up to lead Israel when it was attacked by its neighbors. The period of Joshua and Judges is sometimes called the "tribal confederacy." It lasted from 1250 B.C. to around 1020 B.C., the beginning of the monarchy under King Saul.

Geographically, the land of Israel was (and is today) very small—roughly 150 miles long and 75 miles wide—about the size and shape of the state of Vermont. Why did God desire that Israel possess a *land* of its own? Perhaps because God wanted the Israelites to be a settled people, rather than to live as nomads. Why the land of *Canaan*? Perhaps because it was located at the crossroads of the world (Europe, Asia and Africa), a place where Israel would be God's "light to the nations" (Isa. 42:6).

THE MONARCHY (RUTH, 1–2 SAMUEL, 1 KINGS AND 1 CHRONICLES)

During the period of the judges, the Philistines were Israel's principal enemy. They were ambitious and militaristic, and they began to push inland from the Mediterranean coast where they had landed from the Isle of Crete in the 1100s B.C. The Philistine threat to the Israelites was the reason Israel wanted "a king over us . . . like other nations" (1 Sam. 8:19–20). Israel's first king was Saul (c. 1020–1000 B.C.). He was anointed by Samuel, the greatest Old Testament figure between Moses and the monarchy. Saul was a great warrior, but he was unstable and a disappointment as God's "anointed."

King David: Israel's Greatest Hero (2 Samuel, 1 Kings and 1 Chronicles). God told Samuel to anoint David as the one who should follow Saul (1 Sam. 16). David was the youngest son of Jesse, a Judean farmer. He was born in Bethlehem in the year 1030 B.C. David ruled over Judah, then over all of Israel, for forty years—from age thirty to age seventy (from 1000 to 961 B.C.). He was a charismatic leader; a great military commander who broke the power of the Philistines and extended and secured Israel's borders; a political genius who united the northern and southern tribes by locating Israel's capital in the neutral city of Jerusalem (the City of

David); and a religious figure who brought the Ark of the Covenant to Jerusalem, wrote psalms of worship to God and prayed for forgiveness and cleansing after his adultery with Bathsheba and the murder of Uriah (Ps. 51).

God's plan of salvation becomes more specific in the Davidic narrative. God, through the prophet Nathan, promises that from David's *house* (descendants) will come one whose "kingdom shall be made sure forever" (2 Sam. 7:16). Matthew and Luke carry this promise forward by showing in their genealogies of Jesus that Joseph, Jesus' legal father, was a descendant of David (see Matt. 1:6 and Luke 3:31). Luke, in his birth narrative, reports that Gabriel said to Mary, concerning Jesus, "He will be great . . . and the Lord God will give to him the throne of his ancestor David. He will reign . . . forever, and of his kingdom there will be no end" (Luke 1:32–33).

Solomon: The Great Monarch (1 Kings and 2 Chronicles). Solomon was the second child born to David and Bathsheba. Solomon had many wives, including foreign wives, whom he married to forge political alliances. For some of these wives he erected altars and idols to their pagan gods. He also taxed the people and compelled them to work in his government and on his building projects, including his temple—Solomon's temple—his most famous legacy, located on the present site of the Dome of the Rock in Jerusalem.

Solomon was given the gift of wisdom (1 Kings 3:5–12), as demonstrated in the story of the two women and the baby (1 Kings 3:16–28), but he "did what was evil in the sight of the Lord, and did not . . . follow the Lord, as his father David had done" (1 Kings 11:6). Solomon died in 922 B.C. Solomon's son, Rehoboam, could not hold the twelve tribes together, and Israel split into two halves. The ten northern tribes became the nation of Israel, with its capital at Samaria; the two southern tribes, Judah and Benjamin, became the nation of Judah, with its capital at Jerusalem.

THE DIVISION AND DEFEAT OF ISRAEL AND JUDAH (2 KINGS AND 2 CHRONICLES)

The stories of the Northern Kingdom of Israel and the Southern Kingdom of Judah are sorry chapters in the history of Israel. Many kings—there were nineteen in the North and twenty in the South—and priests paid hom-

age to the fertility gods and other deities of the Canaanites, and they persecuted and oppressed their own people, especially the weak and the powerless.

The corruption, oppression and faithlessness of the kings and priests in
the North and South led to the decline and demise of both kingdoms. In
721 B.C. the Northern Kingdom was defeated by the Assyrians, with most
of the Israelites deported or assimilated into the Assyrian population, resulting in the Ten Lost Tribes of Israel. In 586 B.C., the Southern Kingdom was
defeated, Solomon's temple was destroyed by the Babylonians and many
Judeans were hauled off in chains to Babylon. The Southern Kingdom of
Judah became the surviving "remnant," whose members were called "Jews"
(see, for instance, Esther 2:5). After the Exile, the term *Jew* became a designation for those from or identified with Judah.

With the siege and impending defeat of Jerusalem by the Babylonians,
many Jews left Judah and resettled in North Africa, Asia Minor and Europe,
in what is called the *Diaspora,* a Greek word meaning "dispersion." It is
estimated that 80 percent of the Jews in the first century A.D. lived outside
of Israel, which is why the apostle Paul had little trouble finding a synagogue
in which to preach.

EXILE, RETURN AND RESTORATION
(2 KINGS, 2 CHRONICLES, EZRA, NEHEMIAH
AND ESTHER)

The next chapter in Israel's history is the Exile or Captivity in Babylon.
The Exile severely tested Israel's faith: Solomon's temple, the sign or symbol
of God's presence among his people, had been destroyed, and David's
dynasty, which was to last forever, had apparently come to an end. *What
happened?* What happened had been foretold by the prophets: God would
judge and punish Israel if it was faithless and disobedient, if it had "other
gods," if it did not live as a people of "justice and righteousness."

In the year 539 B.C., the Persians defeated the Babylonians. The Persian
king, Cyrus, issued an edict that allowed the Jews to return to their homeland—Israel's new or second Exodus. (When the United States recognized
Israel as an independent state in 1948, giving the Jews a homeland of their
own, President Truman said: "I am Cyrus.") The exiles who returned (many

chose to remain in Babylon) found Judah in shambles. It took men like Governor Nehemiah, who rebuilt the walls around Jerusalem, and Ezra, who reinstituted Jewish religious life in Judah, to strengthen the faith of those who returned and took up residence in the Promised Land.

THE VOICE AND MESSAGE OF THE PROPHETS

During the periods of the monarchy and the divided kingdoms, Israel became increasingly faithless and disobedient. God called prophets to exhort the Israelites to return to the covenant he made with them at Mount Sinai and to prophesy dire consequences if they refused to do so.

THE PROPHETS

The main Hebrew word for *prophet* can either mean "the one who calls or is called" or "one who speaks for another" ("Thus says the Lord"). Prophets were not usually from priestly families, and most had a special feeling for Israel's election by and covenant with God. The prophets came on the scene during the period of the kings as a check and balance to the kings; they faded out in the postexilic period when there were no longer kings in Israel. According to Jewish tradition, with the death of Malachi (c. 440 B.C.), God's spirit departed from Israel.

The prophets spoke to the people of Israel and Judah in the context of their everyday lives and times, calling them to change their ways and return to the covenant. We often think of Israel's prophets as speaking to or about the future, but this was only a minor part—perhaps no more than 10 percent—of their message.

THE BOOKS OF THE PROPHETS

In the Old Testament, the lives and words of prophets such as Nathan, Elijah and Elisha were woven into the biblical narratives. They are sometimes called "speaking" or "narrative" prophets. Other prophets' words and sermons were written down and collected by their disciples in order to be remembered and passed on. These prophets are sometimes called "writing" or "canonical" prophets.

In the Christian Old Testament, the books of the prophets are divided into four major and twelve minor prophets—"major" meaning longer and "minor" meaning shorter. In the Hebrew Scriptures, there are three major prophets (Daniel is included among the Writings, not the Prophets), each of which was one scroll in length, like the Isaiah scroll mentioned in Luke 4:17–20. The twelve minor prophets comprised one scroll, referred to as the Book of the Twelve. In Christian Bibles, the majors are first, followed by the minors. And among the minors, Hosea is first because it is the longest of the preexilic prophetic writings, though Amos was the first book to be written.

CHRONOLOGY OF THE PROPHETS

The following is a list of the prophets of Israel and the dates of their ministries from various Bible dictionaries and commentaries and John Drane's *Introducing the Old Testament*.

Narrative Prophets	Elijah (c. 870–845)
	Elisha (c. 850–800)
Preexilic Prophets (760–586 B.C.)	Amos (c. 770–750)
	Hosea (c. 750–722)
	Isaiah (c. 740–690)
	Micah (c. 740–685)
	Zephaniah (c. 635–620)
	Jeremiah (c. 626–586)
	Habakkuk (c. 615–590)
	Nahum (c. 612)
	Obadiah (c. 605–590)
Exilic Prophets (586–538 B.C.)	Ezekiel (c. 593–571)
	Daniel (c. 500s)
Postexilic Prophets (538–440 B.C.)	Haggai (c. 520)
	Zechariah (c. 520–518)
	Malachi (c. 440)
	Jonah (most likely postexilic)
	Joel (most likely postexilic)

IMPORTANT PROPHETS AND PROPHECIES

The following are some of the more important prophets and their prophecies.

Elijah. Elijah was the forerunner and the most important of the pre-literary prophets (those for whom books are named). He prophesied in the North in the 800s B.C., did battle with King Ahab and Queen Jezebel, and defeated the prophets of Baal at Mount Carmel. According to the prophet Malachi, Elijah, who was taken up to heaven in a whirlwind (2 Kings 2:11), will return to announce the coming of the Messiah (Mal. 3:1; 4:5). In the New Testament, John the Baptist is described in language reminiscent of Elijah (compare 2 Kings 1:8 and Matt. 3:4) and is identified as the "Elijah figure" who heralds the coming of the Messiah (see Matt. 17:12–13 and Luke 7:24–27).

Amos. Amos is the first prophet whose words were recorded in a book that was named for him. Amos is considered to be the greatest of the minor prophets in terms of style, message and personality. Amos prophesied in the North beginning in the 770s B.C. He spoke out against Israel's empty, ritualistic worship and its unjust treatment of the poor, saying that God does not want Israel's false offerings; he wants "justice [to] roll down like waters, and righteousness like an ever-flowing stream" (5:24).

To Amos, to sin or do evil against another person was to sin against God, a refrain the apostle John echoes in his first letter: "Those who do not love a brother or sister whom they have seen, cannot love God whom they have not seen" (1 John 4:20).

Hosea. Hosea was an Israelite who spoke out against Israel ten or more years after Amos. In contrast to Amos's message of doom and destruction, Hosea was a prophet of hope, if only Israel would be faithful. The book opens with God commanding Hosea to "take for yourself a wife of whoredom" (1:2). Hosea marries Gomer, who bears two sons and a daughter, and then, again, becomes a prostitute. There is little agreement as to whether this is meant to be understood autobiographically or allegorically, but a persuasive view is that God told Hosea to marry Gomer so that Hosea would know and could speak about the pain of unfaithfulness in personal terms, the pain that God suffered from Israel's unfaithfulness—its corrupt priests, its idolatry, its ingratitude.

The marriage *motif* or theme is a powerfully symbolic one: God's covenant with Israel at Mount Sinai is like a covenant of love and fidelity in marriage. A similar motif is found in Paul's description of Christ as the bridegroom and the church as his bride (Eph. 5:23). Another motif in Hosea is that of resurrection, which some scholars see in verse 6:2: "On the third day he will raise us up."

Isaiah. Isaiah was a Judean who lived in Jerusalem in the 700s B.C. He is the most frequently quoted prophet in the New Testament. Many scholars believe that the book of Isaiah has two authors—chapters 1–39, written by "Isaiah, son of Amoz" in the late 700s during the reigns of four Judean kings, and chapters 40–66, written by an unknown prophet (designated Second or Deutero Isaiah) in the 540s, toward the end of Israel's Babylonian exile. Whether Isaiah is written by one author or two, it is clear that chapters 1–39 assume an Assyrian, and chapters 40–66 a Babylonian historical context. Yet to quote the nineteenth-century American evangelist Dwight L. Moody: "What is the use of talking about two Isaiahs when most people don't know there is one?"

The book of Isaiah contains prophecies that the New Testament interprets as messianic: The one sent from God will be born of a virgin and called "Immanuel" (Isa. 7:14; Matt. 1:23); the Holy Spirit will come upon him and he will "bring good news" (Isa. 61:1–2; Luke 4:16–21); he will establish the throne of David and reign forever (Isa. 9:6–7; Luke 1:32–33). The most important prophecies, however, are those relating to a *suffering servant* who would come as an "intercession for the transgressors" and bear "the sin of many" (Isa. 53:12). Jesus understood these verses as referring to himself. He said that he came to give his life as "a ransom for many" (Mark 10:45); he told his disciples that the prophecies in Isaiah 53 "must be fulfilled in me" (Luke 22:37); he told the two on the road to Emmaus that he was the one who had come to "suffer these things" (Luke 24:26).

Jeremiah. Jeremiah lived some one hundred years after Isaiah in the last years of the Southern Kingdom. His ministry lasted for forty years. More is known about Jeremiah than any other prophet because of the autobiographical material in his book. Jeremiah was rejected by the people because he prophesied the coming judgment of God, which led to much personal suffering. Some call him the "father" of the saints. According to William Neil, "Jeremiah's chief contribution lies in the witness of his own life. He is the incarnation of the prophetic message, and it is this that makes him at once the most human and sympathetic figure in the Old Testament. . . . [His] life bears a closer resemblance to that of Jesus than any other Old Testament figure" (*Harper's Bible Commentary*).

What is most remembered about Jeremiah, however, is his prophecy of a *new covenant*: "The days are surely coming, says the Lord, when I will make a new covenant" (Jer. 31:31), which the New Testament interprets as having been instituted by Jesus at the Last Supper: "This cup that is poured out for you is the new covenant in my blood" (Luke 22:20).

Jonah. The story of Jonah and the whale—actually, a large fish—is one of the best-known stories in the Old Testament. The book of Jonah is a story *about* a prophet (though probably not the prophet mentioned in 2 Kings 14:25), not just the *words* of a prophet. Some see the book as teaching the universality of God's love, showing that we cannot run away from God when we are called to announce this love to others—even when the "others" are our most hated enemies, our "Assyrians."

MESSIANIC PROPHECIES

By some counts there are more than four hundred messianic prophecies in the Old Testament. We need to be cautious when looking at these prophecies, because some are open to more than one interpretation—that is, we should not press them to say more than they do. What we can say, and with great confidence, is that the Old Testament prophecies clearly point to something more to come, something still ahead, something yet to happen, which the New Testament interprets as having occurred in Jesus of Nazareth: his virgin birth, his Davidic heritage, his wondrous acts, his claims and promises, his suffering death for the sins of the world, and his resurrection, which confirmed his "person" (who he was) and his "work" (what he came to do).

THE WRITINGS: ISRAEL'S WISDOM AND DEVOTIONAL LITERATURE

The Writings contain the last books in the Jewish Bible. Two of them are collections, without a single author (Psalms and Proverbs); the other three are not central to the salvation-history story of Israel (Job, Ecclesiastes and the Song of Songs). As to the order of the books, Job is first, because its setting is earlier than the other four books. Psalms and Proverbs are next, and in this order because David, the patron of psalmic literature, lived before Solomon, the patron of wisdom literature.

The book of Ecclesiastes begins, "Vanity of vanities . . . all is vanity" (1:2). All of life is futile and has no meaning—the just and the unjust suffer equally. The author of the book, who calls himself "the Teacher" (1:12), says that only in God, the maker and creator of all things, can one find meaning in life. How does one do this? By fearing (revering) God and keeping "his commandments, for that is the whole duty of everyone" (12:13). A famous passage in Ecclesiastes is the Teacher's observation that "For everything there is a season . . . a time to be born, and a time to die . . . a time to plant, and a time to pluck . . . a time to weep, and a time to laugh . . . a time to mourn, and a time to dance . . . a time to keep silent, and a time to speak . . . a time for war, and a time for peace . . ." (3:1–8).

The Song of Songs had a hard time winning its way into the Hebrew canon, because its concerns seemed to be the celebration of love between a man and a woman and because it contains no mention of God. It was eventually received into the canon because of its references to Solomon, whose name is mentioned seven times in the book, and because Rabbi Akiba, one of the founders of rabbinic Judaism, argued that the book was not about human love but an allegory about God's love for Israel.

THE BOOK OF PSALMS

The Psalms have been called Israel's *soul music* (in ancient Israel, psalms were meant to be sung). In contrast to other writings in the Old Testament, the Psalms are the words of Israel speaking to God rather than the words of God speaking to Israel. A unique feature of the Psalms, which also occurs in the Proverbs, is the parallelism and rhyming of thoughts rather than words. The book of Psalms—or Psalter—is the longest book in the Bible, is the most quoted book in the New Testament, is used in church worship services for responsive readings, and is widely used for personal devotions.

It is difficult to date the Psalms because most do not deal with events in Israel's history to which they can be related. The dates range from the time of David down to and through the Exile. David is given credit for writing seventy-three of the Psalms, but a Psalm *of* David can also mean a Psalm *for* or *dedicated* to David. The Psalter is divided into five "books": 1–41, 42–72, 73–89, 90–106, and 107–150, each of which ends with a short doxology. Some believe this was done to parallel the Pentateuch—the five books of David and the five books of Moses.

Broadly speaking, the Psalms are laments, prayers and petitions to God for help; hymns of praise to God for choosing Israel and for delivering Israel from her enemies; and hymns that extol God's greatness and holiness. Some of the more well-known Psalms are Ps. 1, which talks about the "two ways" or outcomes in life; Ps. 8, a psalm of praise of God as the Creator ("O Lord . . . how majestic is your name over all the earth"); Ps. 9, which contains words we often hear from pastors: "Let the words of my mouth and the meditation of my heart be acceptable to you, O Lord, my rock and my redeemer"; Ps. 22, which opens with Jesus' words from the cross: "My God, my God, why have you forsaken me?"; Ps. 23, the best known and best loved of the psalms, which portrays God as the Good Shepherd; Ps. 46, which underlies Martin Luther's hymn "A Mighty Fortress Is Our God"; Ps. 51, David's prayer for forgiveness and cleansing after his adultery with Bathsheba and the death of Uriah; Ps. 110, which the New Testament interprets as a prophetic psalm that points to Jesus as the promised Messiah; and Ps. 119, a long acrostic poem of twenty-two eight-verse stanzas about the Word of God, which the psalmist says, "is a lamp to my feet and a light to my path."

THE BOOK OF PROVERBS

The book of Proverbs is dedicated to Solomon (1:1) because of his legendary wisdom (see 1 Kings 4:29–34); he is also the author of 375 proverbs in chapters 10–22 and another 135 or so in chapters 25–29 (including some duplications: for instance, 12:11 and 28:19). Scholars do not regard the book of Proverbs as a single composition, but rather as collections of sayings and proverbs (there are eight discernible *collections* in the book), dating back to "wisdom schools" during the reign of King Solomon in the tenth century B.C. Proverbs flourished in the ancient world, especially in Egypt and Mesopotamia. Israel claimed that her wisdom and sages were superior to those of other cultures and nations.

The following comments are more than might seem warranted by the book of Proverbs, which for many people is a seldom read book, and rarely read in church, in contrast to the book of Psalms. The book offers wonderful advice on how to live as God's children in the everyday world—even the twenty-first-century world. Also, the book is fun to read, perhaps more so than any book in the Bible; it is easy to read: one chapter per day on the corresponding day of the month; and it is a good introduction to the Bible because its wisdom is universal.

The theme of the book of Proverbs is *wisdom,* a term which is used some forty times. What is wisdom? Eugene Peterson, in his preface to the book of Proverbs in *The Message,* says that wisdom is "being skillful in honoring our parents and raising our children, handling our money and conducting our sexual lives, going to work and exercising leadership, using words well and treating friends kindly, eating and drinking healthily, and cultivating emotions within ourselves and attitudes that make for peace." Peterson says that the book of Proverbs concentrates on these matters more than any other book in the Bible, distilling everything "into riveting images and aphorisms that keep us connected in holy obedience to the ordinary."

The book of Proverbs has two broad sections—chapters 1–9 and chapters 10–31. The first section contains short homilies addressed to young men ("my son/sons"; inclusive language: "my child/children"). Some view the two parties as father-and-son, others as teacher-and-student or master-and-apprentice. These chapters contain instructions about wisdom, which comes from "the fear [meaning extreme awe or reverence] of the Lord" (1:7); following in the ways of the righteous and not the wicked (5:18–19); warnings that those who plot evil will reap ruin and disaster (6:12–15); warnings about the danger of pursuing illicit sexual pleasure (6:32–34), a frequently repeated theme in these chapters; and the belief that discipline and hard work are essential for success (6:6–1).

The second section—chapters 10–31—contains six collections of proverbs and wisdom sayings, plus an acrostic poem. The proverbs in 10–22 (thought to be the earliest "collection") and 25–29 are attributed to Solomon, though many are probably anonymous. In addition to the Solomonic proverbs, there are two collections of an unnamed author's "Sayings of the Wise" (22–24) and the sayings of Agur and Lemuel (30–31). The proverbs in these chapters are short, pithy, memorable sayings that are rooted in practical experience and universal in nature to help one navigate through life.

Most are written as two-line couplets, a noted feature of biblical poetry. The two lines are not meant to say the same thing twice; rather, the second line strengthens and interprets the first by sharpening and intensifying its thought or theme. The book's proverbs are general principles, not absolutes; for instance, some promise that the righteous will prosper (13:21), but this is not always the case. Also, proverbs are "situation-sensitive," meaning that they are to be understood in the context of the particular circumstances to which they apply. The epilogue to the book—the final twenty-two verses (31:10–31)—is an acrostic poem, with the first letter of each verse corresponding to successive letters in the Hebrew alphabet, about the perfect or ideal wife. The epilogue ends where the prologue began, lifting up "the fear of the Lord" as the beginning of knowledge.

THE BOOK OF JOB

Job is a timeless book, one of the great classics of literature and the most intellectually demanding book in the Bible. It is a story about (rather than by) a wealthy chieftain, Job, who probably lived during the patriarchal period. (A person named Job is mentioned in Ezekiel 14:14, 20, but there is no consensus as to whether this is the same person.) The narrator tells us that Job is wise, just, righteous and reveres God, but as a result of a wager between God and Satan to test Job's love for God, he loses everything—his flocks, his children, even his health (painful, festering sores). We often hear about the "patience" of Job, but as the story unfolds, Job is anything but patient.

The book of Job is a theological discussion of the question of suffering: If God is all-powerful and all-loving, how is it that the righteous suffer? And why do some suffer more than others? Job's three friends represent what is called retribution theology: Good things happen to good people and bad things to bad people. Job is suffering, so he must be a sinner. But we are told at the beginning of the book that Job is not a sinner. Then why does he suffer? Job pleads with God for an explanation. God speaks to Job, out of a storm, asking questions of his own: Where was Job when God laid the foundations of the earth, made light and darkness and wind and rain, and made the creatures of the world? Who is Job to question God's justice? Humbled, Job steps back, saying, "I have uttered what I did not understand"

and puts his trust in God, echoing back, perhaps, to the first chapter in the narrative: "Naked I came from my mother's womb, and naked shall I return; the Lord gave, and the Lord has taken away; blessed be the name of the Lord" (1:21).

JUDAISM TODAY

Judaism is the religion of the Jews. The Jewish scholar Jacob Neusner defines Judaism as "God's will conveyed in the Torah to Israel." There are three distinct branches of Judaism.

Orthodox Judaism holds to the strict observance of the Torah, which it believes God dictated to Moses on Mount Sinai. Orthodox Judaism is the most rigid and legalistic of the three branches of Judaism and the only form of Judaism recognized by the State of Israel. The Orthodox forbid all work on the Sabbath, such as commerce, cooking, travel and writing, and follow the Old Testament dietary laws regarding kosher food and the separation of meat and milk products. Orthodox worship services are conducted by male rabbis in Hebrew; men and women sit in separate pews; and men are required to wear head coverings. Orthodox Jews look forward to reestablishing the temple in Jerusalem (now a Muslim mosque and shrine), to the resumption of ancient sacrificial rituals, and to the coming of a personal Messiah.

Reform Judaism began in Germany in the early 1800s as an effort to "reform" Judaism and bring it into the mainstream of society. Reform Judaism is sometimes called Liberal or Progressive Judaism. Reform Jews do not regard the Torah as law but as teaching, and open to interpretation. Worship services are in the everyday language of the people; there are female rabbis; men and women may sit together; and some services have instrumental music and mixed choirs (forbidden in Orthodox Judaism). The rules regarding the Sabbath are relaxed and the dietary laws are generally not observed. Reform Judaism believes in the coming of a future messianic age rather than in a personal Messiah.

Conservative Judaism began in Europe at the end of the nineteenth century but is largely an American phenomenon—a corrective or middle course between the legalism of Orthodox Judaism and the liberalism of

Reform Judaism that seeks to "conserve" the traditions of Judaism on the one hand while adapting to changes in society on the other. In recent years, Conservative Judaism has moved more to the left (Reform) than to the right (Orthodox), leading some to speculate that eventually Judaism will be divided into two branches—Orthodox and Reform.

According to the new *World Christian Encyclopedia* (Second Edition, 2001), from which most of the numbers for religions and denominations in this book are derived, there are an estimated 14 million Jews in the world. Forty percent live in the United States and 30 percent live in Israel. The first Jews came to the North American continent in 1654, but the real influx came following the pogroms (organized massacres) in Russia in the 1880s. According to the 1997 *American Jewish Yearbook,* 38 percent of U.S. Jews are Reform, 40 percent are Conservative, 7 percent are Orthodox and 15 percent are unaffiliated.

JUDAISM AND CHRISTIANITY

Judaism and Christianity have many similar beliefs. They both believe in a single, sovereign, supreme God, in the centrality and authority of Scripture, and in resurrection and an afterlife. The principal differences between the two religions are as follows: First, Judaism believes that God revealed himself in the Torah, not, as Christians believe, in a person (Jesus). Second, Judaism believes that God is one (Deut. 6:4), not, as Christians believe, triune (Father, Son and Holy Spirit). Third, Judaism regards God as pure spirit, which precludes his incarnation in human form; Christians believe that "the Word became flesh [in Jesus of Nazareth] and lived among us" (John 1:14). Fourth, Judaism believes that Adam's fall affected only Adam, not his progeny. Men and women have "inclinations" to do good and evil, but are not, as Christians believe, innately fallen or sinful. Fifth, Judaism believes that salvation comes through righteous living and faithfulness to the Mosaic covenant; Christians believe that salvation is by "grace through faith" in Christ's salvific death on the cross (Eph. 2:8).

Another difference between the two faiths is their formal day of worship. Jews worship on Saturday, the seventh day of the week, because "on the seventh day God finished the work he had been doing . . . [and] he rested" (Gen. 2:2). The word *sabbath* means "rest." When the Roman emperor

Constantine became a Christian in the early 300s, Sunday was officially recognized as the formal day of worship for Christians, because "on the first day of the week" (Luke 24:1) Jesus was raised from the dead (Easter Sunday).

CHAPTER 3

JESUS OF NAZARETH

He grew up in an obscure village, the child of a peasant woman. He worked in a carpenter shop until he was thirty, and then for three years he was an itinerant preacher. He never owned a home. He never had a family. He never went to college. He never traveled more than two hundred miles from where he was born. He didn't do any of the things usually associated with greatness. He had no credentials but himself.

While he was still a young man the tide of public opinion turned against him. His friends ran away. He was turned over to his enemies. He went through the mockery of a trial. He was nailed to a cross between two thieves. While he was dying his executioners gambled for the only piece of property he had on earth, his coat. When he was dead he was laid in a borrowed grave through the pity of a friend.

Twenty centuries have come and gone, and all the armies that ever marched, and all the navies that ever sailed, and all the parliaments that ever sat, and all the kings that ever reigned—put together—have not affected the life of men and women on this earth as much as this one solitary life.

SOURCE UNKNOWN

THE WORLD, LIFE AND MINISTRY OF JESUS

People have managed to do away with many things down through the ages, but not Jesus. He remains a potent figure—often misunderstood, sometimes ridiculed, but always there. We date our calendar from his birth, capture him in art and music, and use his teachings as a reference point in talking about faith and ethics. In this chapter we will look at the first-century Greco-Roman-Jewish world in which Jesus grew up and lived out his ministry. Then we will look at Jesus' birth, baptism by John, public ministry, teachings, betrayal, arrest, trials, crucifixion, burial, resurrection and ascension. This will provide us with important background information for our study of the Gospels, the written testimonies to the person and work of Jesus.

THE INTERTESTAMENTAL PERIOD

The period between the return of the exiles from Babylon (538 B.C.) and the birth of Jesus is a period of religious history about which very little is known. A modest temple was built at the urging of the prophets Haggai and Zechariah (520–515), referred to as the Second Temple. The walls around Jerusalem were rebuilt under Governor Nehemiah (c. 445). Jewish religious life was reestablished by Ezra. The Hebrew Scriptures were collected, though the final canon was not confirmed until some time later. And the Jews regained control of their land from the Syrians (Seleucids), only to have it taken away a century later by the Romans.

ALEXANDER AND THE GREEKS

In the year 336 B.C. Alexander the Great—one of the greatest generals and conquerors in all of history—at the age of twenty, succeeded his father, Philip II, King of Macedonia (northern Greece), who was assassinated. Alexander was a brilliant military tactician and a bold, courageous leader. After solidifying his throne, he defeated the Persians and moved east, conquering Egypt, Palestine (in 332) and Babylon. He wanted to go farther, into India, but his war-weary generals rebelled and refused, ending his conquests.

Alexander was a pupil of Aristotle and he loved everything Greek. His dream was to unify East and West. He induced his soldiers to marry women from among the peoples he conquered; he introduced Greek language, culture and religion wherever he was victorious; and he built a number of Greek cities, such as Alexandria in Egypt. An example and consequence of Alexander's program of Hellenization (*Hellas* was the ancient name for Greece) was the Jewish community in Alexandria. It became so Hellenized that the Hebrew Scriptures had to be translated from Hebrew to Greek in order to be read, resulting in the *Septuagint* (chapter 1).

In the year 323 B.C., at the young age of thirty-three, Alexander died of a fever (typhoid or malaria) in Babylon. Because he had no legal heir, his empire was divided among his generals, among whom two are particularly notable. In the East, *Ptolemy* became the ruler of Egypt and Palestine, with his capital at Alexandria. (Cleopatra, the wife of Marc Antony, who committed suicide in 30 B.C., was the last of the Ptolemies.) *Seleucus* became the ruler of Syria and Babylonia, with his capital at Antioch. There were many battles between the Seleucids and the Ptolemies because the Seleucids wanted access to the Mediterranean Sea. The Seleucids finally triumphed and became the rulers of Palestine in 198 B.C.

THE MACCABEAN REVOLT

Antiochus IV, who took the title *Epiphanes,* meaning "God Manifest," became king of the Seleucid or Syrian Empire in 175 B.C. In an effort to stamp out Judaism, he banned sacrifices at the temple, Sabbath observances, the teaching of the Scriptures and the circumcision of newborn males—all "on pain of death." He also desecrated the temple by offering a swine as a sacrifice to Zeus, the principal Greek god.

This provoked a Jewish uprising under the leadership of Mattathias, a priest, and his five sons, the most famous of whom was Judas, whose nickname was *Maccabeus,* a word meaning "the hammer." The Maccabees (Jewish guerrilla forces) defeated the Syrians in December 164 B.C. and purified the temple, an event which Jews celebrate as the Feast of Lights or Hanukkah ("dedication"), an eight-day festival that occurs around the same time of year as Christmas. Following the Maccabean revolt (recorded in 1 and 2

Maccabees in the Apocrypha), and with the Syrians falling victim to Rome's expansion to the east, the Jews for a short time regained control of their homeland (160–63 B.C.).

THE ROMAN EMPIRE

The Romans wanted to control the perimeter of the Mediterranean Sea in order to have a safe land route during the winter months from Egypt— the breadbasket of the Roman Empire—to Rome. In the year 63 B.C. the Roman army, under Pompey, marched into Jerusalem, and Israel again became subject to foreign rule, this time to the mighty Roman Empire.

Jesus was born during the reign of Octavian, better known as *Augustus,* "the August One" (who died in the month we now call August), the grand-nephew and adopted heir of Julius Caesar, who was assassinated in 44 B.C. Augustus was the first Roman emperor, and most historians consider him to be Rome's greatest emperor because of his organization of the administration of the empire. He ruled from 27 B.C. to A.D. 14. Augustus issued the decree that "all the world should be registered" for tax purposes (Luke 2:1), which sent Joseph and Mary to Bethlehem, where Jesus was born. Augustus was succeeded by *Tiberius,* his adopted stepson, during whose reign (A.D. 14–37) Jesus began his public ministry ("In the fifteenth year of the reign of Emperor Tiberius...," Luke 3:1) and was crucified.

Other emperors of note during the balance of the first century were *Claudius* (41–54), who expelled Jews and Jewish Christians from Rome in 49 (they returned after his death in 54); *Nero* (54–68), who persecuted Christians and, according to tradition, was responsible for the deaths of Peter and Paul; *Vespasian* (69–79), who put down the Jewish revolt of 66–70 and built the famous Colosseum in Rome; *Titus* (79–81), Vespasian's son, who destroyed Jerusalem at the end of the First Jewish War; *Domitian* (81–96), who some scholars believe may be the emperor behind chapters 4–22 of the book of Revelation; and *Trajan* (98–117), the first non-Italian (Spanish) emperor.

ISRAEL/PALESTINE

Israel was part of the Roman province of Syria (the Roman Empire had fourteen provinces) and was ruled by local kings such as the Herods, and by governors such as Pontius Pilate, who ruled Judea and Samaria from 26 to 36, and Antonius Felix and Porcius Festus, who are mentioned in the book of Acts.

The Jews' influence waned after the First Jewish War, an uprising that was brutally crushed by Rome. The temple was burned and thousands of Jews were killed; thousands more were sold into slavery; and the city was razed, with only the Western or "Wailing" Wall of the temple platform, now the holiest site in Israel, left standing. The Romans also defeated pockets of Jews elsewhere in Israel, including the Essenes at Qumran near the Dead Sea. Some sixty years later there was another uprising, the Second Jewish War (132–135), which also was crushed, after which Rome changed the name of the land to *Palestinia*—"Land of the Philistines"—to remove the name of Israel from the land. The Jews did not regain control of the territory until the United Nations established the State of Israel in 1948.

THE HOUSE OF HEROD

The founder of the House of Herod was Antipater, a half-Jew from Idumaea, the Old Testament land of Edom, south of Judea. (Edom was the name given to Esau in Genesis 25:30; his descendants became the Edomites.) During Julius Caesar's Egyptian campaign against Pompey for the sole control of Rome (48–47 B.C.), Antipater sided with Caesar, who rewarded him with the governorship of Judea (in 47 B.C.) and with Roman citizenship. Caesar also granted the Jews two special privileges: exemption from military service and the freedom to worship their own God.

HEROD THE GREAT

Antipater was assassinated in 42 B.C. At the time of his death his son, Herod, was military overseer of Galilee. In the year 40 B.C. Marc Antony, the ruler of the eastern half of the Roman Empire, gave Herod the title "King of the Jews" (actually, he was a vassal king). Herod was called "the Great" by the Romans (*not* by the Jews) because of his great architectural achievements: the temple in Jerusalem, which he dismantled and began rebuilding in 20 B.C. to win favor with the Jews (Herod's temple was even grander than Solomon's); his palace in Jerusalem, where Jesus was "tried" by

Pontius Pilate; Antonia Fortress (named for Marc Antony) in Jerusalem, where Jesus was mocked and scourged by the soldiers; Caesarea, a town in northwest Palestine on the Mediterranean Sea (named for Caesar Augustus), which was Herod's capital city and later Pilate's official residence, where Paul was imprisoned in the late 50s; Herodium, Herod's residence south of Bethlehem, where some believe he is buried; Machaerus in Perea, east of the Dead Sea, where John the Baptist was imprisoned and beheaded; and a string of fortresses, such as Masada on the west side of the Dead Sea, which was destroyed by the Romans at the end of the First Jewish War.

Herod ruled Palestine from 37 to 4 B.C. He was paranoid about others claiming his throne and ordered the executions of two of his ten wives and three of his seven sons, whom he considered potential rivals. He also ordered the killing of "all the children in and around Bethlehem who were two years old or under" upon learning that Jesus, Israel's hoped-for Messiah—and thus a potential rival—had been born there (Matt. 2:16). Whatever we might think of Herod, he must have been an efficient and effective administrator, because Rome allowed him to rule the ever-turbulent land of the Jews for thirty-three years.

HEROD'S SUCCESSORS

Upon Herod's death, his kingdom was divided and bequeathed to three of his sons.

Archelaus ruled Judea and Samaria from 4 B.C. to A.D. 6. He was an evil and oppressive ruler, like his father, and the Jews sent a delegation to Rome to protest against him. Emperor Augustus removed Archelaus and banished him to Gaul (modern-day Belgium and France), after which Judea and Samaria were ruled by governors appointed by the emperor (Pontius Pilate was the fifth governor after Archelaus). In Matthew's nativity narrative, Joseph is warned about Archelaus and takes his family to Nazareth, which was beyond Archelaus's control (Matt. 2:19–23).

Herod Antipas (or simply *Antipas* to avoid confusion with his father) ruled the regions of Galilee and Perea from 4 B.C. until he was removed by Emperor Caligula in A.D. 39. Antipas was the ablest of Herod's sons. He imprisoned and beheaded John the Baptist (Mark 6:14–29) at his fortress-palace at Machaerus (according to the Jewish historian Josephus) and had a brief encounter with Jesus on Good Friday (Luke 23:6–12).

Philip the Tetrarch ("ruler of a fourth") ruled the northeastern territories from 4 B.C. until his death in A.D. 34. His rule was one of moderation and justice. Philip was responsible for rebuilding the ancient city of Panion, which he renamed Caesarea Philippi, combining his name with that of Caesar. Caesarea Philippi was the location of Peter's great confession to Jesus: "You are the Messiah" (Mark 8:27–30).

Herod Agrippa I, called *King Herod* in the book of Acts (12:1), was a grandson of Herod the Great. He ruled over the former territories of Antipas and Philip, and from 41 to 44 over all of Israel. He was responsible for the execution of the apostle James, the brother of John (Acts 12:2), and for the arrest and imprisonment of Peter (Acts 12:3–19). In the year 44 he was struck down by "an angel of the Lord" (Acts 12:23). King Herod was succeeded by his son, *Herod Agrippa II,* called King Agrippa or *Agrippa* in the book of Acts. Agrippa II, who died in the year 93, was the last Herodian ruler. He heard Paul's defense at Caesarea in the late 50s (Acts 25:13–26:32) and sided with Rome against his own people in the First Jewish War.

JEWISH POLITICAL AND RELIGIOUS COMMUNITIES IN THE FIRST CENTURY

In the first century, the majority of the Jews lived in Judea, in the south. Galilee, in the north, was heavily Gentile ("Galilee of the Gentiles," Matt. 4:15). The Sadducees were the ruling hierarchy; the Pharisees and the Essenes were the "religious" of Israel, to which the scribes were attached or related; and the Zealots were the "freedom fighters." The following are some comments about each of these groups.

THE SADDUCEES

The Sadducees were Israel's priestly party. They controlled the temple and the Sanhedrin, the ruling council. The name *Sadducee* comes from Zadok (Greek: *Saddouk*), a priest during David's reign whose descendants held office in Israel from the time of Solomon (1 Kings 2:35). The Sadducees gave priority to the Torah over the rest of the Jewish Scriptures and did not believe in bodily resurrection. Their focus was on the temple and maintaining the status quo. It is believed that the Sadducees were responsible for the arrest and death of Jesus, whom they regarded as a dangerous revolutionary who might provoke a riot that would bring down the heavy hand of Rome. The Sadducees were linked with the temple; after its destruction in the year 70 they disappeared from the scene.

THE PHARISEES

The Pharisees were the "religious" of Israel. It is believed that the term *Pharisee* meant "separated one" because they avoided or separated themselves from anything that was impure. The Pharisees came to prominence in the years following the Maccabean uprising. In the first century A.D. they were middle-class fundamentalist laymen, and few in number—only six thousand, according to Josephus. In contrast to the Sadducees, they were much admired, especially for their learning and piety. The Pharisees believed in the whole of Scripture, not just the Torah; in an expanded law or "fence around the Torah" (stringent rules and regulations concerning the Sabbath and other matters); and in the resurrection of the dead (see Acts 23:8). It was the Pharisees who led the Jewish community after the fall of the temple and who determined the books that were accepted into the Jewish canon.

The Pharisees believed the best way to reflect God was to keep the law. They challenged Jesus when they felt he did not do so—for instance, when he ate with sinners, healed lepers and broke the Sabbath. Jesus countered by saying the Pharisees paid more attention to the law than to matters of "justice and mercy and faith" (Matt. 23:23).

THE ZEALOTS

The Zealots were Jewish resistance fighters ("heirs" of the Maccabees) who wanted to overthrow Rome. Galilee was a hotbed of Zealot activity. One of Jesus' disciples was called Simon the Zealot, which may mean that he had been a Zealot. Some think that Judas Iscariot was a Zealot who became disillusioned with Jesus. It was the Zealots who provoked the uprising against Rome in the year 66, which precipitated the First Jewish War.

THE ESSENES

The Essenes, a term some believe means "pious one," lived celibate lives in small semi-monastic communities (the "monks of Judaism") like the one at Qumran on the northwest shore of the Dead Sea (see map on p. 300). They believed they were Israel's true remnant. Although a peaceful people, the Essenes were destroyed by the Roman Tenth Legion in the year 68 in the First Jewish War. Fortunately, they first hid their "library"—some eight hundred manuscripts, including every book of the Old Testament except Esther—in clay jars in eleven caves near Qumran west of the Dead Sea, which were accidentally discovered by a Bedouin shepherd boy in 1947. The Qumran documents are the oldest extant Jewish Scriptures, some dating back to 250 B.C.

THE SCRIBES

The scribes were not a political party or religious community but professional people who could read and write. Their principal function was to copy, interpret and teach the Scriptures. They are variously referred to in the New Testament as scribes, "scribes of the Pharisees," teachers and experts in the Law (of Moses).

THE FIRST-CENTURY NEW TESTAMENT WORLD

The following are some brief comments on the first-century economic, social, domestic and religious world into which Jesus was born and lived out his ministry.

ECONOMICS

Palestine was an agrarian economy, with a rich variety of grains, vegetables and fruits, and sheep and goats. Wealthy landowners farmed their lands by leasing them out to tenants, sharecroppers and day laborers. In addition to farmers, there were stonemasons, carpenters, butchers, bakers, weavers, potters and other craftsmen and merchants. Village life was primitive and never easy. Travel was by foot and very slow (fifteen to twenty miles a day). Rome levied taxes on crops and imposed tolls and duties on people and merchandise; Jewish law required both tithes and grain offerings to be made at the temple. Civil taxes and religious tithes could amount to as much as 40 to 50 percent of one's income.

SOCIETY

Jewish society was less rigid than Roman society. At the top were hereditary priests who officiated at the temple and offered sacrifices for the people; they were assisted by Levites. The priestly group and the lay aristocracy—wealthy individuals who were not members of priestly families—formed a socio-religious political group that exercised control over the lives of the people. Below the priests, Levites and aristocracy were the common people (farmers, craftsmen and merchants), and below them slaves who ended up on the wrong side of a conflict or who were born to women in slavery or who could not pay their debts. Those living in rural villages in Galilee and elsewhere were more conservative than those who lived in large cities like Jerusalem, and there was constant tension between the two groups.

DOMESTIC LIFE

The family was the basic unit. Marriage and procreation were considered religious obligations ("Be fruitful and multiply"). Marriages were normally arranged by parents, frequently when children were quite young, and often to family relatives like cousins. Girls were married between the ages of twelve and fourteen and males between the ages of eighteen and twenty. Women were restricted to the home and were second-class citizens, excluded even from certain areas of the temple. It was unusual for men to converse with women in public, even their wives. Sons were more highly favored than daughters, but boys were "nobodies" until the age of twelve or thirteen.

RELIGIOUS LIFE

Jews were either full-blooded Jews (those born Jewish) or proselytes (those who converted to Judaism). Two other groups were "God-fearers," those attracted to Judaism but who never converted to Judaism, and Gentiles, a term for anyone who was not Jewish, including the God-fearers. The most important Jewish institution was the temple in Jerusalem, the center of the Jewish sacrificial system. Two other important institutions were the Sanhedrin, the chief judicial and legislative body within Judaism, and the synagogue, from a Greek word meaning "place of assembly." The synagogue was more important than the temple for people living outside Jerusalem; it functioned as a place of worship, prayer, study and fellowship.

JESUS OF NAZARETH: IN "THE FULLNESS OF TIME"

There are two Greek words for time. One is *khronos,* which denotes linear time, from which we get the word "chronology." The other is *kairos,* which denotes the "right time" or "perfect time." Jesus came in *kairos* time—in "the fullness of time" (Gal. 4:4)—which made it possible for the good news to spread throughout the Roman Empire.

- There was universal peace, prosperity and stability in the world—the *Pax Romana* ("Peace of Rome")—which began with the reign of Augustus in 27 B.C.
- There was a *lingua franca* or common universal language, Greek, which made it possible for the good news to be preached everywhere in the Greco-Roman world, and a road system and safe sea routes, which allowed Paul, Barnabas and others easy access to important cities in the Mediterranean world.
- There was a *spiritual hunger* for something other than Roman mythology and emperor worship. People wanted a faith that could give meaning and hope to life.
- There was a growing, widespread belief in *one God,* partly as a result of the Diaspora, the dispersion of Jews who left Palestine following the fall of Jerusalem in 586 B.C. Wherever the Jews settled—more than one hundred fifty cities in the Roman Empire are known to have had synagogues in the first century—they witnessed to their faith in a single, supreme, sovereign God.

In the "fullness of time"—a one-hundred-year window between the beginning of Augustus's reign in 27 B.C. and the final mopping-up operation at Masada in 73 at the end of the First Jewish War—the "Word became flesh" and entered human history in the person of Jesus of Nazareth.

THE BIRTH OF JESUS

The four gospels deal with Jesus' public life from his baptism by John in the Jordan River to his death and resurrection in Jerusalem. To their gospels, Matthew and Luke added birth (or nativity) narratives. There are several possible reasons for their doing so. First, it is reasonable to assume that there was an interest in Jesus' *origins.* Second, Jesus' legal or earthly father, Joseph, was from the *line of David,* which was important to establish because the Messiah was to be a "Son of David" (2 Sam. 7:12–16). Third, it was important to show that Jesus' birth in *Bethlehem* fulfilled the prophecy in Micah 5:2 regarding the Messiah's birthplace. Last, Matthew and Luke wanted to begin their gospels with Jesus' conception to show that he was, from the very first moment, *divine.*

JOSEPH AND MARY

Joseph and Mary were the "parents" of Jesus. Joseph was his legal father and Mary his natural mother. We know very little about Joseph, other than that his ancestors were from the tribe of Judah (Matt. 1:1–2; Luke 3:33–34). He drops out of the picture after the story of Jesus in the temple when Jesus was twelve years old (Luke 2:41–52). Most scholars believe that Joseph died while Jesus was still in Nazareth. We also are not told much about Mary, other than that she was young, a virgin, the cousin of Elizabeth and that she found favor with God (Luke 1:28). By all accounts, she must have been a remarkable woman and mother. According to Roman Catholic teaching, Mary "was preserved immaculate from all stain of original sin by the grace of God." The doctrine of *Immaculate Conception*—which refers to Mary's conception, not that of Jesus—is an attempt to explain how Jesus was born of a human without the taint of original sin.

To understand the birth narratives and the possible disgrace that Joseph and Mary faced as a result of Mary's pregnancy, one needs to know something about marriage relationships in first-century Israel.

Betrothal. In ancient times, couples would enter into betrothals at very young ages because life-spans were short. Mary was probably thirteen or fourteen when she was betrothed to Joseph, much younger than the mature, matronly Mary we are used to seeing in Renaissance Christian art. The betrothal or engagement was entered into before witnesses and, for all intents and purposes, the betrothed couple was married. If one party died, the other was deemed a legal widow or widower. Until formally married, however, the bride and groom continued to live with their respective parents.

Marriage. After a period of betrothal, usually one year, the couple would be married, sometimes in a lavish ceremony like the wedding at Cana (John 2:1–11). After the wedding, the bride left her parents and her husband assumed responsibility for her support.

Between betrothal and marriage, an angel came to Joseph in a dream in Matthew's gospel, and to Mary in person in Luke's gospel, to announce that Mary would conceive a son through the power of the Holy Spirit and that they were to "name him Jesus" (Matt. 1:21; Luke 1:31), meaning "God saves" (us from our sins).

THE BIRTH NARRATIVES

Matthew's birth narrative (1:18–2:18) is told from Joseph's perspective. It contains the account of the "wise men from the East" who, led by the star of Bethlehem, come to pay homage to Jesus, after which the holy family takes refuge in Egypt. Luke's narrative (1:26–38; 2:1–20) is told from Mary's perspective. It contains the account of Augustus's decree that those living in Roman provinces "should be registered," which sends Joseph and Mary to Bethlehem (a five-day journey) where Jesus is born in a stable and is visited by shepherds.

Although the two accounts are different, it is not difficult to harmonize them. Take, for instance, the *Annunciation* ("announcement") that Mary was to conceive a child through the agency of the Holy Spirit. The announcement comes to Mary in Luke's gospel and to Joseph in Matthew's gospel. Why two separate and different revelations? One explanation is that Mary did not want to tell Joseph of her pregnancy because they were not yet married. When Joseph found out, he made plans to break the engagement (see Matt. 1:19), but an angel appeared to him in a dream and told him that the child in Mary's womb was conceived by the Holy Spirit.

The most striking thing about the two narratives is not their differences but their complete agreement on all essential points: the principal characters are Joseph and Mary; the revelations are made by an angel; conception takes place between betrothal and marriage (Mary's virginity is emphasized in both accounts) and occurs through the agency of the Holy Spirit; the child's name is to be Jesus; the birth takes place in Bethlehem during the latter years of the reign of Herod the Great; and the family settles in Nazareth. It is hard to imagine how these two accounts of Jesus' conception and birth, with such important similarities, might have arisen if they were not true. The importance of the birth narratives, though, is not the details of Jesus' birth but the *inbreaking* of God into human history.

Where did the material in the birth narratives come from? According to tradition, Mary, the mother of Jesus, died in the early 60s. If so, Luke, who tells us that he "investigated everything carefully" (Luke 1:3), would have had ample time to visit with Mary while he was in Caesarea during Paul's imprisonment (c. 59–60).

WHEN WAS JESUS BORN?

We think of Jesus being born at the zero hour between B.C. and A.D. His birth, though, was much earlier, because he was born during the reign of Herod the Great, who died in 4 B.C. and had earlier ordered all of the children in Bethlehem up to two years of age to be killed when he learned that Jesus had been born there. Most scholars believe that Jesus was born in 6 or 5 B.C. If so, Jesus lived approximately thirty-five years, because most scholars believe that he died in A.D. 30. The person responsible for the error in Jesus' birth date was a sixth-century monk named Dionysius. He updated the calendar in 533 to shift the center of history from the founding of Rome in 753 B.C. to the birth of Christ. Unfortunately, he made a calculation error. Today, in many parts of the world, the terms B.C. (*Before Christ*) and A.D. (*Anno Domini*: "In the Year of our Lord") are being replaced by B.C.E. (*Before the Common Era*) and C.E. (*Common Era*).

As for the celebration of Christmas, many suppose that Jesus' birth may have been in the spring (shepherds and sheep in the fields, the wise men traveling to Jerusalem) rather than winter. Christians have been celebrating

Christmas ("Christ's Mass") on December 25 since the year 336, when the emperor Constantine combined Christ's birth with the celebration of the winter solstice, the day on which the sun is "reborn," because Jesus was "the light of the world" (John 8:12). *Epiphany*, from a Greek word meaning "manifestation," celebrates the presentation of Jesus to the wise men (or "magi") who came to Bethlehem. Epiphany occurs twelve days after Christmas on January 6.

THE INCARNATION OF GOD

The Christian faith rests on two key beliefs, one at the beginning of the Jesus story, the other at the end. The belief at the beginning is the *Incarnation*—God becoming incarnate in Jesus (John 1:14)—the merger of the divine and the human. The belief at the end of the story is the *Resurrection*, which confirms everything that Jesus said and did during his life, the most important being his saving death on the cross.

The story of the virginal conception of Jesus is about the incarnation of God *in* Jesus, not about the virgin birth *of* Jesus. The Incarnation distinguishes Christianity from Judaism and Islam, the other two monotheistic religions. Only Christianity believes that the eternal, transcendent God of the universe became incarnate in a human being, namely, Jesus of Nazareth.

BRIEF OUTLINE OF JESUS' MINISTRY

The following is a brief chronology of the principal events in the public ministry of Jesus in the first three gospels.

- John the Baptist, the Elijah-like "messenger" prophesied by Malachi (3:1; 4:5), announces that Jesus is the one Israel has long been waiting for. Jesus is baptized in the Jordan River, receives God's Spirit and is led into the wilderness where he is tested by Satan.
- Following his baptism and temptation, Jesus returns to Galilee, saying, "The time is fulfilled . . . the kingdom of God has come near; repent, and believe in the good news" (Mark 1:15).
- Jesus calls twelve disciples and begins his ministry, much of which occurs

in and around Capernaum, a fishing village and commercial center on the northwest shore of the Sea of Galilee, which became Jesus' home after he was rejected at Nazareth (Luke 4:24–30). The people are amazed by Jesus' teachings and healings, but don't understand him to be the hoped-for Messiah.

- Conflicts erupt between Jesus and the religious leaders having to do with Jesus' association with sinners (tax collectors, lepers, the unclean), his nonobservance of certain Jewish rituals and his breaking of the Sabbath.

- At Caesarea Philippi, Jesus asks the disciples, "Who do you say that I am?" Peter answers, "You are the Messiah" (Mark 8:29). Peter and the others, however, do not understand that Jesus' messiahship means suffering and death, which is why they abandon him after his arrest: they think that he and his mission have failed. It is only after his resurrection that they understand.

- After Peter's confession, Jesus turns his attention from the crowds to his disciples to prepare them to take the good news to "the ends of the earth" (Acts 1:8).

- Jesus predicts his suffering and death and then sets out for Jerusalem where he is betrayed, arrested, denied, tried, beaten, crucified and buried—and then raised from the dead to confirm that he was and *is* who the Gospels claim him to be: the only begotten Son of God.

JESUS' BAPTISM, TESTING AND CALLING TWELVE TO BE HIS DISCIPLES

Most of what we know about Jesus occurred during his public ministry—probably the years A.D. 27 to 30—as reported in the Gospels. We know almost nothing about his life before he was baptized by John, other than that he grew up in Nazareth, a small town (of perhaps five hundred people in the first century) in the hills of Lower Galilee; that he had four half brothers—James, Joseph, Judas and Simon—and unnamed half sisters (Mark 6:3); and that his father's vocation was carpentry. The years between his birth in 6 or 5 B.C. and the beginning of his public ministry in A.D. 27 are referred to by scholars as Jesus' "hidden years."

JESUS' BAPTISM

The event that launched Jesus on his mission was his baptism by John the Baptist (or Baptizer), the last great Israelite prophet. John and Jesus were related through their mothers (Luke 1:36). John had disciples, and Andrew and Peter were John's disciples before they joined Jesus (John 1:35). John was killed early in Jesus' ministry by Herod Antipas (Mark 6:14–29) at Machaerus, east of the Dead Sea. He died for his outspoken criticism of Antipas's marriage to Herodias, the wife of his half brother, Herod Philip (not to be confused with Philip the Tetrarch). The marriage of Antipas to his sister-in-law was a violation of Mosaic Law (Lev. 20:21).

Malachi prophesied that Elijah, who was taken to heaven in "a chariot of fire" (2 Kings 2:11), would return to announce the coming of the Lord (Mal. 3:1; 4:5). Orthodox Jews still believe this. In the Gospels, John the Baptist is understood as the Elijah figure who announces Jesus as the Anointed One of God. In Matthew's gospel, Jesus says, referring to John, "He is Elijah who is to come" (Matt. 11:14). In Luke's gospel, Jesus refers to John as the one prophesied in Malachi (Luke 7:27). John the Baptist was not "Elijah-returned," that is, he was not the reincarnation of Elijah, as some who believe in reincarnation claim the Bible teaches (see John 1:21–23). Rather, he was the one sent to fulfill Elijah's mission to announce the coming of the Messiah.

John baptized Jesus in the Jordan River (see map on p. 300). When Jesus came up out of the water, "He saw the heavens torn apart and the Spirit descending like a dove on him. And a voice came from heaven, 'You are my Son, the Beloved; with you I am well pleased'" (Mark 1:10–11). The baptism accounts in the Gospels are very terse (only two verses in Luke: 3:21–22). The emphasis in the New Testament is not on the *beginning* of Jesus' public life, his baptism, but on the *end* and climax of his life—his death and resurrection.

Some have wondered why Jesus was baptized, because John's baptism was "a baptism of repentance for the forgiveness of sins" (Mark 1:4) and Jesus was sinless. There are several possible answers. One is that Jesus' baptism was his consecration by the Holy Spirit (Mark 1:10), which empowered him for his messianic ministry. Another is that Jesus' baptism for the forgiveness of sins was his first step in identifying with and bearing the sins of those for whom he came to give his life. Still another is that Jesus' baptism was a signal of the coming of the kingdom of God, which he came to proclaim (Mark 1:15).

JESUS' TESTING IN THE WILDERNESS

After his baptism in the Jordan, Jesus is led by the Spirit into the wilderness, where he is tempted (or tested) by Satan. The Gospels tell us that Jesus was tested for *forty* days, which is biblical shorthand for a long period of time. (Other examples of *forty* in the Bible are the forty days of rain during the flood, Moses' forty days on Mount Sinai, the spies' forty-day reconnaissance mission in Canaan, Israel's forty years in the wilderness, Elijah's forty-day trek to Horeb, and the forty days between Jesus' resurrection in Jerusalem and his ascension.) Jesus demonstrates in his testing his perfect obedience to the will of God and his superiority over Satan.

Inasmuch as Jesus was alone in the wilderness, the account of his testing must have been told to the disciples at a later date, along with other *personal* material in the Gospels (see Mark 4:34). Some have asked, Why did God allow Satan to tempt or test Jesus? The answer may be to let us identify with Jesus' *humanness,* as when the author of the letter to the Hebrews writes, "Because he himself [Jesus] was tested . . . he is able to help those who are being tested" (Heb. 2:18).

JESUS' DISCIPLES

The word *disciple* comes from a word denoting "learner"—so a disciple is a student or an apprentice. There were disciples in the Old Testament: Isaiah, for instance, had disciples (Isa. 8:16). But the term owes its popularity to the New Testament, where it often refers to one of "the Twelve." And among the Twelve, Peter, James and John have a special or unique relationship with Jesus (the "inner circle"): they are always first in the lists of the disciples, they go with Jesus to see Jairus's daughter, they are taken by Jesus up on the Mount of Transfiguration, and they are asked by Jesus to pray with him in the Garden of Gethsemane.

Jesus' disciples came from Galilee, with the possible exception of Judas Iscariot, who many scholars believe came from southern Judea. They were working men, probably middle class, and included two sets of brothers. Jesus chose his disciples from among his many followers—Luke mentions seventy (Luke 10:1)—which he appointed and commissioned to be the new "patriarchs" of Israel, which is the reason, some say, why the Twelve were men.

The names of the Twelve are set out in the Synoptic Gospels and in the book of Acts. *Simon Peter* is always listed first among the disciples. Simon was his Hebrew name; after his confession of Jesus as the Messiah at Caesarea Philippi, Jesus calls him Peter, from the Greek work *petra,* meaning "rock" (Matt. 16:18). Peter was married and he and his wife had a daughter, whose name comes down to us as Petronilla. Peter's wife accompanied him on his missionary journeys (1 Cor. 9:5); they both were martyred in Rome in the mid-60s. Peter is often the mouthpiece for the disciples, and two New Testament letters bear his name. According to the Catholic Church, Peter was the first bishop of Rome (reign: 30–67), a belief which has no support among non-Catholic scholars, and even prominent Catholic scholars such as Raymond Brown.

In John's gospel, the first disciple whom Jesus calls is *Andrew,* who then leads Peter to Christ (John 1:41–43). The two brothers were fishermen in Capernaum. Jesus calls them to "fish for people" (Mark 1:16–18). Andrew became the patron saint of Scotland in the year 750; he is also the patron saint of Russia.

The other set of brothers are *James* and *John* (in this order because James was the older of the two), the sons of Zebedee, who had a successful fishing business with boats and employees. Jesus gave them the name "sons of thunder" (Mark 3:17). James was beheaded in the year 44 by Herod Agrippa I (Acts 12:2). John was exiled to the Isle of Patmos in the 80s; he is believed to have died in Ephesus at the end of the first century. John is the author of the fourth gospel, three letters that bear the Johannine name (1 John, 2 John and 3 John) and the book of Revelation.

The other eight disciples are less prominent in the Gospels. They are as follows: *Philip,* who is mentioned three times in John's gospel. *Bartholomew,* who most scholars believe is Nathanael in John's gospel (John 1:45–51). *Matthew,* also called Levi, the tax collector, the author of the first gospel in the New Testament canon. *Thomas* Didymus (the "twin"), commonly called "doubting Thomas" because he refused to believe in Jesus' resurrection until he saw and felt Jesus' scars (John 20:24–28). According to legend, Thomas took the gospel to India, where he was martyred. *Thaddaeus,* who some believe is "Judas son of James" in Luke 6:16 and Acts 1:13. *James,* the son of Alphaeus, about whom nothing is known. *Simon the Zealot* (which may mean that he was once a Zealot). And *Judas Iscariot* (possibly meaning "from Kerioth" in Judea), the only disciple with a second name (to distinguish him from several other Judases in the Bible), the treasurer of the disciples (John 12:5–6), who betrayed Jesus, after which he hanged himself (Matt. 27:3–5).

JESUS' PUBLIC MINISTRY

Jesus' public ministry is sometimes divided into three periods. First, the period of *obscurity*—Jesus' baptism in the Jordan, his testing in the wilderness and calling the Twelve to be his disciples. Second, the period of *popularity*—Jesus' healing the sick, performing great miracles and preaching and teaching "with authority." Third, the period of *opposition*—Jesus' challenges to the religious authorities, especially in Jerusalem (chasing the money changers out of the temple), resulting in his arrest and crucifixion.

JESUS' MISSION

What was the mission or "work" of Jesus? That is, what did Jesus come to do?

- First, he came to *reveal* God, who is beyond human comprehension. In John's gospel, Jesus says, "The Father and I are one" (10:30) and "Whoever has seen me has seen the Father" (14:9). The writer of the letter to the Hebrews says that Jesus is "the exact imprint of God's very being" (Heb. 1:3). So Jesus came to reveal God; he came as "the image of the invisible God" (Col. 1:15); he came as the "human face" of God; he came to speak for God (Heb. 1:2).
- Second, he came to *redeem* humankind through his faithful life and saving death, which was prophesied by Isaiah, who said "the righteous one, my servant" would bear "the sin of many [and be made an] intercession for the transgressors" (Isa. 53:11–12). Jesus said that the words of Isaiah would be fulfilled in him (Luke 22:37), the "suffering servant" who came to die for—to atone for—our transgressions against God's commandments to love him and to love one another. Judas's betrayal of Jesus

to the ruling authorities, which led to his crucifixion, set in motion God's plan of salvation. Jesus' death was not a meaningless tragedy; it was the capstone in God's plan to redeem humankind.

JESUS' DEATH

Why was Jesus killed? This is a two-part question. *First,* why did Jesus go to Jerusalem, knowing that he would be killed there (see Mark 10:32–34)? Jesus went to Jerusalem to die a one-time-forever sacrificial death for the sins of the world (Heb. 10:1–18). If Jesus had not died sacrificially—for instance, if he had died of old age—he would not have "died for our sins." Jesus went to Jerusalem to fulfill his mission.

Second, why, shortly after he arrived in Jerusalem, did the authorities put him to death? That is, why did the Sadducees want him killed? And why did Pontius Pilate, knowing that he was innocent (Luke 23:13–15), have him crucified?

The Sadducees. The Sadducees were the keepers of the status quo. They were afraid that Jesus' preaching and actions might incite a riot that would bring a swift, brutal response from Rome, so Jesus had to be dealt with. (The Christian writer Frederick Buechner, paraphrasing John 11:49–50, said that Caiaphas, the chief priest, decided "it would be better for one man to get it in the neck for the sake of many than for many to get it in the neck for the sake of one man.") The Sadducees' concern was based on the Jews' opposition to Roman rule; on the upcoming Passover festival, which celebrated Israel's deliverance from foreign rule, and the belief and hope that the Messiah would appear during Passover; on Jesus' popularity and his coming from Galilee, an area seething with anti-Roman feeling; and Jerusalem being swollen to overflowing with a multitude of pilgrims and others (estimates range as high as two hundred thousand) who had come to Jerusalem to celebrate Passover.

Did the Sadducees have reason to be concerned? Yes, because the Roman army's mission was to quash all disturbances. (In the Jewish uprising in A.D. 66, Rome destroyed the temple and killed thousands of priests and others.)

Pontius Pilate. Why did Pilate allow the innocent Jesus to be crucified? Pilate had already offended the Jews by erecting Roman emblems ("graven images") of Emperor Tiberius in Jerusalem and by diverting funds from the temple treasury to build an aqueduct. And when the Jews were seriously offended, they went to Rome and complained, and they threatened to do the same again if Pilate did not hand Jesus over to be crucified: "If you release this man, you are no friend of the emperor" (John 19:12).

Did Pilate have reason to be concerned? Yes, because a Jewish delegation had been successful in having Archelaus removed in A.D. 6. (In the year 36, after ordering his soldiers to attack a crowd of defenseless Samaritans at Mount Gerizim, Pilate himself was removed from office.) We have a very negative image of Pilate—"crucified under Pontius Pilate"—but there is a legend that Pilate and his wife later became Christians, and the Egyptian Orthodox Church reveres them as martyrs.

JESUS' ARREST, TRIALS, CRUCIFIXION, DEATH, BURIAL, RESURRECTION AND ASCENSION

Jesus' public life ends with his *passion,* a word that has changed in meaning over the centuries. In the New Testament sense it means "suffering." It was first applied to Jesus' suffering on the cross, then took on a broader meaning to include Jesus' agony beginning in the Garden of Gethsemane and ending with his death on the cross. The passion narrative is included in all four gospels, and is the longest self-contained segment in each of the Gospels.

JESUS' FINAL WEEK

There are large gaps in the Jesus story, but in the final week we get a day-by-day, then an hour-by-hour, account.

- Palm Sunday: Jesus' entry into Jerusalem on the colt of a donkey (Zech. 9:9b), with people waving palm branches (John 12:13) and crying "Hosanna!" (Palm branches were symbols of victory; *Hosanna* means "Lord, save us.")
- Monday: Jesus overturns the money changers' tables and drives the merchants out of the temple.

- Tuesday: The Pharisees and others ask Jesus about his "authority"; whether or not Jews should pay taxes to Caesar; marriage in heaven; and which of the commandments is the most important.
- Wednesday: The plot against Jesus.
- Maundy Thursday: The Last Supper, the Garden of Gethsemane and Jesus' arrest and indictment.
- Good Friday: The Jewish and Roman "trials" and Jesus' scourging, crucifixion, death and burial.
- Holy Saturday: Jesus in the tomb.
- Easter Sunday: Resurrection Day (the Lord's Day). Christ is risen! He is risen indeed!

THE EVENTS OF JESUS' FINAL WEEK

The following are some events in the last days of Jesus' life, which for Christians are the most important days in the history of the world.

The Last Supper. According to tradition, the Last Supper—so called because it was Jesus' last meal with his disciples—took place in an "upper room" at Mary's house (Mary, the mother of Mark) on what is now called Maundy Thursday. The word *maundy* comes from the Latin *mandatum,* meaning "mandate" or "command," because Jesus gave his disciples "a new commandment, that you love one another . . . as I have loved you" (John 13:34). The earliest account of Jesus' Last Supper appears in Paul's first letter to the Corinthians (11:23–25). At this meal, Jesus instituted the new covenant. When we eat the bread and drink the wine (or grape juice), we remember and reaffirm this covenant.

Judas's Betrayal. Judas betrayed Jesus by leading the Jewish authorities to him in the Garden of Gethsemane. (Judas knew where to find Jesus at night and could lead the guards to him without attracting public attention.) The gospel writers indicate that Judas was driven by Satan to betray Jesus and that he was given money for doing so (Luke 4:13; 22:3–5).

Peter's Denials. Jesus predicted that Peter would deny him, which he did. This incident highlights the honesty of the gospel accounts because Peter was highly regarded in the early church. Jesus returned to Peter after his resurrection and "reinstated" him, summoning him to "feed my sheep" (John 21:15–19).

Jesus' Arrest and Jewish Trial. On Thursday evening, in the Garden of Gethsemane, Jesus was arrested by the temple guards. He was formally charged by the Sanhedrin (from a Greek word meaning "council"), the seventy-member Jewish ruling body (Num. 11:16), plus the chief priest, which had authority over religious matters. On Friday morning Jesus was tried and found guilty of blasphemy, a grave offense in which the name or essence of God is cursed or reviled. Jesus' blasphemy was not that he claimed to be the Messiah—many claimed to be such, both before and after Jesus—but that he claimed to be divine, by saying, "You will see the Son of Man seated at the right hand of the Power, and coming with the clouds of heaven" (Mark 14:62).

Jesus' Roman Trial. Rome denied capital punishment powers to local authorities throughout the empire (see John 18:31b), so the Jews took Jesus to Pontius Pilate, the Roman governor, who resided at Antonia Fortress in Jerusalem during Passover Week to keep peace and order. (As mentioned above, Passover was a celebration of the liberation of Israel from foreign rule, dating back to the Exodus.) Pilate gave in to the leaders of the Sanhedrin and sentenced Jesus to death as a political revolutionary. This was a trumped-up charge because the Sanhedrin's guilty verdict on the grounds of blasphemy would not have warranted Roman execution.

Jesus' Crucifixion. Jesus' death sentence was crucifixion, the cruelest and most shameful method of capital punishment. Roman citizens could be crucified only for high treason, which is why, according to tradition, Paul, who was a citizen, was beheaded. (Crucifixion, because of its inhuman cruelty, was abolished by Emperor Constantine in 316.)

Crucifixion was usually preceded by flogging or scourging with whips containing bones and metal in the lashes. This was done to weaken the victim's resistance and shorten the time it would take him to die. The accused was then made to carry his crossbeam to the spot of execution, which for Jesus was the "Place of the Skull" (*Golgotha* in Greek, *Calvary* in Latin), so called either because the area was shaped like a skull or because it was a place of execution. When Jesus fell en route, Simon of Cyrene (an ancient city in present-day Libya) was forced by the Roman soldiers to carry Jesus' beam the rest of the way.

Crosses were put in a public place, with a sign or notice of the accused's crime as a warning to others. Jesus' sign read: "The King of the Jews" (Mark 15:26), implying that Jesus claimed to be a king who opposed the emperor. The victim was then stripped naked (humiliated) and nailed or bound to the cross to prevent any movement. Death was by asphyxiation and was slow and agonizing; some lived and suffered for days. The final disgrace came at the end: the body of the deceased was left to birds of prey, who often picked it clean.

Jesus' Death and Burial. Most scholars believe that Jesus died on April 7 in the year 30. According to Mark, Jesus was crucified at 9:00 A.M. (Mark 15:25) and remained on the cross until 3:00 P.M. (Mark 15:33). The Gospels report that Jesus' disciples and closest friends abandoned him, except for his mother and a few other women and John. After Jesus died, Joseph of Arimathea (a town northwest of Jerusalem), a member of the Sanhedrin and "a disciple of Jesus" (Matt. 27:57), placed him in his family tomb. Some women followed Joseph so they would know where to go on Sunday (Easter) morning to anoint Jesus' body with oils and spices for burial (Luke 23:55–24:1).

Jesus' Resurrection. On the third day Jesus was raised from the dead. There are several accounts of Jesus' resurrection appearances in the New Testament, but there is no uniformity with regard to sequence, place or names and numbers of people. If the four Resurrection accounts were exactly the same, we should be suspicious, not convinced, as we would be if the testimonies of four witnesses in a murder trial were identical in all respects.

An illustration of different accounts of the same event occurs in two different stories of Hannibal crossing the Alps—one by the Greek historian Polybius, the other by the Roman historian Livy—which New Testament scholar Bruce Metzger says "can by no stretch of the imagination be harmonized, yet no one doubts that Hannibal most certainly arrived in Italy. . . . Discrepancies in the accounts of Jesus' resurrection cannot be used to prove that the resurrection did not take place" (*The New Testament: Its Background, Growth, and Content*).

The Resurrection accounts are written as *fact*—as something that actually happened—not as theology. And they emphasize the element of surprise: no one expected what happened on Easter morning, even though Jesus had said that he would be raised on the third day (see Mark 8:31). And they struggle to describe Jesus' risen body, which was clearly a body, with wounds that could be felt . . . but somehow transformed: Jesus was not immediately recognized; his body was physical but it could pass through doors; and he was able to eat and drink as he did before his crucifixion. According to Frederick Buechner, "Unless something very real took place on that strange, confused morning, there would be no New Testament, no church and no Christianity" (*The Magnificent Defeat*).

Jesus' Ascension. After forty days, Jesus was "taken up . . . into heaven" (Acts 1:11). Jesus' ascension ended his earthly life. Jesus' ascension is mentioned by Luke at the end of his gospel (24:50–51) and at the beginning of the Acts of the Apostles (1:9–11). It is also mentioned in Mark's "longer ending" (see next chapter) and is alluded to by John in verses such as 20:17 ("ascended . . . ascending"). Although the word *ascend* means "to rise," Jesus' ascension is not meant to be understood as if heaven were a *place* in space and time. It is meant to be understood as Jesus' coming into the presence of God, and being seated "at the right hand of God" (Rom. 8:34), where he now reigns over all things.

JESUS' NAMES, TITLES AND SYMBOLS

THE NAMES AND TITLES OF JESUS

We often think of *Christ* as Jesus' surname or second name, but this is a title, not a name. In the ancient world there were no surnames. People were named with their father's name or by geography (Joseph of Arimathea) or by their vocation. Jesus' name would have been *Jesus bar Joseph,* meaning "Jesus, son of Joseph." Altogether there are some fifty names or titles for Jesus in the New Testament, among them *Savior, Son of the Most High, Immanuel* ("God with us"), *Lord, Master* (a title of respect), *Teacher, Rabbi, Son of David* (a messianic title), the *Galilean,* the *Nazarene,* the *Carpenter,* the *Prophet,* the *Lamb,* the *Word,* the *Lion of Judah,* the *Great High Priest* and the *Alpha and the Omega.* The three most common titles are the following:

Messiah. The title *Messiah* comes from the Hebrew word *mashiah,* meaning "one who has been anointed." Israel's expectation was that the Messiah—the Anointed of God—would come from the House of David and would, like David, lead Israel in the defeat of its enemies. The Greek word for Messiah is *Christos,* thus the English "Christ." Because of the word's political connotation, Jesus himself seldom used the title *Messiah.* He came as a suffering servant to redeem humankind, not as a military leader to win a victory for Israel over Rome. Following his resurrection he is called *Jesus Christ* or *Christ Jesus,* combining his name and his title. Paul merges the person and work of Jesus into one term when he refers to Jesus as *Christ* or *the Christ,* as when he says "we proclaim Christ crucified" (1 Cor. 1:23).

Son of Man. The term *Son of Man* is used by Jesus in referring to himself, as when he says, "The Son of Man came . . . to give his life" (Mark 10:45) and "The Son of Man [must be] lifted up" (John 3:14). Interestingly, no one else uses this term to refer to Jesus, that is, no one says, "There is the Son of Man." Why did Jesus use this phrase to describe himself? Perhaps because it had no known or precise meaning, as did the term Messiah. Or perhaps because of the use of the term in Daniel 7:13–14, where the prophet speaks about "a son of man, coming with the clouds of heaven" (NIV) whose kingdom would have no end (see Mark 14:62), which many Jews interpreted as messianic.

Son of God. The term *Son of God* is used in the Gospels to express Jesus' unique relationship to God and his true identity: "Whoever has seen me has seen the Father" (John 14:9). This term did not require any special knowledge for Gentile readers, as did Messiah. The term Son of God is the title or designation used by the early church in referring to Jesus in the Apostles' and Nicene Creeds.

SYMBOLS FOR JESUS

The most sacred and universal Christian symbol is the cross, which symbolizes Jesus' sacrifice for our sins and his victory over death. Crosses with Jesus hanging from the crossbeam—which symbolize his sacrificial death (universal in Roman Catholic churches)—are called *crucifixes,* from the Latin word for "crucify." Crosses in most Protestant churches are without the figure of Jesus, symbolizing his resurrection and triumph over death.

Other symbols that we often see in Christian churches, and also in Christian art, are the following:

- **INRI** are the first letters of the four words Pontius Pilate inscribed on the plaque over Jesus' head on the cross in John's gospel (John 19:19), confirming his execution as a political rebel or revolutionary. The words in Latin are *Iesus Nazarenus Rex Iudaeorum* and in English "Jesus of Nazareth, King of the Jews" (in Latin and Greek, there is no letter "J"). This abbreviation is often used in Christian art depicting Jesus on the cross.

- X and P are the first two letters—*Chi* (X) and *Rho* (P)—of the Greek name for Christ (*Christos*), which became a monogram (a design composed of one or more letters or initials of a name) for Christ. These letters allegedly appeared to Constantine, the first Christian emperor of the Roman Empire, in a vision before his victory at the Milvian Bridge in Rome in 312 (see chapter 6). The two letters are often superimposed, with the P coming between the upper arms of the X.

- **IHS** are the first three letters of the name of Jesus in Greek—I (iota), H (eta) and Σ (sigma). This monogram often occurs in Christian art and on church banners and vestments and is the emblem of the Jesuits, the Society of Jesus.

- A and Ω are the first and last letters of the Greek alphabet. They refer to Jesus, who in the book of Revelation calls himself "The *Alpha* and the *Omega* . . . who is and who was and who is to come" (1:8); and later in the book as "The first and the last, the beginning and the end" (22:13).

- IXΘYE is a word made from the first letters of the words *Jesus Christ, God's Son* (and our) *Savior* ("Iesous Christos Theou Uios Soter"), pronounced "ickthoos." The letters spell the Greek word *fish*, which became and is still a popular Christian symbol.

CHAPTER 4

THE GOSPELS

In Jesus the promise is confirmed,

the covenant is renewed,

the prophecies are fulfilled,

salvation is brought near,

sacred history has reached its climax,

the perfect sacrifice has been offered and accepted,

the great priest over the household of God

has taken his seat at God's right hand,

the prophet like Moses has been raised up,

the Son of David reigns,

the kingdom of God has been inaugurated,

the Son of Man has received dominion from

the Ancient of Days,

the Servant of the Lord, having been smitten to death

for his people's transgressions and borne the sin of many,

has accomplished the divine purpose,

has seen light after the travail of his soul,

and is now exalted and extolled and made very high.

F. F. BRUCE
The New Testament Development of Old Testament Themes

THE GOSPEL TESTIMONIES TO JESUS

In chapter 3 we looked at the first-century Greco-Roman-Jewish world and the high points in Jesus' life, especially the last week of his life. In this chapter we will look at the recorded testimonies to the person and work of Jesus. To see and understand how Mark, Matthew, Luke and John crafted their narratives—which are both similar and different—we will look at each gospel's structure, audience and message, and then offer a side-by-side comparison of the Gospels. Also, we will look at unique features in each gospel: Jesus' miracles in Mark, which play a larger part in his gospel than in the other three; Jesus' Sermon on the Mount in Matthew, which is found only in Matthew; Jesus' parables in Luke, which are more numerous and better known than those in the other gospels; and Jesus' "I am" sayings in John, which are unique to the fourth gospel.

THE GOSPELS: THE "GOOD NEWS"

After Jesus' resurrection and ascension, stories of and about Jesus—who he was and what he came to do—were written down and organized into books. They were written so that readers and hearers of the Gospels would "know the truth" concerning Jesus (Luke 1:4) and "have life in his name" (John 20:31).

WHAT IS A "GOSPEL"?

The word *gospel* comes from the Old English word *godspel*—"God's [good] story"—which derives from the Greek word *euangelion*, a compound composed of the adjective *eu*, meaning "good" (as in eulogy, euphemism and euphoria), and *angelion*, meaning "message" or "news." In the New Testament, the gospel or good news is that the Son of God died that we might not perish but have eternal life (John 3:16). From the second century on, the word *gospel* has also been applied to the first four books of the New Testament—the books *containing* the good news.

Many people read the Gospels as biographies. Though they contain biographical material, they are not biographies, at least not in the modern sense, because they are anonymous, they cover only 10 percent of Jesus' life (his last three years or so), and they provide little information about Jesus' family, his growing-up years or his physical appearance, though he would have been much more Middle Eastern looking than the fair-skinned, blue-eyed Jesus we are used to seeing in Western religious art. The Gospels' primary concern is not with the *facts* of Jesus' life—so we should not be surprised by occasional differences—but with the *meaning* of his life.

THE DATING AND WRITING OF THE GOSPELS

It is often thought that the Gospels were the first Christian books to be written, because they appear first in the New Testament. As we saw in chapter 1, however, the letters of Paul, which were written during and after his missionary journeys (c. 50–64), predate all four of the Gospels. It is believed that Mark was the first gospel to be written (65–70), followed by Matthew and Luke (mid-80s), and finally John (mid-90s). A minority view is that all four gospels were written before 70 because they fail to mention the destruction of the temple in Jerusalem in the year 70 (see Luke 21:5–6).

The stories about Jesus were transmitted, initially, in oral form. The move from oral to written stories—the Gospels—occurred because of the need for a written account of Jesus' life (his followers were dying). The intention of the gospel writers was not to write historical accounts of the life of Jesus, but to present their understanding of the person and work of Jesus for their audiences.

Also, the Gospels were written to answer a number of questions in the first-century world; two of the most important were the following:

- If Jesus was the Messiah, why did the Jews not recognize and accept him as such? *Answer:* Most Jews were looking for a king to lead Israel in the overthrow of Rome, not a suffering servant.
- If Jesus was the Son of God, why was he crucified as a common criminal on a cross? *Answer:* God sent his Son to die a public sacrificial death for the sake of the world.

THE GOSPEL AUDIENCES

We read the Gospels as we do other written works. In the first century, however, which had a literacy rate of only 2 or 3 percent, the Gospels were read aloud rather than privately. To help listeners follow their narratives, the writers used repetition, especially triads—repeating ideas and themes three times—which are found throughout the Gospels. Also, though each gospel has a primary audience (as we will see), they were read by Christians throughout the Mediterranean world, as Luke implies in his preface. Further, we are used to hearing the Gospels read in church. There were no churches, as such, until the third century. At the outset, the Gospels were read aloud in house groups.

THE AUTHORSHIP OF THE GOSPELS

It is assumed that because the Gospels are named—"The Gospel According to . . ."—that we know who wrote them. The Gospels, however, are anonymous; that is, the authors did not add their names to their writings as Paul and others did to their letters. The fact that the writers did not autograph their works, however, does not mean that we have no idea who wrote them. They were "named" very early to differentiate them one from another and for liturgical reading. Further, according to British scholar R. T. France, "There is no evidence that any of the Gospels ever existed [without their present names], nor is there any variation in the names of those to whom they are attributed," so there is no reason to quarrel with the naming. Further, the truth and authority of the Gospels does not depend on knowing with absolute certainty who wrote them but, as with other books in the Bible, their inclusion in the canon.

THE STRUCTURE OF THE GOSPELS

Each of the Gospels has a twofold structure. The first half has to do with Jesus' public ministry—his sermons, parables, discourses and teachings to the crowds, which are interspersed with healings and miracles to authenticate his message (validating the message through the messenger). The second half has to do with Jesus' disciples—his teaching that the way of salvation is through the Cross (Mark 10:45), followed by his arrest, trials, beatings and crucifixion, and then his resurrection to again confirm his message. The writers of the Gospels were very sophisticated in developing and structuring their narratives, as we will see when we look at the individual gospels.

WHY ARE THERE FOUR GOSPELS?

Why are there four gospels—or we might ask, why are there *only* four gospels, because there were "gospels" other than those we have in the New Testament (some two dozen in all), such as the gospel of Peter, the gospel of Thomas, the gospel of Nicodemus and the gospel of Philip. With regard to this question, the gospels that did not make it into the New Testament were judged by the early church not to have been written by an apostle of Jesus, or someone closely associated with an apostle (like Mark and Luke), and did not enjoy church-wide acceptance and usage.

With regard to why there are four gospels and not one, the early church fathers believed that each of the four testimonies was an authentic, distinctive, valuable witness to Jesus and that our understanding of him would be richer and deeper with all four rather than only one, or with a harmonized, composite gospel such as Tatian's *Diatessaron* ("fourfold"), which appeared in the latter half of the second century (c. 170).

If the Gospels are written testimonies to Jesus, why are they different? The reason they *seem* different is that the authors were writing to different communities or audiences and each chose to emphasize, in shaping his narrative, different aspects of the Jesus story. Mark wrote to Christians suffering persecution in Rome; Matthew wrote to Jewish Christians that Jesus was the long-awaited Messiah; Luke wrote to Gentile Christians that Jesus was the Savior of the world; John wrote a theological reflection on the meaning of the One in whom "the Word became flesh."

SYMBOLS FOR THE GOSPELS

The four gospels have been represented by symbols, though more so in earlier times than today. The symbols are as follows (see Ezek. 1:10):

- Matthew is represented by a *man,* symbolizing Jesus' humanness, because his gospel begins with the human ancestry of Jesus.
- Mark is represented by a *lion,* which lives in the wilderness, because his gospel opens with "the voice of one crying in the wilderness." The lion symbolizes Jesus' mighty power.
- Luke is represented by an *ox,* a sacrificial animal symbolizing Jesus' sacrificial death, because his gospel starts with Zechariah entering the

temple to burn incense before the daily sacrifices.

- John is represented by an *eagle,* a bird that can soar higher than any other bird, because the first words in his gospel are "In the beginning," meaning "In the heavens," which symbolizes Jesus' divinity.

THE HISTORICAL JESUS

Two final matters concerning the Gospels have to do with the *historical* Jesus. The first has to do with the historicity of Jesus: Did such a person ever live? The second has to do with the gospel accounts of Jesus: Do they present a true and accurate witness to the Jesus of history? The first question has been put to rest because no serious scholar doubts the historical existence of Jesus. The second question is more troublesome because the Gospels present different portraits of Jesus. Biblical scholars in the mid–1800s began to view the Gospels as collections of fictitious stories. The decades that followed saw an obsessive quest to find the *real* Jesus, which many thought could be done by stripping away the supernatural aspects of the gospel stories. This movement came to an end with the publication of Albert Schweitzer's classic study, *The Quest of the Historical Jesus* (1906). Schweitzer's conclusion, after reading more than sixty "lives" of Jesus, was that "he comes to us as one unknown."

In the early 1950s, the pendulum swung back to a more positive view of Jesus (the New Quest) and to the view that much more could be known about Jesus than was previously suspected. In the late 1970s, a further quest began, called the Third Quest by British scholar and now Bishop of Durham N. T. (Tom) Wright. Scholars such as Wright take seriously the Jesus we find in the Gospels (which the first two quests did not) and ask: If Jesus was a mere teacher and healer, as some claim, how are we to account for the fact that within a generation of his death there were large, thriving, culturally diverse communities of believers (in Jesus' saving death and resurrection) throughout the Roman Empire?

In the 1980s a new challenge surfaced from the Jesus Seminar, a small group of liberal scholars organized in 1985 to debate the historicity of the words and acts of Jesus in the Gospels. The Jesus Seminar errs in reading the Gospels as if their authors intended them to be read as historical biographies. The Gospels are not "histories." They are carefully crafted theological narratives written to present each writer's understanding of the person and (saving) work of Jesus for his readers and audience.

The Jesus Seminar, using its own in-house rules of historiography, believes that only 18 percent of the *words* and 16 percent of the *acts* of Jesus are authentic. This is contrary to the widely held belief that people in Jesus' day had exceptional memories, which was how information was passed along. Also, important details in the Gospels have been confirmed by careful research. These facts, and the Bible being the inspired Word of God, give us good reason to be confident that the Gospels are true, reliable testimonies to the public life and ministry of Jesus.

THE SYNOPTIC GOSPELS

Since the late nineteenth century, Matthew, Mark and Luke have been called the Synoptic Gospels. The word *synoptic* comes from *syn* ("with" or "together") and *optos* ("seeing," as in *optic*), meaning that these three gospels see things in much the same way.

THE PRIORITY OF MARK

Most scholars believe that Mark was the first gospel to be written. The reasons for this are as follows.

- First, Matthew and Luke *include* much of Mark's material in their own gospels: more than 90 percent of Mark appears in Matthew and more than 50 percent appears in Luke. Also, they *follow* Mark's "story line," whereas in their handling of common non-Markan stories and sayings, referred to by scholars as "Q" (next section), they often disagree with one another in their placement of the texts.
- Second, if Mark was first, it is easy to see why Matthew and Luke were written; but if Matthew and Luke were first, it is hard to see why Mark was needed: Mark has no birth narrative, his "shorter ending" includes no resurrection appearances, and he has no Sermon on the Mount or Sermon on the Plain and very few parables.
- Third, Matthew and Luke are more *systematic* than Mark in telling their story; they are more *polished* than Mark—they smooth Mark's grammar and his choppiness, they soften his statements about the disciples and

their failure to understand Jesus, and they clarify difficult passages; and they speak more *reverently* of Jesus—all of which argues for Mark coming before Matthew and Luke, rather than the other way around.

THE FORMATION OF THE SYNOPTIC GOSPELS

Mark and Peter were together in Rome at the end of Peter's life (1 Peter 5:13). According to tradition, Mark's gospel is based on Peter's recollections of his years with Jesus, which Mark organized into what became the first gospel. Later, Matthew and Luke, using Mark as a source document, wrote their own gospels. Today we might call this plagiarism. In the ancient world, where there were no copyright laws or controls, the use of other people's writings was a normal, accepted practice.

In addition to Mark's gospel, it is believed that Matthew and Luke had in their possession another source, referred to by scholars as "Q" for the German word *quelle,* meaning "source," though no Q document, if it ever did exist, has been found. The rationale for a Q hypothesis is that Matthew and Luke contain *in common* some 230 verses not found in Mark. Finally, Matthew and Luke had materials that each gleaned independently of the other. Some examples are their different birth narratives, the different details in Matthew's Sermon on the Mount (Matt. 5–7) and Luke's Sermon on the Plain (Luke 6), and their use of different parables. Scholars refer to Matthew's special or unique materials as "M" (some 300 verses) and Luke's as "L" (some 500 verses).

If Mark was the first gospel to be written, as most scholars now believe, it was the first of a new literary genre—the pulling together of sermons, stories and other materials to tell the good news in story form. To Mark we owe an enormous debt of gratitude. Without his gospel, and the other three that followed, we would know almost nothing about Jesus' birth, his parables and teachings, his healings and miracles, his passion and crucifixion, his resurrection appearances and final instructions, and his promise of eternal and everlasting life. Some have called Mark's gospel the "single most important book ever written."

THE KINGDOM OF GOD

In the Synoptic Gospels, Jesus' principal teaching has to do with the *kingdom of God,* which is mentioned some fifty times in the first three gospels and hardly at all in John. What is the kingdom of God? Strange as it might seem, Jesus never explains the term. Stranger still, he uses the term in several different ways: "The kingdom of God has come *near*" (Mark 1:15), "The kingdom of God is *among you*" (Luke 17:21), "There are some standing here who will not taste death *until* they see that the kingdom of God has come with power" (Mark 9:1).

The kingdom of God does not mean a *kingdom*—that is, a geographical place, like the United Kingdom—but *kingship,* as in the kingly rule or reign of God. It is a spiritual concept, not a political one. Is the kingdom here, or is it coming in the future? And how does one enter the kingdom?

As to the first question, Jesus came to inaugurate the kingdom; the "kingly rule" of God will come when Jesus returns. So the kingdom of God has two dimensions: it is *already* (among us) and *not yet* ("thy kingdom come"). As to the second question, one enters the kingdom by repenting and believing the good news (Mark 1:15); and being in the kingdom is so important that one should sell all that he or she has to obtain (enter) the kingdom (Matt. 13:44–46). A final question has to do with the church: Is the church the kingdom of God on earth? No, it is the witness to the future *coming* of the kingdom.

The New Testament scholar Oscar Cullmann said that Jesus' first coming was like D Day—the day the Allied Forces landed at Normandy in June 1944, which signaled the beginning of the end of the war in Europe. Jesus' second coming will be V Day—the day when he comes in power and glory to reign over his kingdom. As Christians, we know that the decisive day has come (D Day). The only uncertainty is the date of the final victory (V Day), as it was when the Allied Forces first landed in France.

MARK: THE FOUNDATION GOSPEL

Mark's gospel was long neglected because of its alleged incompleteness, and because many, beginning with Augustine in the late fourth century, thought it was a summary of Matthew. Today the opposite is the case because it is now believed that Mark was the first gospel—the first attempt to put the oral stories about Jesus into a written narrative—and because it was a source document for Matthew and Luke.

According to church tradition, Mark's gospel was written from Rome, most likely in the years immediately following Peter's death in the mid–60s. It is the shortest gospel, with only 661 verses; it is mostly narrative, with very few teachings; and it is the most lively and action-oriented of the Gospels. Also, Mark has two endings: a "shorter ending," which stops at verse 16:8—the oldest manuscripts, the codices *Sinaiticus* and *Vaticanus,* end at 16:8—and a "longer ending" (16:9–20) that was added later to complete Mark's sudden ending, which contains no resurrection appearances (most Bibles have a line between 16:8 and 16:9).

Mark's gospel has a short prologue—Jesus' baptism and testing—and then a three-part structure: Jesus' ministry in *Galilee* (1:14–7:23), Jesus' *journey* to Jerusalem (7:24–10:52), and Jesus' final week in *Jerusalem* (11:1–16:8/20). Matthew and Luke generally follow Mark's outline, but modify it for purposes of their own story. Jesus' journey to Jerusalem in Luke, for instance, is ten chapters long—from 9:51 to 19:27.

JOHN MARK

As noted earlier, none of the Gospels has a "signature." According to Papias, the bishop of Hierapolis, "Mark became Peter's interpreter and wrote down accurately all that he remembered of the things said and done by the Lord, but not, however, in order" (the graphic details in Mark's gospel suggest an eyewitness source). There is no reason to suppose that Mark did not write the gospel that bears his name, because it is unlikely that it would have been attributed to someone who was neither a disciple nor an apostle unless he was, in fact, the author.

According to tradition, then, the author of the first gospel was Mark, also called John Mark (Acts 12:12, 25), John being his Hebrew name and Mark or Marcus his Greco-Roman name. He was the son of Mary, a widow of some means who lived in Jerusalem, whose house was a center for the early church in Jerusalem (Acts 12:12). If Mary's house was the location of the Last Supper, Mark could have followed Jesus and the disciples into the Garden of Gethsemane and may have been the "young man" in the garden in Mark 14:51–52. (Some think that each gospel has a "secret autograph" and see these two verses, which have nothing to do with Mark's "arrest narrative," as his autograph; others consider such views to be silly speculation.)

Mark was the cousin of Barnabas (Col. 4:10), and together they accompanied the apostle Paul on Paul's first missionary journey in the late 40s. For some reason, at Perga, Mark "left them and returned to Jerusalem" (Acts 13:13). Mark and Paul were later reconciled (see 2 Tim. 4:11). Mark is thought to have founded the church in Egypt and died in Alexandria. According to legend, in the year 829 Venetian merchants smuggled Mark's bones out of Egypt and brought them to Venice and buried them in San Marcos Square.

Mark was with Peter in Rome, and his gospel has a definite *Petrine* focus: Peter is the first disciple to be called, he is listed first among the disciples, he is mentioned more often and more prominently than the other disciples, and he is the one who "confesses" Jesus as the Messiah. Mark, though, must have had sources other than Peter; and even if Peter was a source, it was Mark, not Peter, who organized the "Jesus Story" into its present format.

MARK'S STRUCTURE, AUDIENCE AND MESSAGE

Mark's gospel is more concerned with theological order than with chronological order: the Cross is ever before his eyes. The German theologian Martin Kähler called Mark's gospel "a passion narrative with an extended introduction."

Structure. Mark is in a hurry to get his message across, as if writing a revolutionary tract for people in the catacombs and on the run, as can be seen in his frequent use of the word "immediately" (some forty times)—immediately Jesus did this, then immediately Jesus did that, and then immediately he did something else. The opening line in Mark's gospel proclaims Jesus to be "the Son of God," which is repeated three times to an ever-expanding audience. At his baptism, the heavens open up and God's voice says to Jesus, "You are my Son" (1:11). In the middle of the story, three disciples go with Jesus up on the Mount of Transfiguration and hear for themselves God say, "This is my Son" (9:7). At the end of the story, at the foot of the cross, a Roman centurion declares for all to hear, "Truly this man was God's Son" (15:39).

Jesus is the one prophesied by Isaiah to call Israel to repent and believe the good news. In the first half of Mark's gospel, Jesus preaches throughout

Galilee and performs miracles to show his divine power: healing the blind, feeding the multitudes, raising Jairus's daughter from the dead. In the second half Jesus tells his disciples that he did not come to be served but "to give his life as a ransom for many" (10:45), an important foundation verse for the doctrine of *substitutionary* ("for us") *atonement*. Jesus said this "good news must be proclaimed to all nations" (13:10), meaning "to all peoples." The hinge on which Mark's gospel turns is Peter's confession of Jesus as the Messiah (8:27–30).

Audience. Mark's readers, it seems, are Gentile Christians. There is no Jewish genealogy; there are very few Old Testament references; Jewish words and customs are explained (see 7:3–4); and it is a Gentile, a Roman centurion at the foot of the cross, who declares Jesus to be God's Son (15:39).

Message. Mark's readers were probably wondering whether Jesus was good news or a false hope. Jesus' forerunner, John the Baptist, had been beheaded; Jesus himself had been crucified; two of the church's leading figures and greatest heroes, Peter and Paul, had just been martyred; and the persecution of Christians in Rome, as scapegoats for the burning of Rome, was on the increase. Mark writes to strengthen the courage and faith of his readers. He tells them that hoping in Jesus is a real hope, just as it was for Jesus' disciples when he assured them that if they lost their lives "for my sake" they would be saved (8:35).

JESUS' MIRACLES

An important feature of Mark's gospel is the passion narrative, which had circulated in oral form long before he wrote it down. Another feature is Mark's use of miracle stories: one-third of his gospel has to do with miracles, compared to only 20 percent in the other three gospels.

There are some thirty-five miracles in the Gospels. When Jesus calms the storm, the disciples say to one another, "Who then is this, that even the wind and the sea obey him?" (Mark 4:41). In Luke's gospel, the disciples of John the Baptist ask Jesus, "Are you the one who is to come, or are we to wait for another?" Jesus says, "Go and tell John what you have seen and heard: the blind receive their sight, the lame walk, the lepers are cleansed, the deaf hear, the dead are raised . . ." (Luke 7:22).

A miracle has been described as "an event that happens in a manner contrary to regularly observed processes of nature." In the Bible, Jesus' miracles are of two kinds. The vast majority are *healing* miracles: exorcising demons, curing lepers and giving sight to the blind. The others are *nature* miracles: stilling the wind, feeding the multitudes and raising people from the dead.

MIRACLE FORMAT

The miracles in the Gospels have a threefold structure—setting, miracle and proof of miracle (validation)—as illustrated in the intertwined double-miracle of the woman with the hemorrhage and Jairus's daughter (5:21–43), referred to as Mark's "sandwich."

Setting. "There was a woman who had been suffering from hemorrhages for twelve years" (v. 25). Some people came to Jairus and told him, "Your daughter is dead" (v. 35).

Miracle. The woman with the hemorrhage came up behind Jesus and "touched his cloak" (v. 27). Jesus went to Jairus's home and took the girl by the hand and said to her, "Little girl, get up" (v. 41).

Validation. The woman with the hemorrhage "was healed of her disease" (v. 29). After Jesus spoke to Jairus's daughter, she "got up and began to walk about" (v. 42).

The healing agent in both of these stories was Jesus, but there were also acts of *faith.* To the woman, Jesus said, "Daughter, your faith has made you well" (v. 34). To Jairus, Jesus said, "Do not fear, only believe" (v. 36). In the first miracle, it was the faith of the woman being healed; in the second, it was the faith of the child's father, which should encourage us to pray for others.

People today, especially those who do not believe in the supernatural, are skeptical of miracles. In Jesus' day people believed in miracles. Even Josephus, the first-century Jewish historian (thus not a Christian), recorded that Jesus performed miracles. If Jesus was the incarnate Son of the God, who "created the heavens and the earth," there is no reason to be hesitant about his performing numerous spectacular miracles. C. S. Lewis said, "Who, after swallowing the camel of the Resurrection, can strain at such gnats as the feeding of the multitudes?"

MATTHEW: THE JEWISH-CHRISTIAN GOSPEL

Matthew was the most popular gospel in the early church and the gospel most often quoted by the church fathers. The reasons for Matthew's early popularity are that its author was believed to have been a disciple of Jesus, which Mark was not; it is more comprehensive than Mark, with both birth and resurrection narratives; and its organized teaching materials, like the Sermon on the Mount, made it ideal for teaching new believers.

Matthew's gospel has long been a favorite of Catholics (Catholics are sometimes called Matthew-Christians). It underlies the Catholic Church's claims that Peter was the vicar of Christ and the head of the church on earth ("You are Peter, and on this rock I will build my church," Matt. 16:18) and that Peter's successors, the popes, continue in this role or capacity today. Matthew's gospel, which most scholars believe was written in the mid–80s, has 1,068 verses, making it the second longest gospel.

Some scholars view Matthew as the most anti-Jewish of the gospels, as in his seven *woes* against the Jewish leadership in chapter 23. Further, some see Matthew 27:24–25 as responsible for Christian anti-Semitism down through the ages. In these verses, Pilate says, regarding Jesus, "I am innocent of this man's blood." The people answer, "Let his blood be on us and our children."

MATTHEW'S PLACEMENT

If Mark was the first gospel to be written, as most New Testament scholars believe, why does Matthew have pride of place? First, it was once believed that Matthew *was* the first gospel. Second, it is much more *complete* than Mark (Matthew is 60 percent longer than Mark). Third, it has good teaching materials and it addresses church problems, such as *disciplining* members who have sinned (18:15–20). Fourth, it is the best *bridge* between the two testaments, because Matthew's message is that Jesus is the One promised in the Old Testament.

MATTHEW, THE TAX COLLECTOR

The early church believed the Matthew identified with Matthew's gospel was "Matthew, the tax collector" (10:3), one of Jesus' disciples. Interestingly,

Mark and Luke refer to him as Levi (a second name?) when he is called by Jesus, and do not add the words "the tax collector" after his name in their lists of the twelve disciples (as Matthew does in 10:3). Tax collectors were despised by the Jews because they collaborated with Rome and because they allegedly had no principles, so it is strange that Matthew calls himself "the tax collector" (his "secret autograph"?). Some commentators believe that Matthew may have worked for Herod Antipas near Capernaum collecting custom taxes on merchandise carried through Galilee on the road from Damascus to Acre, a city on the Mediterranean Sea. As a customs official, Matthew would have known how to write and keep records and could have written down many of Jesus' teachings, which are a central feature of his gospel.

There is more disagreement regarding the authorship of Matthew's gospel than the other three: it follows Mark's order very carefully; it uses or incorporates 90 percent of Mark's material, in some places word-for-word (why would one who was an eyewitness borrow so heavily from one who was not, including the account of his own call?); and it does not have the sense or feel of firsthand reporting. Some believe that Matthew's gospel was written by his followers or disciples, which is why they had to rely so heavily on Mark. They took Mark's gospel, Matthew's collection of Jesus' teachings such as the Sermon on the Mount, and special materials such as the Matthean birth narrative, and wrote an expanded gospel, which they attributed to their teacher or master, a common, accepted practice in ancient times. Perhaps this is the meaning of the term *according to,* that is, Matthew's gospel was written "according to" Matthew (the principal source) rather than "by" Matthew (the final author).

MATTHEW'S STRUCTURE, AUDIENCE AND MESSAGE

Matthew follows Mark's story, to which he adds several teachings and a different emphasis: Jesus as the promised Messiah.

Structure. Matthew begins his gospel with a long genealogy, which may seem like a strange way to start a story, but it would have been very meaningful to his hearers/readers. It tells the long story of Israel, beginning with father Abraham, moving through the generations to King David, from which the Messiah was to be descended, and ending with Joseph, Mary and Jesus.

Matthew's Jesus comes to bring a new word from God, which Matthew inserts as five *discourses* into Mark's narrative. (Matthew, like Luke, feels the need to expand Mark's narrative.) Some commentators see Matthew's Jesus as the *new* Moses, based on the many similarities between the two: Moses was saved from death by Pharaoh's daughter, Jesus was saved from Herod's "slaughter of the innocents" by an angel of the Lord; Moses went from Midian to Egypt, Jesus went from Bethlehem to Egypt (a story that appears only in Matthew); Moses wandered in the wilderness for forty years, Jesus was in the wilderness for forty days; Moses expounded the law he received on Mount Sinai, Jesus gave a new exposition of the law in the Sermon on the Mount ("You have heard it said, but I say . . ."). Jesus as the "new Moses" would have helped Matthew's readers remain connected with their Jewish roots. Some see still another connection: Matthew's five discourses and Moses' five books of the Torah.

Each of the discourses ends with a concluding statement ("When Jesus had finished saying . . .") and with Jesus moving, geographically, to a new location. The discourses have to do with *discipleship* (the Sermon on the Mount: 5:1–7:28), *mission* (apostleship, persecution, confessing Christ: 10:1–11:1), *the kingdom of God* (the growth and end-times parables: 13:1–53), *community life* (humbleness, forgiveness, wherever two or three are gathered: 18:1–19:1) and *the coming judgment* (the seven woes, signs of the end of the age and for the least of these my brethren: 23:1–26:1).

Audience. It is believed that Matthew's readers are Jewish Christians because Jewish words and customs are not explained; it is assumed that his readers know what he is talking about. According to tradition, Matthew was written to Christians in Antioch, because the first reference to Matthew is by Ignatius, the third bishop of Antioch.

Message. In Matthew, Jesus is the long-awaited Messiah whom the Jewish leaders fail to recognize and refuse to acknowledge. Matthew's claim that Jesus is the Messiah is set forth in two ways. First, his genealogy from Abraham to David to Joseph shows that Jesus was a *descendant* through Joseph, his "legal" father, of the House of David. Second, his numerous references to the *prophecies* of Isaiah, Micah, Hosea, Jeremiah and others regarding the

Messiah. With regard to the latter, Matthew uses what are called "fulfillment citations" to show that various events took place in the life of Jesus to fulfill what had been spoken or written about the Messiah.

JESUS' SERMON ON THE MOUNT

The Sermon on the Mount—it is not called a "sermon" in Matthew (the term comes from Augustine)—summarizes the essence of Jesus' teachings about how Christians are to live in the world, which even non-Christians such as Gandhi have acclaimed. The sermon contains some of the most beautiful images in the New Testament: parallelisms such as the eight Beatitudes and the six antitheses; wonderful rhythms of thought such as the Lord's Prayer; exaggerated figures of speech such as the beam in the eye; and contrasting images such as the two gates, the two trees and the two house builders.

The Sermon on the Mount may have been preached on a hillside near the Sea of Galilee, possibly near the Church of the Beatitudes on the western side of the sea. Matthew presents the "sermon" as a single continuous teaching. Many, however, believe that Matthew collected and combined a number of Jesus' teachings into a unified whole because of the length of the sermon and the complexity of the topics and because there is a different order in Luke, with the Beatitudes in chapter 6, the Lord's Prayer in chapter 11 and seeking first the kingdom of God in chapter 12.

THE BEATITUDES

The Sermon on the Mount opens with eight beatitudes or "blesseds." Some have conjectured that the Beatitudes are the "bottom lines" of sermons that Jesus preached time and again throughout Galilee, which Matthew combined into a series of eight teachings. The individual Beatitudes, in their opening and closing, reflect the "already but not yet" dimensions of the kingdom of God, which we looked at earlier in the chapter: "Blessed are . . ." (the already dimension) "for they *will* . . ." (the not-yet dimension).

The eight Beatitudes apply to all Christians; they summarize the Christian ethic, which should be seen in the lives of those who call themselves "Christians." With regard to the Beatitudes themselves, the single most important Beatitude is the first: "Blessed are the poor in spirit, for theirs is the kingdom of heaven" (Matthew often uses kingdom of "heaven" rather than kingdom of "God" because he was writing to *Jewish* Christians, who did not audibly speak God's name). When we recognize our spiritual poverty—our helplessness to save ourselves—and cast our souls on the mercy of God, we are "blessed." Chapter 10 contains comments on all of the Beatitudes and the rest of Matthew's "sermon."

LUKE: THE UNIVERSAL GOSPEL

Luke's gospel is the longest book in the New Testament (1,149 verses), and Luke–Acts (Luke also wrote the book of Acts) comprises one quarter of the New Testament. Luke has been called "the first Christian historian"—the only writer, according to Boston University scholar Howard Clark Kee, to present the story of Jesus as would an historian, which allowed it to be taken seriously by nonbelievers. Luke's storytelling is superb and his gospel is, for many people, their favorite "Life of Christ." The Scottish scholar James Denney was once asked to recommend a good book on the life of Christ. Denney said, "Have you read the one that Luke wrote?" Luke tells us that he wrote his gospel so that his readers "may know the truth" (Luke 1:4).

Luke was a second-generation Christian, that is, he did not know or claim to have known Jesus during his public life. He based his gospel on the writings and eyewitness accounts of others (see 1:1–3). In his writing he is careful to name people (such as emperors) and to date events ("In the fifteenth year of . . .") as though he is writing history, which he continues in the Acts of the Apostles. His intent, however, is theological: to show God working out his purposes on the plane of history. It used to be thought that Luke was primarily an historian; since 1950 he has been seen primarily as a theologian.

We are not certain where Luke wrote his gospel. One possibility is Rome because Paul, his "father" in the faith, was martyred in Rome. Other possibilities are Antioch, which according to tradition was Luke's hometown, and someplace in Greece, given the book's dedication and audience and the tradition that Luke died in Boeotia (Greece). Luke's "secret autograph" may be the "we" references in his companion work, the book of Acts (see Acts 16: 9–17; 21:1–17; 27:1–28:16).

LUKE, THE PHYSICIAN

From the beginning, tradition has assigned the authorship of the third gospel to Luke. There must have been compelling reasons for doing so, because Luke was neither a disciple nor an apostle. (Mark probably had some exposure to Jesus, and certainly Matthew did, but Luke had none.) It is generally assumed that Luke was a Gentile, but some dispute this because of his knowledge of things Jewish, which could easily have come from Paul. And he seems to have been a doctor, given his use of precise medical language and terms and Paul's reference to him as "the beloved physician" (Col. 4:14).

It is believed that Luke met and joined Paul at Troas on Paul's second missionary journey (Acts 16:9–10) in the early 50s; that he helped Paul start a church in Philippi, which he then served as pastor; and that he later rejoined Paul (Acts 20:5–15), accompanying him to Caesarea when Paul was imprisoned there, and then sailing with him to Rome (Acts 27:1). According to an ancient prologue to the gospel: "Luke was a disciple of the apostles. . . . He accompanied Paul until the latter's martyrdom, serving the Lord without distraction, for he had neither a wife nor children. He died at the age of eighty-four, full of the Holy Spirit."

LUKE'S STRUCTURE, AUDIENCE AND MESSAGE

Luke also follows Mark's story line, but he is more polished and literary, and also more expansive, in telling his story.

Structure. Luke wants to be sure that Theophilus—perhaps his "patron," who would see to the publication of his two writings—knows "the truth concerning the things about which [he has] been instructed" (1:4). How does Luke do this? That is, how does he tell his story? By writing a first-century historical narrative with names, dates and places. As to structure, the Irish scholar David Gooding says Luke's gospel has two great "movements"—*coming* and *going*—Jesus coming from heaven to earth, which begins in the manger, and his going from earth to heaven, which ends with his resurrection and ascension; the turning point or hinge is verse 9:51.

Luke's story begins in Jerusalem, with Zechariah in the temple, and ends in Jerusalem, with the disciples waiting for the Holy Spirit, which comes on Pentecost. The centerpiece of Luke's gospel is the ten-chapter journey from Samaria to Jerusalem (9:51 through 19:27). A journey of this length would take only three or four days; in Luke, it takes several months. Here we get the story of Mary and Martha; the parables of the Good Samaritan, the Rich Fool, the Prodigal Son, the Rich Man and Lazarus and the Pharisee and the Tax Collector; and the story of Zacchaeus.

Audience. Whereas Matthew wrote to convince his readers that Jesus was the promised Messiah, Luke wrote that Jesus was the universal Savior. His genealogy, for example, goes beyond David and Abraham to Adam: Jesus did not come to save only Israel, he came to save *all* who are lost. It is believed that Luke's readers are Christians who lived in northern Mediterranean cities.

Luke wrote for a Greco-Roman audience, which knew little about the Old Testament or Judaism. This can be seen in Luke's dedication to Theophilus; his literary style and vocabulary; his frequent use of Greek rather than Hebrew words such as *Master* rather than Rabbi, *Mount of Olives* rather than Gethsemane and *Place of the Skull* rather than Golgotha; his general avoidance of Semitisms such as *Messiah* and *Son of David;* and his limited reference to Jewish customs.

Message. Some scholars see Jesus' homily in the synagogue at Nazareth (4:16–21), which marks the beginning of Jesus' Galilean ministry, as Luke's gospel in a nutshell: Jesus understood himself to be the One anointed by the Spirit (4:18)—the One who came to bring the good news of salvation to the poor, the sick and the demon-possessed; to tax collectors such as Matthew and Zacchaeus; to adulterers and adulteresses; to women as well as men (women receive more attention in Luke than in the other gospels); to the lost, like the one stray sheep and the Prodigal Son; and to outcasts and the despised such as lepers and Samaritans, and even Roman soldiers (7:1–10).

Luke is not as terse as Mark, nor as harsh as Matthew, nor as otherworldly as John. Luke's message is that salvation is now: "*Today* [in the synagogue in Nazareth] this scripture has been fulfilled in your hearing"

(4:21); "*Today* salvation has come to this [Zacchaeus's] house" (19:9); "*Today* you [the penitent thief] will be with me in paradise" (23:43).

JESUS' PARABLES

A parable has been described as "an earthly story with a heavenly meaning"—a story with details from everyday life told to present a religious or spiritual truth. The parables in the Gospels are of three kinds: *similitudes,* in which Jesus begins by saying, "The kingdom of God [or heaven] is like . . ." (as in Mark 4 and Matt. 13); *narratives,* such as the Prodigal Son and the Good Samaritan, many of which have a surprise ending; and *allegories,* in which each detail symbolizes something else, as in the parable of the sower.

Historically, at least up to the end of the nineteenth century, Jesus' parables were viewed as allegories. The most famous allegorical treatment is Augustine's interpretation of the story of the Good Samaritan. The man on the road was Adam; Jerusalem was the city of God and Jericho was the city of evil; the robbers were Satan; the priest and the Levite were the Law and the Prophets; the Samaritan was Jesus; and the inn was the church and the innkeeper was Paul. Since the turn of the last century, scholars have concluded that Jesus' parables were meant to convey a single or main point, and sometimes a secondary point, as in the story of the father and the younger son and the older brother in the parable of the Prodigal Son.

Fuller Seminary's George Vanderlip classifies Jesus' parables into four broad groups:

- The dawning of *the kingdom of God* in and through the ministry of Jesus, as in the sower, the mustard seed and other "growth" parables.
- God's gracious *love and compassion,* as the waiting father showered upon his "prodigal" son.
- Warnings about *the coming judgment,* as in the parable of the rich man (who wanted to warn his five brothers) and the beggar Lazarus.
- The nature of *discipleship,* as illustrated in parables such as the Good Samaritan.

There are some forty-five parables in the Gospels, all of which appear in the synoptics (John uses discourses rather than parables). Of the synopticists, Luke has the most parables (and Mark the least), and he extends them over several chapters, whereas Mark and Matthew lump them together. Also, Luke has some of the best-remembered parables, such as the Good Samaritan and the Prodigal Son. Chapter 10 contains brief expositions of the parable of the Good Samaritan, generally regarded as Jesus' most memorable parable, and the parables of the Rich Farmer (or Fool) and the Rich Man and Lazarus.

THE PARABLE OF THE SOWER

The parable of the sower (Luke 8:4–15) is a unique parable: it is one of only five parables that is found in all three Synoptic Gospels, it is one of only a handful of allegorical parables, and it is one of only two parables with an explanation. In Luke's gospel, the sower is the first of some thirty parables that Jesus uses as a means of instruction. In the parable, the *sower* is Jesus, the *seed* is the gospel, the *soil* is the hearer of the gospel, and the *different soils* are different responses to the gospel. Jesus says that some "may not understand" his parables (Luke 8:10), meaning that the truth always remains hidden from those who do not care to see and hear what God has revealed.

In its allegory form, the four kinds of soils and people are as follows:

- The *hard path* (walking paths): Those who shut their minds to God's Word; those who see and hear but refuse to believe, like the Pharisees.
- The *thin soil* (thin soil over rock): Those who receive God's Word and then fall away; those whose faith is shallow and rootless, like Peter before Jesus' resurrection, who confessed Jesus as the Messiah and then denied him.
- The *thorny soil* (soil where seeds and weeds grow together): Those who believe God's Word but never give it first place in their lives; those whose faith is choked by the goods, comforts and pleasures of the world, like the rich young ruler (18:18–25).
- The *good soil* (deep, fertile, well-prepared soil): Those who hear God's Word as a "saving" word; those who believe, like Jairus and the woman with the hemorrhage, and are richly blessed.

Bible scholars have interpreted the parable of the sower in two different ways. Some see it as a *warning*: Only those who plant the gospel in their lives (the rich soil) will be saved. Others see it as an *encouragement*: "For to those who have [faith], more will be given" (Luke 8:18), that is, gathered up in God's final "harvest."

JOHN: THE SPIRITUAL GOSPEL

John's gospel is perhaps the most popular book in the Bible, having been translated into more languages than any book in either the Old or New Testament. John tells us that he wrote his gospel "so that you may come to believe that Jesus is the Messiah, the Son of God, and that through believing you may have life in his name" (John 20:31). John probably wrote his gospel in Ephesus in the mid–90s; it has 878 verses, midway in length between Mark, the shortest, and Luke, the longest.

DIFFERENCES BETWEEN JOHN AND THE SYNOPTIC GOSPELS

John's gospel stands apart from the synoptics in terms of style, structure and content; the overlap is only about 10 percent. Some differences between John and the synoptics are as follows:

Omissions. John's gospel has no birth narrative or baptism, no temptation or testing in the wilderness, no exorcisms, no parables or beatitudes, no transfiguration, and no agony in the Garden of Gethsemane.

Additions. John's gospel adds the story of the wedding at Cana, the discourse between Jesus and Nicodemus, the stories of the woman at the well and the man born blind whose sight was restored, the washing of the disciples' feet on Maundy Thursday, the raising of Lazarus, and several Jewish feasts and festivals.

There are also many geographical and chronological differences between John and the synoptics: Jesus' ministry is principally in Judea (John's focus is on Jerusalem, not Nazareth and Capernaum); Jesus' ministry extends over three years (three Passovers) rather than what appears to be only one year in the synoptics; and the ministries of Jesus and John the Baptist overlap (they are clearly separate in the synoptics). Because of the many differences between John and the Synoptic Gospels, John's gospel is often referred to as the fourth gospel.

Some say that John's gospel differs from the synoptics because he never saw the writings of Mark, Matthew and Luke. This is hard to believe, given John's leadership position in the church and the late writing of his gospel. Others say that John's intention was not to write a fourth *synoptic* gospel but, instead, to supplement the other three with a theological reflection on the One in whom "the Word became flesh" (1:14).

JOHN, THE BELOVED DISCIPLE

John was the younger brother of James ("the sons of thunder") and a member of the inner circle of Jesus' disciples. Many identify him with the disciple whom Jesus *loved* (or had a special relationship with) in the fourth gospel, who is not named, probably out of modesty (John's "secret autograph"?). John may have been Jesus' half cousin, because it appears that his mother (Salome) and Mary were sisters (see Mark 15:40, Matt. 27:56 and John 19:25). This may be the reason why John, rather than Jesus' siblings, who do not seem to have believed in him (see comment in John 7:5), was asked to care for Mary after Jesus' death (19:27). John was the leader of the church in the latter decades of the first century. According to tradition, he lived out the final years of his life in Ephesus, where he died in his nineties at the end of the first century.

There are five books that bear the name of John in the New Testament: the fourth gospel, the three letters of John, and the book of Revelation. Although the language and style of these books occasionally differs, the theology is the same and the five are collectively called the Johannine Literature. With regard to the fourth gospel, Irenaeus and others in the early church held that John, the son of Zebedee, is "the disciple who is testifying to these things" (21:24). Many, however, believe the fourth gospel did not come from the "hand" of John but from his followers, called by Catholic scholar Raymond Brown the Community of the Beloved Disciple.

JOHN'S STRUCTURE, AUDIENCE
AND MESSAGE

As seen above, John does not follow Mark's story line, nor is it clear— at least not as clear as with the synoptics—to whom his gospel is addressed. *Structure.* John opens his gospel with an echo from Genesis 1:1: "In the *beginning . . ."* At the very beginning was God, who has now come in the person of Jesus to usher in a *new* beginning. John weaves his narrative around seven signs, which are followed by discourses. The end comes with Jesus' crucifixion, followed by his resurrection, which is the sign of the new creation.

John's structure is much like the synoptics in the sense of having two halves or parts, a public ministry and a private ministry. The first half (1–12), dealing with Jesus' public ministry, has been called the Book of Signs (or Miracles): turning water into wine at Cana, healing the cripple at the pool of Bethsaida, feeding the multitudes, healing the man born blind, raising Lazarus from the dead. The second half, dealing with Jesus' ministry to his disciples (13–17) and his passion (18–21), has been called the Book of Glory: Jesus' *hour,* his death and resurrection, his "glorification."

Audience. John says that he has written his gospel "so that you may come to believe [in Jesus]" (20:31). According to Mercer University professor of religion Alan Culpepper, John's readers are Greek-speaking Jews, because some Jewish terms have to be translated (see, for instance, 1:41); they have a general knowledge of the Old Testament (3:14) and Jewish beliefs and practices; they have some familiarity with Jesus' public life and ministry, and his death and resurrection; and although they live outside of Palestine (Ephesus?), they appear to have some understanding of the geography of the gospel story.

Message. John's gospel is simple yet profound, one in which, Clement of Alexandria said, "A child can wade and an elephant can swim." John does not begin his gospel with a genealogy reaching back to Abraham (as in Matthew) or Adam (as in Luke) but with the language of Genesis 1:1: "In the beginning was the Word" (John 1:1) who "became flesh and lived among us" (1:14). William Barclay, the popular Scottish Bible commentator, said, "This might well be the greatest single verse in the New Testament." In John's gospel, Jesus is much more outspoken about who he is ("I am the way") than in the other gospels. He is the Son of the Father, who sent him—the very Son of God, the incarnate Word of God, the revealed and living presence of God. Jesus did not come to *bring* the message of eternal life; he *is* the message—the very incarnation of the message. He was not the one who *spoke* God's Word, as the prophets had done; he *is* the Word—the living Word.

JESUS AND NICODEMUS

In John 3, Jesus receives a visit from Nicodemus, a distinguished Pharisee, "a leader of the Jews" and a secret admirer of Jesus, though there is no indication that he was a "believer," at least during Jesus' lifetime, perhaps to avoid being "put out of the synagogue" (9:22). Nicodemus appears three times in John's gospel, but nowhere in the other three.

Jesus tells Nicodemus that he must be "born from above" or anew or again (3:3). Our first birth is our biological birth—our birth from "below." Our second birth is our spiritual birth—our birth from "above." When we are born again—when we turn *away* from sin and *toward* Jesus and *experience* him in our lives—we become a new creation, with a new purpose and a new will. The apostle Paul, in talking about his rebirth, says, "It is no longer I who live, but it is Christ who lives in me" (Gal. 2:20).

Jesus goes on to talk about "eternal life," one of John's favorite themes (Nicodemus seems to fade out of the narrative at 3:15). Eternal life is given a fuller interpretation in John's gospel than in the other three. In the synoptics, it means "life everlasting"—life beyond the grave. In John it means this too, but also the enjoyment of God's blessings in this life—the quality of life, not merely the duration of life.

JESUS' "I AM" SAYINGS

The center chapters of John's gospel (6–15) contain seven "I am" sayings—seven metaphors from everyday life that Jesus uses to describe himself as "the way of salvation." The Greek words *ego eimi*—"I am"—in John are the same Greek words in the Septuagint when God said to Moses: "I AM WHO I AM."

- After feeding the multitudes with physical bread, Jesus says, "I am *the bread of life* [the bread from heaven that sustains life forever]. Whoever comes to me will never be hungry, and whoever believes in me will never be thirsty" (6:35).
- Referring to himself as the true, everlasting light, he says, "I am *the light of the world.* Whoever follows me will never walk in darkness but will have the light of life" (8:12).
- Speaking to the crowds, Jesus says, "I am *the gate* [to eternal life]. Who-

ever enters by me will be saved" (10:9).

- Using the Old Testament image of God as "shepherd," as in the Twenty-third Psalm, Jesus tells his listeners: "I am *the good shepherd.* The good shepherd lays down his life [to protect and save] his sheep" (10:11).
- After the death of Lazarus, Jesus tells Mary and Martha: "I am *the resurrection and the life.* Those who believe in me, even though they die [physically], will live [spiritually], and everyone who lives and believes in me will never die" (11:25–26).
- Speaking to Thomas and the disciples, Jesus says: "I am *the way, and the truth, and the life* [the true way to eternal life]" (14:6).
- Using familiar agricultural imagery, Jesus says to the disciples: "I am *the vine* [the life-source], you are the branches. Those who abide in me and I in them bear much fruit" (15:5).

The story is told of a missionary traveling through an unknown country at night. His guide was up ahead. The missionary, looking down, could not find the road. He said to the guide, "I can't see the way." The guide replied, "I am the way; just follow me and you will reach your destination." The Christian's destination is a more perfect union with God the Father. How is this possible? Through Jesus, our guide. He is "the way"—the way we have access to God, the way we come into the presence of God—and this way is open to all who choose to follow the One whom God has sent to lead and guide us.

THE GOSPELS: FOUR STORIES, ONE JESUS

John's gospel contains the fourth and final recording of Jesus' words. Some think that because the Gospels present different stories and portraits of Jesus, they are fiction rather than fact. Not at all. We read multiple biographies of a person we are interested in, and because they are written from different angles and at different points in time, they each help us to know the person better than if we had read only one biography. Matthew, Mark, Luke and John have given us four different portraits of Jesus, but they are all about the same Jesus, who lived and died and rose again. Those who were imprisoned, thrown to the lions, sawed in half and burned at the stake went to their deaths because they believed that the gospel testimonies to Jesus were true.

SUMMARY COMPARISON OF THE FOUR GOSPELS

The chart at the end of this chapter is a comparison of the four gospels. It contains the following information:

- The number of verses in each gospel, the estimated dates of writing, church traditions regarding authorship, and the intended readers or audience.

- Each author's understanding of Jesus' mission and each author's picture or portrait of Jesus.

- The beginning of the Jesus Story, which is different in each of the gospels. For Mark, it is Jesus' baptism, because Peter, his "source," began his association with Jesus at this point. For Matthew, it is Jesus' birth and his Davidic genealogy to establish his messianic credentials. For Luke, it is also Jesus' birth, but with a genealogy back to Adam to show Jesus' universal saviorship. For John, it is Jesus as the preexistent *Logos* or Word, which became flesh.

- Jesus' first important (recorded) public act, which some commentators claim is a clue to where each gospel writer is headed with his story. In Mark, it is Jesus healing the man with the evil spirit, which shows Jesus to have supernatural power. In Matthew, it is Jesus' Sermon on the Mount, which shows Jesus bringing a new teaching from God ("You have heard that it was said . . . but I say . . ."). In Luke, it is Jesus' claim in the synagogue in Nazareth that "This scripture has been fulfilled in your hearing," which shows Jesus to be the one anointed with the Spirit to bring good news to the poor, the maimed and the oppressed. In John, it is the One in whom the Word became flesh and turned water into wine at Cana, the first of seven signs that show Jesus to be the incarnate Son of God.

- The structural midpoints between Jesus' preaching and teaching to the crowds about the kingdom of God, and teaching his disciples about what lies ahead in Jerusalem (for him) and beyond (for them).

- Some highlights from the gospel narratives.

- Some special features of each gospel and the Gospels' individual symbols.

	Mark	Matthew	Luke	John
Verses	661	1,068	1,149	878
Date	65–70	Mid–80s	Mid–80s	Mid–90s
Author	John Mark, a follower of Peter	Matthew, the disciple, or his followers	Luke, a companion of the apostle Paul	John, the disciple and apostle
Audience	Gentile Christians in Rome	Jewish Christians in Syria/Galilee	Christians in the Greco-Roman world	Christian community in Ephesus
Jesus' Mission	"To give his life as a ransom for many" (10:45)	"To fulfill what has been spoken" (1:22)	"To seek out and to save the lost" (19:10)	To do "the will of him who sent me" (6:39)
Portrait of Jesus	Crucified Son of God	Promised Messiah	Universal Savior	The Word Incarnate
Beginning of the Jesus Story	Baptism by John the Baptist	Birth and Jewish genealogy	Birth and universal genealogy	Before Creation (the divine *logos*)
Jesus' First Important Public Act	Capernaum: Jesus' first healing (1:21–28)	Sea of Galilee: Jesus' first sermon (5–7)	Nazareth: Jesus' first self-claim (4:16–21)	Cana: Jesus' first sign (2:7–11)
Structural Centerpoint	Peter's confession of Jesus as the Messiah (8:27–31)	Peter's confession of Jesus as the Messiah (16:13–21)	Start of Jesus' journey to Jerusalem (9:51)	Jesus' washing the disciples' feet (13:1)
Unique Jesus Materials/Stories in the Narratives	Jesus' action and urgency ("immediately"); Jesus' humanness; Jesus' miracles (one-third of gospel); Jesus' passion (first written account)	Jesus as the fulfillment of Israel's hopes; Jesus' Sermon on the Mount; Jesus' "end-times" discourse (24–25); Jesus' Great Commission	Jesus' birth narrative; Jesus' concern for sinners, outcasts and women; Jesus' parables (most in number and most unique); Jesus' ascension	Jesus as "the Word made flesh"; Jesus' "born again" dialogue with Nicodemus; Jesus' seven signs; Jesus' seven "I am" sayings
Special Features	• Earliest • Shortest • Straight-forward • Two endings	• Pride of Place • Systematic • OT references and citations • Catechetical	• Historical • Sophisticated • Holy Spirit • Book of Acts sequel	• Independent of Synoptics • Eyewitness • Theological • Most Popular
Symbol	Lion	Man	Ox	Eagle

CHAPTER 5

THE OUTWARD MOVEMENT

No one observing the itinerant fishermen and village craftsmen trying to launch an apocalyptic movement in Palestine in the name of an executed Galilean troublemaker would ever have supposed that by the end of the first century there would be flourishing communities of Gentile adherents in the major Mediterranean cities and in Rome itself. [The book of Acts] is the story of the geographical shift of Christianity from Galilee to Rome. . . . The author's detailed and accurate knowledge of the Roman world—including names, titles and functions of the colonial administration of the empire—lend to his work an air of authority and learning.

HOWARD CLARK KEE
Understanding the New Testament

THE ACTS AND LETTERS OF THE APOSTLES

Jesus' final charge or commission to his disciples in Matthew's gospel was to take the good news to "all nations" (28:19), meaning to all peoples, and in the book of Acts to "the ends of the earth" (1:8), meaning throughout the Roman Empire (in the first century there was little or no knowledge of sub-Saharan Africa, the Americas or the Far East). The book of Acts—the story of how the gospel moved from Jerusalem to Rome—tells how this was done by Paul, Barnabas, Timothy and others. In this chapter we will look at the coming of the Holy Spirit on Pentecost, the early church in Jerusalem, the apostle Paul and his planting of churches throughout the northern Mediterranean world, and the letters that were written to these and other churches by Paul, James, Peter and John. We will also look at the book of Revelation and some ways this book has been understood down through the centuries. Last, we will ask, Why didn't the Jews accept Jesus as the Messiah?

THE ACTS OF PETER AND THE TRAVELS OF PAUL

The book of Acts is the second half of Luke's two-volume work on the origins of Christianity, the story of how the good news spread throughout the Roman Empire in the decades immediately following Jesus' death. Although the book is called the Acts of the Apostles, so named by Irenaeus in the latter half of the second century, only three disciples who were with Jesus during his lifetime are mentioned by name—Peter, James and John. Luke's gospel and Acts were separated in the second century to combine the four gospels into one collection, and to give Acts a place of its own as the story of "the outward movement" of the good news.

LUKE'S AUTHORSHIP OF ACTS

Luke's authorship of Acts has never been seriously challenged, though some have wondered why, if he was Paul's traveling companion, he never mentions that Paul wrote letters to his churches. The answer may be that Luke chose to emphasize Paul's preaching (there are nine Pauline *speeches* in Acts), which is how history was sometimes written in antiquity, that is, through the spoken words of the principal characters in the narrative. Also, some have wondered why, if Luke–Acts is a two-volume work, he reintroduces Theophilus at the beginning of Acts and repeats the story of Jesus' ascension. Perhaps it is because his gospel and Acts were separate scrolls and this was Luke's way of tying them together.

THE IMPORTANCE OF ACTS

The book of Acts was initially considered to be of secondary importance, because it was written by a second-generation Christian and because it was viewed as *history* rather than as *gospel*. Some think the only reason Acts was admitted into the canon was that its author wrote one of the four canonical gospels. How much poorer we would be if this work had been omitted. We would not have known about Pentecost and the early church in Jerusalem, or the Jewish persecution of the disciples and the early Christians, or the conversion of Paul and his travels in Asia Minor and Europe.

An important feature of Acts is the credibility it lends to Jesus' resurrection: the changed lives of the apostles, who feared for their lives on Good Friday but fifty days later, on Pentecost, began preaching the risen Christ on the streets of Jerusalem; the martyrdom of those who chose to die for their faith rather than renounce it, such as Stephen and the apostle James; and the risen Jesus' call of Paul, who had been a bitter opponent of Christianity. At the end of Luke's gospel, after Jesus' ascension, Luke says that the disciples "were continually in the temple blessing God" (24:53). Soon, however, Jewish Christians—Jews who believed that Jesus was the Messiah—were forced out of the temple, and over time out of Jerusalem as well. At the outbreak of the First Jewish War in 66, most of the Christians had already left. The Jewish persecution of the Christians did not enfeeble or destroy the church but rather strengthened it, dispersing it far and wide, resulting in the good news being proclaimed throughout the Roman Empire.

THE MESSAGE OF ACTS

The book of Acts is Luke's account of the first thirty years of the Christian church—the story of how Christianity moved from Jerusalem, the center of the Judeo-Christian world, to Rome, the center of the socio-political world. In Acts, as in his gospel, Luke has taken care to give us an "orderly account," as set forth by Colin J. Hemer, among others, in his defense of Luke's historicity in *The Book of Acts in the Setting of Hellenistic History.*

Some think that Luke had three purposes in writing Acts. First, to show how the apostles and others implemented the Great Commission. Second, to state that Christianity was not opposed to Rome by telling how Roman officials refused to persecute Christians when provoked by Jews and others to do so (a great deal of Acts is devoted to this subject). Third, to "defend" Paul, who was the early church's greatest missionary, but not one of the original apostles; who had a burden for Israel at a time (the final decades of the first century) when the church was becoming increasingly Gentile; and who was known to have had difficulties with some of his churches, most notably the church at Corinth.

Structurally, the book of Acts has two easily divisible sections: a *Petrine* section (1–12), extending from Jerusalem to Antioch, with an interlude telling how Paul became the apostle to the Gentiles (9:1–19); it ends with the death of Herod Agrippa I in 44 (12:23). The second half (13–28) is the *Pauline* section; it begins with the sending of Paul and Barnabas to Asia Minor in the year 46 (13:1–3). It was at Antioch, which became the center of Gentile Christianity, "that the disciples were first called 'Christians'" (11:26).

PENTECOST: THE CHURCH'S "BIRTHDAY"

The book of Acts opens with Jesus and the disciples in Jerusalem. In Acts 1:8—a key verse in understanding the structure and message of Acts—Jesus says, "You will receive power when the Holy Spirit has come upon you; and you will be my witnesses in Jerusalem, in all Judea and Samaria, and to the ends of the earth" (that is, in expanding concentric circles). In the Gospels, Jesus promised to send the Holy Spirit (John 14:26), who came on *Pentecost,* a Greek word meaning "fiftieth," so named because it was the fiftieth day after Passover. Originally, Pentecost was a Jewish harvest festival; later, it commemorated the giving of the Ten Commandments to Moses on Mount Sinai.

In Acts, on the first Pentecost after Jesus' death (ten days after his ascension), "there came a sound like the rush of a violent wind . . . tongues, as of fire, appeared among them . . . all of them were filled with the Holy Spirit and began to speak in other languages" (2:2–4). The Spirit of God appeared audibly and visibly, wind and fire being biblical symbols of God's presence. Those filled with the Spirit began to speak in strange tongues (fifteen are mentioned). As the Spirit at baptism launched Jesus on his ministry to Israel ("repent and believe," Mark 1:15), the Spirit at Pentecost launched Jesus' apostles on their ministry to the ends of the earth ("repent and be baptized," Acts 2:38).

THE EARLY CHURCH IN JERUSALEM

Several important events in the life of the Christian church are reported in the book of Acts following Jesus' ascension: the replacement of Judas, with the "lot" (thus God's choice) falling to Matthias, to bring the number of Jesus' disciples again to twelve (the new or true Israel); the arrest and persecution of the apostles by the Jewish authorities; the appointment of "the seven" to help with the work of the church, among them, Stephen, the first Christian martyr; Philip's baptism of the Ethiopian eunuch; and the conversion of Cornelius, the Roman centurion and God-fearer, the first Gentile convert. Peter's speech to Cornelius's household (10:34–43) is an outline of the early church's preaching of the good news. Space does not allow us to cover these and other events in the Jerusalem church. We have to move on to the next episode in the outward movement: the call, travels and letters of the apostle Paul.

THE DEATHS OF PETER AND PAUL

The book of Acts was probably written in the 80s, after Peter and Paul had been martyred in Nero's persecution of the Christians in the mid–60s, following the burning of Rome in July 64. (Nero set fire to a large residential section of the city where he later built himself a palace. To counter rumors that he was responsible for the fire, Nero blamed the Christians, many of whom were executed.) Some have wondered why there is no account of the deaths of Peter and Paul in the book of Acts. One speculation is that Acts was written before Peter and Paul died, which seems unlikely. Another is that Luke intended to write a third volume. Still another is that Luke wanted to end with Paul "teaching about the Lord Jesus Christ with all boldness and without hindrance" (28:31) to show the gospel being proclaimed in the capital of the Roman Empire.

According to Dionysius, Peter was crucified upside down in the city of Rome, claiming that he was not worthy to be crucified in the same manner as Christ. Paul was beheaded outside the city walls at *Tre Fontane* ("Three Fountains"). Constantine, the first Christian emperor of the Roman Empire (reign: 312–337), initiated the building of Saint Peter's Basilica, now the largest church in Christendom, to mark the burial spot of Peter (it is said that Peter's bones lie beneath the altar in Saint Peter's Church) and the Church of Saint Paul Outside-the-Walls to mark the burial spot of Paul.

THE APOSTLE PAUL: AMBASSADOR FOR CHRIST

The book of Acts introduces us to the apostle Paul, the most important—though not the first or only—of the church's early missionaries. Well before Paul's first journey, in the year 46, churches had been established in *Damascus,* where Ananias and others were active; in *Antioch,* which had a large Christian community and served as Paul's mission base; in *Cyprus,* Barnabas's native land; in *Rome,* which had a thriving church years before either Peter or Paul arrived there; and in *Alexandria* (Egypt), the home of Apollos, who is mentioned later in Acts and in Paul's first letter to the Corinthians.

PAUL'S CALL AND CONVERSION

The call of Paul is the most dramatic conversion story in the Bible. According to the account in Acts 9, Paul went to Damascus, the current capital of Syria, to hunt for "any who belonged to the Way" (those who followed "the way" of Jesus). As Paul approached the city, "a light from heaven flashed around him. He fell to the ground, temporarily blinded, and heard a voice say to him, 'Saul, Saul, why do you persecute me?'" (Luke uses Saul, Paul's given name, until Paul's first missionary journey.) Saul asks, "Who are you, Lord?" Jesus answers, "I am Jesus, whom you are persecuting" (because Paul was persecuting Jesus' followers). Paul is told to go into the city to meet Ananias, who tells him that he is the one Jesus has chosen "to bring [Jesus'] name before Gentiles."

Luke's narrative of Paul's call in 9:1–19 is followed by two parallel accounts, one in Paul's speech to the Jews in Jerusalem following his arrest at the end of his third journey (22:3–16), another in his speech to Festus and Agrippa II during his imprisonment in Caesarea (26:9–18).

PAUL OF TARSUS

We know a lot about Paul from Luke's narrative in the book of Acts, and also from Paul himself (see Gal. 1:13–24 and Phil. 3:4–6), but there is no scholarly consensus as to the dates of his birth, travels, activities, imprisonments, letters or death. Paul was born in the first decade of the first century in Tarsus, the capital of Cilicia in southeastern Asia Minor. Tarsus was an important Greek city, famous for its schools (the "Athens of Asia Minor") and a prosperous Mediterranean port and trade center.

Paul's family was from the tribe of Benjamin, and they named him after King Saul, the Benjaminites' most famous hero (Paul or Paulus was his Greco-Roman name). Paul had a sister, whose son warned Paul of a plot against him following his arrest in Jerusalem (23:16). Paul's family were Roman citizens, although it is not known how they obtained their citizenship (perhaps for some important service to Rome); Paul says that he inherited his citizenship (22:27–28). Paul's father's vocation was leatherworking and tentmaking, as was Paul's.

When he was old enough, Paul went to Jerusalem to study under Gamaliel (22:3), considered by most scholars to be the greatest rabbinic teacher in the first century. In Jerusalem, Paul became a strict, zealous Pharisee who persecuted Christians whom he thought were undermining Judaism. In the year 33 or 34, when Paul was in his late twenties, he "met" Jesus on his way to Damascus.

Paul was the ideal man in the ideal place at the ideal time to launch God's worldwide mission to the Gentiles: A *Pharisaic Jew* who was firmly grounded in God's Word; a *Diaspora Jew* who was able to translate the good news into the language and thought-forms of the Greco-Roman world; a *Roman citizen* who was protected by his rights of citizenship; and a *religious zealot*, first on behalf of Judaism, then Christianity. During his dozen years on the mission field (c. 46–58) Paul established churches in Thessalonica, Corinth, Ephesus, Philippi and other important Greco-Roman cities.

PAUL'S MISSIONARY JOURNEYS

It is not known how many missionary journeys Paul undertook, but three are well documented in the book of Acts (see map on p. 299).

First Journey (13:1–14:28). Paul's first journey (c. 46–48) covered about fourteen hundred miles. Paul, Barnabas and Mark (for part of the way) went from Antioch in Syria to Cyprus (Barnabas's homeland), then to Galatia, and back to Jerusalem. Paul visited at least six cities in Galatia on this journey. We have no letters to churches in any of these cities, unless it can be said that his letter "to *the churches* of Galatia" (Gal. 1:2) was a circular letter written to all of them.

Second Journey (16:40–18:22). Paul's second journey (c. 49–53) covered some twenty-eight hundred miles. Paul, Silas (who replaced Barnabas) and Timothy (who replaced Mark) revisited several cities of the first journey, and then were called by the "man of Macedonia" (Greece) to come to Europe (Acts 16:9). Paul visited several important Greco-Roman cities on this journey, among them Thessalonica, Philippi, Athens, Corinth (Paul's second-journey headquarters, where he stayed for eighteen months), Ephesus and Rhodes.

Third Journey (18:23–21:17). Paul's third journey (c. 54–58) covered twenty-seven hundred miles. Paul, Timothy, Luke and others visited churches that Paul had established in Asia Minor and Europe. Paul's headquarters on this journey was Ephesus, where he stayed for more than two years.

At the end of his third journey, Paul returned to Jerusalem with money he had collected from his churches to give to the Christian community in Jerusalem. He went to the temple, which touched off a Jewish uprising. The Roman authorities intervened and arrested Paul and imprisoned him for two years at Caesarea (c. 59–60). Paul, who was a Roman citizen, appealed for a hearing of his case before the emperor in Rome. He and Luke sailed to Rome where, according to tradition, he was acquitted and released, and then rearrested and martyred under Nero in the mid–60s.

PAUL'S WRITINGS

There are twenty-one letters in the New Testament; Paul wrote thirteen of them. Letters were written on papyrus, the name of a plant that grew in the swamps of Egypt. Paper was made from strips from the stalk, which were overlaid and pasted together and smoothed with a piece of ivory or a shell. The Roman scholar and writer Pliny the Younger said the characteristics sought in paper were "fineness, stoutness, whiteness and smoothness." Ink was made from chimney soot, which was mixed with gum water. Writing instruments were made from reeds, which had to be continually sharpened. Pens made from bird's feathers, which were sturdier, did not appear until the seventh century (the word *pen* derives from *penna*, the Latin word for feathers). Letter writers often used professional stenographers, who took dictation by shorthand before putting the writer's words in final form. Letters were sent to recipients—in Paul's case, to church communities and individuals like Timothy and Titus—by a relay system, much like that employed in the early days of the United States, with postal stations and horses that could travel an average distance of fifty miles a day (the word *post* derives from Latin *postus*, the word for "fixed" stations). The terms *letter* and *epistle* originally had two different meanings: letters were personal and private; epistles were public treatises. Today the two are synonymous.

Paul's letters and epistles follow the Greco-Roman form, with the writer's name at the beginning, followed by a formal greeting; then the body of the letter or epistle, which in Paul's case usually included both doctrinal teachings and ethical instructions; and some final greetings at the end. The following are some introductory comments on Paul's letters:

- They were written over a period of fifteen years—from 1 Thessalonians in 50 or 51 to the Pastorals in the early 60s.
- They were usually dictated to trained scribes (see Rom. 16:22, Gal. 6:11 and 2 Thess. 3:17), which may account for occasional differences in wording and phraseology.
- They were carefully written, though some were later edited and combined, as we will see in the Corinthian letters.
- They were more numerous than those we have. For example, two letters mentioned in the Corinthian correspondence (1 Cor. 5:9 and 2 Cor. 2:4) and a letter to the Laodiceans (Col. 4:16) have never been found.

- They were "occasional," meaning some occasion or situation, such as the Judaizers' activities in Galatia, prompted their writing.
- They were both congregational (written for church communities) and personal, like the letter to Philemon.
- They were addressed to cities mentioned in the book of Acts (with the exception of Colossians), which lends credibility both to the book of Acts and to Paul's letters.

We have no letters from the hand of Paul (called "autographs"), only copies of copies, which were made so that his letters could be read by other churches. In modern times, disputes have arisen as to the authenticity of some of Paul's letters. Whether or not all of the letters ascribed to Paul were written by him, they do reflect his understanding of the gospel and his teachings, for which reason they ultimately found their way into the New Testament canon.

THE ORDER AND CLASSIFICATION OF PAUL'S LETTERS

The first collection of Paul's letters included only the nine church letters; sometime before the end of the first century the collection was expanded to include Paul's four personal letters. Some believe that Luke was responsible for assembling Paul's correspondence from copies Paul retained of his letters. Others believe the person responsible for gathering together Paul's letters was Onesimus, the ex-slave mentioned in Paul's letter to Philemon, who later became the bishop of Ephesus.

Paul's letters can be ordered as follows: First, a *biblical* order, based on recipients and length. This is the order in which Paul's letters appear in the canon; they could not be ordered by date because Paul did not date his letters. Second, a *chronological* order, based on the probable date of writing, which allows us to see the flow and development of Paul's thinking. Third, a *classification* order that bunches the letters into groups. The three lists or orders are as follows:

Biblical Order	Chronological Order		Classification Order
Romans	1 Thessalonians	50/51	The First Letters
1 Corinthians	2 Thessalonians	52	1–2 Thessalonians
2 Corinthians	Galatians	49 or 55	The Great Epistles
Galatians	1 Corinthians	55	Galatians
Ephesians	2 Corinthians	55	1–2 Corinthians
Philippians	Romans	57/58	Romans
Colossians	Philippians	55 or 61	The Prison Epistles
1 Thessalonians	Colossians	61	Philippians
2 Thessalonians	Philemon	61	Colossians/Philemon
1 Timothy	Ephesians	62	Ephesians
2 Timothy	1 Timothy	62	The Pastoral Letters
Titus	Titus	63	1–2 Timothy
Philemon	2 Timothy	64	Titus

PAUL'S THOUGHT AND THEOLOGY

Paul grew up believing that the Torah was God's ultimate revelation—and then Jesus appeared to him on the road to Damascus and everything changed. The Law made one aware of sin, but it had no *power* over sin, and it could not *rightly relate* one to God. Only by faith, only by believing in Jesus, the One sent to redeem us from our sins, can we be *justified* (Paul's doctrinal center) and rightly related to God. The bottom line of Paul's theology is the Cross—"Christ crucified and risen."

GALATIANS: THE EPISTLE OF FREEDOM FROM THE LAW

Galatians is one of Paul's most important letters, and it may have been his first letter (possibly as early as 49). Galatians has been called the Magna Carta of Christian Liberty (from Jewish legalism). It has also been called Paul's "letter from the battlefield" because of his attack against the Judaizers, hard-line Jewish Christians who insisted that salvation was not by faith in Christ alone, but by faith *plus* obedience to the Mosaic Law, especially circumcision and observance of the Sabbath. Paul's response was quick and sharp, because the Galatians were "so quickly deserting" the gospel he had just preached to them (Gal. 1:6).

THE JUDAIZERS' ATTACK

Paul established churches in the Roman province of Galatia (present-day Turkey) on his first journey, probably in the years 47 and 48. After he left Galatia, the Judaizers began to create confusion among the new believers. They told the Galatians that in order to become Christians, they had to observe Jewish law and customs. Paul's "salvation by grace through faith" was too simplistic: it needed an additive, it needed to be more firmly grounded in Judaism. (The Judaizers wanted to maintain an ongoing connection with Judaism.) Although the Judaizers were a headache for Paul, we owe them a debt of thanks because they forced Paul to articulate the distinguishing differences between Christianity and Judaism, which made Christianity separate and distinct from, rather than a sect or an extension of, Judaism.

PAUL'S DEFENSE

Paul gives an abbreviated account of his call to show that his "commission" and law-free gospel came directly from Christ (Gal. 1:1, 11–12). He then cites an incident that occurred in Antioch. Peter had associated freely with Gentile Christians, but after the arrival of "certain people . . . from James [the brother of Jesus, who became the leader of the church in Jerusalem] . . . he drew back and kept himself separate" from them (2:12). Paul openly reproved Peter, indicating his independent call and status, saying, "If you, though a Jew, live like a Gentile . . . how can you compel the Gentiles to live like Jews?" (2:14).

JUSTIFICATION BY FAITH

Paul then presents his understanding of the gospel: "A person is justified not by the works of the law [Jewish rules, rituals and customs] but through faith in Jesus Christ. . . . If justification comes through the law, then Christ died for nothing" (Gal. 2:16, 21). Paul bases his "justification by faith" argument on Abraham's belief that God would give him a son. Abraham believed, and God "reckoned [it] to him as righteousness" (3:6, quoting Gen. 15:6)—and this was 430 years before God gave the law to Israel on Mount Sinai. Thus Abraham was justified "by faith," not by observing and practicing the law. Abraham's true descendants are those who share his faith, not those who follow the law, for he was to be the father of many nations, not just Israel.

Then why did God give Israel the law? Paul says the law was meant to be a custodian or guardian until Christ came, like a trustee for someone under age. Now Christ has come, we are no longer under the law.

THE FRUIT OF THE SPIRIT

Paul ends his letter to the Galatians by contrasting "works of the flesh" and "fruits of the Spirit." He says that "God is not mocked, for you reap whatever you sow. If you sow to your own flesh, you will reap corruption from the flesh; but if you sow to the Spirit, you will reap eternal life from the Spirit" (6:7–8). In 5:22–23, Paul lists nine manifestations of the Spirit— collectively, "fruit"—that is or should be evident in the lives of believers: the spiritual fruit of *love* of others, sometimes called the eleventh commandment because of Jesus' command to "love one another" (John 13:34), and *joy* and *peace,* which come from the sure and certain knowledge of salvation and the life to come; the outward fruits of *patience* with difficult people and circumstances, *kindness* in dealing with others and *generosity* in all things; and the inward fruits of *faithfulness* in relationships, *gentleness* and sensitivity and *self-control* of thoughts, words and deeds.

ROMANS: PAUL'S MAGNUM OPUS

Paul's letter to the church in Rome is considered to be his most important writing: the culmination of his thinking after many years on the mission field; the most complete and systematic statement of his understanding of the gospel; his final legacy to the church. Martin Luther called Romans "the purest gospel." The letter to the Romans was written from Corinth on the final leg of Paul's third journey, in late 57 or early 58, before he departed for Palestine with his "collection" for destitute Christians in Jerusalem.

THE CHURCH IN ROME

No one knows who founded the church in Rome. It was not Peter, because many Jews and Christians were expelled from Rome in 49 by

Emperor Claudius (Acts 18:2) while Peter was still in Jerusalem. (The Jerusalem Council mentioned in Acts 15 is dated in the year 49.) Paul did not arrive in Rome until the end of his life. Some think the church was founded by travelers from Rome who were in Jerusalem on the first Pentecost (see reference to "visitors from Rome" in Acts 2:10).

The Roman church was much admired because it was situated in the capital of the Roman Empire. It was a large church—Nero could not have blamed the Christians for burning Rome if they had been a small, insignificant minority—and its membership included both Jewish and Gentile Christians, with the Gentiles being the majority.

Paul's letters were written to churches and people he knew (except for Colossians), but he did not found the church in Rome, nor had he ever been there. Then why did he write to the church of Rome? Some think the answer lies in his desire to "go to Spain" (15:24). He wanted to move his base of operations from the eastern end of the Mediterranean (Antioch) to Rome, so he wrote to the Roman church to introduce himself. But Paul's letter is more than an introductory letter: it is his theological "last will and testament" to the most important Christian church in the world.

"THE GOSPEL ACCORDING TO PAUL"

Some scholars have called Romans 1:16–17 "The Gospel According to Saint Paul." Paul writes that the gospel "is the power of God for salvation to everyone who has faith [in Jesus Christ]. . . . In it the righteousness of God is revealed through faith for faith." The gospel is the good news about how we can, through Christ's saving death, be rightly related to God—and this news is for everyone; the sole condition is faith.

Paul writes that God has revealed himself in creation and to Israel, but "all have sinned and fall short of the glory of God" (3:23). The bad news is that "the wages of sin [the payment to those who serve sin] is death" (6:23). The good news is that God has sent one to rescue us from our sins, namely, Jesus. All who put their faith in him will be "justified" and receive God's "free gift of . . . eternal life" (6:23).

Paul writes that justification by faith is not a new idea but an old one, building on the "Abraham argument" in his earlier letter to the Galatians. Abraham believed God's promises and he was justified—and this was before

Abraham was circumcised. Abraham was justified by *faith* rather than by something he *did.*

THE CHRISTIAN IN THE WORLD

The last chapters in Romans (12–15) have been called "Paul's Sermon on the Mount." He begins by telling the Romans to offer themselves as *living sacrifices* to God (in contrast to Israel's *dead* animal sacrifices) and to be *transformed* by the renewing of their minds (12:1–2). He goes on to write that Christians are to "love one another with mutual affection" (12:10) . . . "rejoice in hope, be patient in suffering [and] persevere in prayer" (12:12) . . . "contribute to the needs of the saints [and] extend hospitality to strangers" (12:13) . . . "bless those who persecute you" (12:14) . . . "rejoice with those who rejoice [and] weep with those who weep" (12:15) . . . "do not be overcome by evil, but overcome evil with good" (12:21) . . . "be subject to the governing authorities" (13:1) . . . "[remember the] commandments" (13:9) . . . "welcome those who are weak in faith" (14:1) . . . "[do not] pass judgment on one another . . . [and] never put a stumbling block in the way of another" (14:13).

THE CORINTHIAN CORRESPONDENCE

Paul and his team visited the city of Corinth on his second journey (c. 50) and stayed for eighteen months. The Corinthian letters are orderly, businesslike answers to a number of problems—and what problems!—that surfaced in the Corinthian church after Paul left. It does not appear that these problems were ever fully resolved, at least according to a letter written by Clement, the third bishop of Rome, in the year 98.

Paul's letters to the Corinthians are important documents because of the light they shed on how the early church struggled to be "Christian" in a pagan environment. Those who say *I wish we could get back to the simplicity of the early Christian church* should read Paul's first letter to the Corinthians.

THE CITY OF CORINTH

Corinth was the capital of the Roman province of Achaia, the southern third of what is now Greece. It was a large city, some believe as large as five hundred thousand people; the second-wealthiest city in the empire (after Rome); a leading seaport and trade center (ceramics); and terribly immoral. Corinth's temple of Aphrodite, the Greek goddess of love, had hundreds of "sacred" prostitutes; and calling someone a "Corinthian" implied that he or she was immoral. The Christian church in Corinth was prone to division and factions, tolerant of promiscuous sexual behavior, ate meat that had been offered to idols, indulged in gluttony and drunkenness at the Lord's Supper, and argued about spiritual gifts.

As mentioned above, the Corinthian correspondence consists of more than the two letters we have in the New Testament. First Corinthians refers to a previous letter (1 Cor. 5:9), and Second Corinthians refers to a letter written "out of much distress and anguish . . . and with many tears" (2 Cor. 2:4), which is not First Corinthians but, more likely, an intermediate letter. And some think that Second Corinthians is a combination of two letters, chapters 1–9 comprising one letter and chapters 10–13 another.

FIRST CORINTHIANS

First Corinthians is a two-part answer to a number of issues in Corinth—by some counts, twelve different issues. First, someone brought news to Paul ("It has been reported to me by Chloe's people," 1:11) that the church was dividing into factions and that there was much immorality among the membership; Paul's responses are contained in chapters 1–6. Second, three members of the Corinthian church brought Paul a letter (thus Paul also *received* letters) asking for advice on a number of issues; Paul's responses begin in chapter 7 with the words, "Now concerning the matters about which you wrote."

Space does not allow for a discussion of the various matters brought to Paul in person and in writing, but they involve many of the same problems the church is struggling with today: cliques and factions, church discipline, conflicts among believers, sexual immorality, marriage and divorce, sensitivity toward new believers, propriety in worship, and the proper exercise of spiritual gifts.

Paul's instructions to the Christians in Corinth are that the church has but one foundation, Jesus Christ; when there is trouble in the fellowship, clean out the old yeast before it ruins the entire batch; bring honor rather than dishonor on the church's witness by being sexually moral; avoid taking civil disputes and conflicts into the public arena; and emphasize spiritual gifts that edify the whole body of Christ rather than those that are only personal in nature.

Paul's "Hymn of Love." What is the *mark* of a Christian? In a word, it is love. Jesus said, "I give you a new commandment, that you love one another. . . . By this everyone will know that you are my disciples" (John 13:34–35).

What is *love?* In the Christian sense of the word, love is not an emotion but an act of the will. We can love someone, in the biblical sense, without "liking" them, as Jesus told his disciples and others in his Sermon on the Mount when he said, "Love your enemies" (Matt. 5:44). The kind of love that Jesus is talking about is called *agape* love, one of four Greek words for love. *Agape* love is self-giving acts of love, the kind of superabundant love shown by the Good Samaritan, the kind of love that does not expect anything in return.

In the thirteenth chapter of First Corinthians, Paul lists fifteen attributes of *agape* love: it is patient and kind; it is not envious, boastful, arrogant, rude or insistent on its own way; it is not irritable, resentful or joyful in wrongdoing; it bears all things, believes all things, hopes all things and endures all things; and it never ends. How are we to *be* Christ in and for the world? By loving those we meet—even those we do not particularly care for—with *agape* love.

Resurrection: Christ's and Ours. First Corinthians 15:3–8 is an outline of the early preaching of the good news: Christ died for us in accordance with the Scriptures (in accordance with God's plan of redemption as revealed in Scripture); he was buried (he really *died*); he was raised on the third day; and he appeared to many people to confirm his resurrection.

To whom did Jesus *appear,* that is, what is the "evidence" for his resurrection? Paul has a sixfold list of Jesus' appearances. First, he appeared to Peter, whom Paul often calls *Cephas.* (*Peter* derives from *petra,* the Greek word for "rock"; *Cephas* is the Aramaic word for rock.) Second, he appeared to *the Twelve,* which is shorthand for the twelve disciples, though Judas was no longer among them. (Paul does not mention that Jesus appeared to the women at the tomb, possibly because women were not considered credible witnesses.)

Third, Jesus appeared to *more than five hundred brothers and sisters,* the only reference in the New Testament to a "mass" appearance. Fourth, he appeared to *James,* his own brother, who does not seem to have been a believer during Jesus' lifetime (see John 7:5). Fifth, he appeared to *all the apostles,* possibly the pre-Pentecost believers, who numbered "about one hundred twenty" persons (Acts 1:15).

Last, Jesus appeared to *Paul* on the road to Damascus, an encounter that Paul understands as no different or less important than Jesus' other appearances. At the midpoint of this great chapter, Paul writes that "Christ has been raised from the dead, the first fruits of those who have died . . . at his coming those who belong to Christ" will be raised (1 Cor. 15:20, 23).

SECOND CORINTHIANS

Paul's second letter to the Corinthians was written to prepare the church in Corinth for his coming visit and to make sure that the collection for the Christians in Jerusalem would be ready when he arrived.

Second Corinthians is the most autobiographical of Paul's letters. In it he defends his ministry against the "super apostles," saying, "Let the one who boasts, boast in the Lord" (10:17). He also tells of his "thorn . . . in the flesh" (12:7), which has fascinated scholars down through the ages. Was it epilepsy? Or cataracts (Paul often refers to his eyes, as in Gal. 4:15)? Or malaria? Or migraines? Whatever the "thorn" was, God did not remove it: he told Paul that his grace was sufficient.

The letter ends with the popular, widely used benediction (blessing): "May the grace of the Lord Jesus Christ, and the love of God, and the fellowship of the Holy Spirit be with you all" (13:14 NIV).

PAUL'S OTHER LETTERS

FIRST AND SECOND THESSALONIANS

Most scholars believe that Paul's first letter was First Thessalonians—which would make it the first New Testament book to be written—a letter that Paul wrote in the year 50 or 51 to a church he founded on his second journey. Paul's preaching brought a strong reaction from some of the Thessalonian Jews and he was forced to leave town before he had finished his teaching (see Acts 17:1–9). Some in Thessalonica were confused about Jesus' return. Had he already come? If not, what would happen to those who had died in the interim? Paul's reflections concerning Jesus' return are the most important feature of these two letters (see 1 Thess. 4:13–18).

THE PRISON EPISTLES

Paul was imprisoned several times: in Philippi, mentioned in Acts 16; in Caesarea for two years (Acts 23–26); and in Rome at the end of his life. It is believed that the following letters were written from prison.

Philippians is Paul's letter of great joy to his favorite church, which he established on his second journey (Acts 16). It contains the Christological hymn or creed: "At the name of Jesus every knee should bend . . . and every tongue should confess that Jesus Christ is Lord" (2:10–11).

Colossians is a letter Paul wrote to a church that he had neither planted nor visited. It addresses a number of heresies in the church in Colossae.

Philemon is the only "personal" letter of Paul and the only letter from the "hand" of Paul (v. 19). Philemon was a wealthy member of the Colossian church. Some think that Paul may have written to him while he was writing to the Colossians, saying, perhaps, to those who came to see him, "And when you get back to Colossae, please give this letter to Philemon." The letter concerns Philemon's runaway slave, Onesimus. It was preserved, so Philemon must have forgiven Onesimus.

Ephesians is the most important Prison Epistle. It was written to the "saints" (Christians) in Ephesus, where Paul stayed for two-plus years on his third journey (Acts 19). Ephesians 2:8 underlies the founding principle of the Protestant Reformation: "For by grace you have been saved through faith, and this is not your own doing [or works]; it is the gift of God." We are saved by grace; "works" are something we do as a *result* of our salvation, not something to *secure* our salvation.

THE PASTORAL LETTERS

Since the early eighteenth century, Paul's two letters to Timothy and his letter to Titus have been called the Pastoral Letters. They contain advice from the pastor Paul to two young pastors, Timothy in Ephesus and Titus in Crete. There is more disagreement regarding Paul's authorship of these three letters than of the other ten: conservative scholars assign them to Paul; others ascribe them to followers of Paul who wrote under his name.

Timothy, who lived in the province of Galatia, met Paul on his first journey; on Paul's second journey he was asked to take Mark's place. Timothy became Paul's constant companion and is mentioned in six of Paul's nine church letters. Titus was a Gentile Christian and a loyal and faithful disciple of Paul. Timothy and Titus are told to establish and maintain orthodoxy, to rebuke false teachers and doctrines, and to be models of Christian conduct; they are also given qualities and characteristics to look for in selecting leaders so as to put their churches in the strongest and ablest hands.

HEBREWS AND THE GENERAL LETTERS: JAMES, PETER, JOHN AND JUDE

THE LETTER TO THE HEBREWS

Hebrews has never been a popular book, perhaps because it deals with ancient Hebraic sacrificial practices and terminology, or because it refers to Jesus as a "high priest." It is sometimes referred to as the "great riddle" of the New Testament: it is not known who wrote the letter (it was once mistakenly thought to have been written by Paul); or when it was written, though most likely before the destruction of the temple in Jerusalem in 70; or from where or to whom, though given its name and its use of the Old Testament it must have been written to Jewish Christians. Hebrews is placed first after Paul's letters because it is the longest of the eight non-Pauline letters.

Hebrews is an important argument in establishing the sufficiency of Jesus' perfect, once-for-all-time sacrifice for our sins. Chapter 11 contains a well-known definition of faith: "Now faith is the assurance of things hoped for, the conviction of things not seen" (11:1). The chapter goes on to list several Old Testament "heroes of the faith"—Abraham, Joseph, Moses, Gideon, David and others—which has led some to call Hebrews 11 the "Faith Hall of Fame."

THE GENERAL LETTERS

Since the early fourth century, the seven short letters between Hebrews and Revelation have been called the General Letters, because they are not addressed to specific churches or readers but to the whole church. (The General Letters are known by the names of their authors, not their address-ees.) The authorship of these letters and their dates have never been agreed upon. Conservative scholars assign them to James, the brother of Jesus; to the apostles Peter and John; and to Jude, another brother of Jesus. Others attribute them to leaders in the early church who wrote under the names of the apostles and brothers of Jesus to give the letters credibility.

The period covered by the General Letters was one of persecution from without and apathy from within. The letters encourage Christians to coop-erate with rather than oppose the government and to suffer quietly the ineq-uities of the world, as Jesus had done. They also urge Christians to oppose false teachings that were creeping into the church. The most important let-ters in this collection are James, First Peter and First John.

James. The early church attributed the letter of James to the oldest of Jesus' four brothers, who was widely respected by the Jewish community. Follow-ing Peter's move to Antioch and to the mission field (1 Cor. 9:5), James became the leader of the Jerusalem church. According to Josephus, he was stoned to death in the year 62. James's letter is written to "the twelve tribes in the Dispersion" (1:1), meaning, to Jewish Christians. It is called the "wis-dom" book of the New Testament. It is also called the *faith plus works* epis-tle, because James writes, "Faith by itself, if it has no works, is dead" (2:17). Paul said to the Ephesians, "You have been saved through faith . . . [not by] works" (2:8–9). James, writing a decade or so later, tells his readers to let the *genuineness* of their faith show forth in their lives, their relationships and their works. We often use the expression "Do not be merely *hearers* of the word, but also *doers* of the word." This comes from James 1:22.

First Peter. The salutation identifies the author of First Peter as "Peter, an apostle of Jesus Christ" (1:1). This letter has been called the "Epistle of Courage"—the courage to suffer as Christ did, in quiet dignity. It was writ-ten to comfort Christians "of the Dispersion" who were being persecuted by the state, called Babylon, most likely a code word for Rome (used also in the book of Revelation). Peter tells his readers to accept their suffering, even undeserved suffering, with cheerfulness, looking to the example of Jesus and following "in his steps" (2:21). He also tells them to answer all who ask about the "hope" they have in Jesus (3:15), an important verse for Christian apologetics.

First John. The author of First John has long been identified with the Johannine Community. He writes against those who denied Jesus' humanity—those who said that Jesus only *seemed* to be human. John says, "We have heard . . . we have seen . . . we have touched with our hands" the crucified and risen Christ (1:1). He tells his readers that Jesus is our "advocate"—one who speaks for us, as in a court of law—with God the Father (2:1–6). John writes that that those who believe that Jesus is the Son of God are assured of eternal life (5:10–12).

THE BOOK OF REVELATION

It goes without saying that the book of Revelation is one of the most difficult books in the Bible, and also one of the most controversial. It is sometimes called the Apocalypse of John, the term *apocalypse* denoting an unveiling of the hidden mysteries of the future: the yet-to-be-written final chapter of the biblical story.

REVELATION'S SYMBOLISM

One reason the book of Revelation is difficult for modern readers to understand is its use of symbolic language: *visions* of the "throne of heaven"; *beasts* with many heads and horns; *numbers* such as 4, 7, 12, 666, 1,000, and 144,000; *strange phenomena* such as "bowls of wrath," a "bottomless pit" and a "lake of fire"; and the use of *colors* such as white (purity), red (violence) and black (death).

In reading Revelation, we need to translate the symbols into ideas without trying to imagine how the things described might look. Also, we need to remember that many of the author's symbols were understood by those to whom he was writing, much like the number "13" would be today. For instance, *horns* (of animals) were a symbol of power; "7" symbolized fullness or completeness (thus 7 horns meant all-powerful and 7 eyes meant all-seeing); and "4" symbolized the 4 "corners" of the earth.

APOCALYPTIC LITERATURE

Apocalyptic literature originated in periods of intense persecution. Chapters 4–22 of Revelation have been dated during the persecutions of the Roman emperor Domitian (81–96), a despotic ruler who demanded that public worship be given to him. The message of apocalyptic literature is that God is sovereign and will save his people, as he did when the pharaoh was oppressing the Israelites in Egypt. Until God intervenes, however, evil will continue—in fact, things will likely get even worse. But God will prevail and all who have been steadfast and faithful will be rewarded.

THE REVELATIONS TO JOHN

It has long been believed that the book of Revelation was written by the apostle John in the mid–90s. This view has been attacked by some because the author refers to himself as a servant and a prophet, rather than the apostle; there is nothing in the book that links the writer to John of the fourth gospel or the letters of John; and there are significant differences in the book's style and language compared to John's gospel and letters. The importance of the book of Revelation, though, is not its authorship but its recording of God's divine revelations. The author tells us that he is writing from the Isle of Patmos (see map on p. 299), a Roman penal colony in the Aegean Sea some forty miles west of present-day Turkey, where "John" was exiled for a short time during the reign of Emperor Domitian. The book of Revelation has two parts.

Messages to the Seven Churches (Rev. 1–3). John is told to write what is revealed to him concerning the seven churches (thus, perhaps, the "whole church") in Ephesus, Smyrna, Pergamum, Thyatira, Sardis, Philadelphia and Laodicea (all located in present-day Turkey). The revelation is one of decline in enthusiasm and of compromise and of apostasy (abandoning one's beliefs). Each church, however, is given a message of hope: All who persevere and keep the faith are assured of eternal life.

Visions of the Future (Rev. 4–22). John is then shown several visions: plagues, famine, wars and death, each described in vivid language, and then a final battle between the forces of good and evil—the Battle of Armageddon.

Rome will fall, Satan will be bound, and there will be "a new heaven and a new earth" (21:1).

MILLENNIALISM

The term *millennialism*—from the Latin *mille,* meaning "thousand"—comes from four references to a "thousand years" in Revelation 20:1–6. It refers to the return of Christ and his thousand-year reign at the end of the age. There are three different interpretations or understandings of Millennialism, as follows.

Premillennialism. Christ's return will be *pre*millennial, that is, he will return before the start of the Millennium. Prior to Jesus' return, there will be famine, wars, earthquakes and great apostasy. When Jesus appears, the Antichrist will be slain, the forces of evil will be defeated in the Battle of Armageddon, and Satan will be bound. Christ will then inaugurate his thousand-year reign of peace and righteousness on earth. Premillennialism is the oldest of the millennial views, dating back to the second century A.D.; it is also the most literal. One form of premillennialism is dispensationalism, which has an elaborate theology concerning the final tribulation before Christ returns and the rapture of believers either before, during or after the Great Tribulation.

Postmillennialism. Christ's return will be *post*millennial, that is, he will return *after* the thousand-year reign of peace and righteousness. This view assumes that the present age will merge into the millennial age, at which time Christ will return to rule over a Christianized world—the kingdom of God on earth. The shift from premillennialism to postmillennialism emerged in the fourth century, following Constantine's Edict of Toleration in 313 (chapter 6). Postmillennialism was very popular in the nineteenth century; in the twentieth century, with two world wars, and today, with ongoing ethnic and political conflicts, few believe that things are getting so much better that Jesus is likely to return at any moment.

Amillennialism. Amillennialism does not regard the Millennium as a literal thousand-year period (the prefix *a* means "no" or "not," as in "atypical"). This view, which goes all the way back to Augustine, interprets the word *millennium* as symbolic or figurative, like other numbers and symbols in the book of Revelation. Amillenialists do not believe in a literal thousand-year period of blessedness, either before or after Christ returns. They believe, instead, that Jesus inaugurated the kingdom of God when he first came; that he will return to perfect the kingdom; and that the Millennium is the period between Jesus' first coming and his return.

In keeping with the rest of the book of Revelation, the phrase "a thousand years" is probably best understood symbolically, meaning, as in Psalm 90:4 and 2 Peter 3:8, a long, indefinite period of time.

UNDERSTANDING THE BOOK OF REVELATION

Some say that the book of Revelation is concerned only with the first-century persecution of the church by Rome. Others say that it is a book of prophecy abou the end of the age—about the consummation of God's plan. Still others say that it has nothing to do with either period but with the ongoing battle between good and evil. There is some truth in each of these views: there is a struggle going on in the world, but there is also order and purpose, and history is headed somewhere rather than nowhere.

The book of Revelation declares that Jesus is the key to the future, to the coming victory and triumph of God, for he alone holds the "book of life" (21:27). Those who are faithful and stand against the world and its ways will partake in the glory of God's kingdom. Martin Luther said, "I don't know *what* the future holds, but I know *who* holds the future." Dietrich Bonhoeffer said that we live in the "now-time"—and we are to live as if every day were our last day, and as if our whole future depended on how we lived our last day.

WHY DIDN'T THE JEWS ACCEPT JESUS?

The prophecies in the Old Testament seem—at least to us today—to clearly point to Jesus. Although many Jews believed that Jesus was the promised Messiah, as reported in the book of Acts (2:41, 47; 4:4), the overwhelming majority, both in Palestine and in the Diaspora, did not. Why not? The following are some possible reasons.

• Jews believed that the Messiah would be a royal figure from Jerusalem, the City of David, not a peasant from an insignificant village in Galilee. And they believed that he would embody the highest purity of Judaism, not someone who ate with tax collectors, healed the unclean and broke the Sabbath.

- Zealot Jews were waiting for a military Messiah like David to lead Israel in the overthrow of Rome. They were not waiting for one whose message was "Love your enemies and pray for those who persecute you" (Matt. 5:44).

- The majority of Jews believed that Elijah himself would return to announce the Messiah. They did not identify any first-century figure with Elijah, as Jesus and the church did with John the Baptist (Matt. 11:14).

- The Jews did not understand that the Messiah would come as a "suffering servant" (as prophesied in Isaiah 53); or that he would be crucified, because one hanged on a tree (on a cross) was under God's curse (Deut. 21:23); or that his death would "save" Israel.

- The Jews did not believe that the Messiah would be raised from the dead in the middle of time; they believed that he would be raised, along with everyone else, at the end of time.

- Most Jews believed that the Messiah would be human only, not divine, as Jesus and his followers claimed him to be (see John 14:9–11).

God's plan is to bring salvation to the whole world, not only the Jews. The centerpiece of this plan is Jesus, the promised Messiah or Christ of the Old Testament, a humble, suffering servant who died a sacrificial death for the sake of the world—"a stumbling block to Jews and foolishness to Gentiles" (1 Cor. 1:23)—who was raised from the dead to confirm his mission and to offer hope "to everyone who has faith" (Rom. 1:16).

CHAPTER 6

THE CHURCH

Your imperial majesty and your lordships demand a simple answer. Here it is, plain and unvarnished. Unless I am convicted of error by the testimony of Scripture, or—since I put no trust in the unsupported authority of popes or councils, for it is plain that they have often erred and contradicted themselves—by manifest reasoning, I stand convicted by the Scriptures to which I have appealed, and my conscience is taken captive by God's word. I cannot and will not recant anything, for to go against conscience is neither right nor safe.

On this I take my stand. I cannot do otherwise. God help me. Amen.

MARTIN LUTHER
Diet of Worms

A BRIEF HISTORY OF CHRISTIANITY

Many introductions to the Bible don't explain how the church of the disciples and apostles became the Catholic, Orthodox, multidenominational Protestant church we know today. In this chapter we will look at the early church; the *schism* or split between Rome and Constantinople, which divided the church into East and West; and the writings of the Reformers, which split the Western church into Catholic and Protestant. Along the way we will look at Constantine, Augustine, Thomas Aquinas, Ignatius of Loyola, Martin Luther, John Calvin and others who helped shape the thinking and theology of the church. We will also look at Francis Xavier, William Carey, David Livingstone, J. Hudson Taylor and others who took the gospel to India, Africa and Asia. Last, we will look at the coming of Christianity to America, the birth and growth of Pentecostalism, and the ever-widening split between Protestant liberals and conservatives.

THE APOSTOLIC ERA (30–476)

The apostolic era opened with the first Pentecost, following Jesus' death and resurrection, when the Spirit came upon Peter and the disciples in Jerusalem (Acts 2). It ended in the fifth century when the Visigoths invaded and sacked Rome. This is the period of the formation of the church by the apostles and their successors; the collection of Christian writings and agreement on the books to be included in the New Testament canon; the "conversion" of Emperor Constantine (312) and the establishment of Christianity as the religion of the Roman Empire; the Councils of Nicea (325), Constantinople (381) and Chalcedon (451), which formulated the basic beliefs of Christianity.

THE APOSTOLIC FATHERS

At the beginning of the second century, the leadership of the church passed to the apostolic fathers, so called because it was believed that at least some, like Polycarp and Clement, had known the apostles. The apostolic fathers were primarily Gentile, in contrast to the apostles and subapostles, like Silas and Timothy, most of whom were Jews. They carried on the apostolic mission, established church government and administrative procedures, wrote catechisms (instructions) for new believers, developed the church's worship and liturgy, and wrote polemical treatises against pagan intellectuals and Jews who were attacking the church.

The following are some important early Fathers.

- *Ignatius* of Antioch (c. 35–107), who was martyred in the Colosseum in Rome, argued for both the deity and the humanity of Jesus.
- *Clement* of Rome (c. 100) set forth the concept of "apostolic succession," the Roman Catholic belief in an unbroken line of bishops from the apostles to the present.
- *Justin Martyr* (c. 100–165), so called because he was beheaded in Rome for his faith, sought to reconcile faith and reason and wrote *apologias* ("defenses") of Christianity.
- *Irenaeus* (c. 130–200), the bishop of Lyons, France, wrote against those who argued that salvation comes through special or secret knowledge, thus only to a select few.
- *Tertullian* of Carthage (c. 150–212), the first North African father, helped develop and formulate the concept of the Trinity.
- *Origen* of Alexandria (c. 185–254), the greatest scholar of the early church, established the intellectual respectability of Christianity.
- *Cyprian* (c. 200–258), the bishop of Carthage, maintained that there was no salvation outside the church.

THE APOSTLES' CREED

The early church developed creeds—from the Latin word *credo*, meaning "I believe"—that summarized essential Christian beliefs. The Apostles' Creed derives its name from a legend that each of the apostles contributed a clause or an article to the creed (the original form of the Apostles' Creed had twelve "clauses"). The creed, though not written by the apostles, does embody the bottom-line beliefs of Christianity. The creed itself is believed to be the end product of several prior creeds and confessions, including a Trinitarian baptismal formula dating from about 200. During the reign of

Charlemagne (ninth century), the Apostles' Creed became the official creed of the Western church.

CONSTANTINE THE GREAT (280—337)

The Roman "Emperor Cult" was a means of unifying the Roman Empire. Those who would not acknowledge the emperor as divine were considered disloyal, the only exception being the Jews, because of their special status (chapter 3), and because they were not considered a threat to the peace of the empire. After Judaism and Christianity split in the latter half of the first century, Rome refused to grant Christianity the same rights and privileges, and Christians were often persecuted and martyred.

In October 312, before entering a crucial battle against his rival, Maxentius, at the Milvian Bridge outside Rome, it is said that Constantine had a vision of the Greek letters *chi* and *rho,* the first two letters of the Greek name for Christ. Constantine won the battle and had Maxentius thrown over the Milvian Bridge into the Tiber River. The following year he issued the Edict of Milan, which gave Christianity legal status in the empire. At the end of the fourth century, in the year 380, Christianity became the official religion of the Roman Empire.

Constantine supported Christianity by exempting the Christian clergy from certain obligations and by declaring Sunday to be a public holiday because it was the day of the week on which Jesus was raised from the dead. During his reign, Constantine generously endowed Christian shrines, both in Rome (Saint Peter's and Saint Paul's churches) and in the Holy Land (the Church of the Nativity and the Church of the Holy Sepulchre).

Constantine moved his capital from Rome to Byzantium, which he renamed Constantinople, the City of Constantine. (In 1930 Constantinople was renamed Istanbul, now the largest city in Turkey.) In the year 325 Constantine convened a council of bishops at Nicea, where he lived during the construction of Constantinople, to resolve the Arian dispute (chapter 7). The council agreed on and formulated the Trinitarian Nicene Creed, the confession par excellence of Christian orthodoxy, which was expanded, strengthened and put into final form at the Council of Constantinople in 381. A modern language version of the Nicene Creed is set out on page 183.

THE NEW TESTAMENT CANON

The New Testament writings were gathered together toward the end of the first century. There seems to have been agreement on most of the books before the end of the second century, except for Hebrews, five of the General Letters and the book of Revelation. According to New Testament scholar I. Howard Marshall, the forming of the canon "was not so much a *confirming* of authority by the church upon the books as it was a *recognition* of the authority the books inherently possessed" (emphasis added). The canon in its present form was first mentioned by Athanasius of Alexandria in the year 367, though final agreement on the canon must have occurred much earlier.

AUGUSTINE (354—430)

Augustinus Aurelius—better known as Augustine—is a hinge figure between the end of the early church and the beginning of the Middle Ages, much as Martin Luther stands between the end of the Middle Ages and modern times. Augustine was born in a small city not far from Carthage in North Africa. His mother (Monica) was a Christian, but Augustine became a Manichaean (below) because he believed it offered a better solution to the problem of evil than his mother's Christianity.

Augustine had a common-law wife for several years, not an uncommon practice in his day, who bore him a son, Adeodatus. At the age of thirty-two, in a garden in Milan, Augustine was convicted by a passage in Paul's letter to the Romans: "Let us live honorably ... not in debauchery and licentiousness ..." (Rom. 13:13–14). He came under the influence of Ambrose, the bishop of Milan, whose clear, reasoned teaching convinced Augustine of the truth of Christianity. Ambrose baptized Augustine and his son on Easter Sunday in 387. In the year 396, at the age of forty-two, Augustine became bishop of Hippo, the modern-day city of Annaba in Algeria.

Augustine waged and won three great battles while bishop of Hippo. First, against the *Manichaeans,* followers of Mani, an eclectic Persian prophet, who believed there were two deities, one good and one evil. Augustine said that there was one God, who was good and all-powerful, and that evil did not come from God but from the misuse of free will.

Second, against the *Donatists,* named for Donatus, the bishop of

Carthage, who believed the validity of the sacraments depended on the personal purity and holiness of the priests who administered them. Augustine said the sacraments are effective *ex opera operato* ("by the act itself"). That is, they impart grace wholly apart from the character of the priest who administers them.

Third, against the *Pelagians,* named after Pelagius, a British monk who lived in Rome, who believed that men and women were not born sinful and that they could, through the exercise of their wills, live sinless lives ("salvation by merit"). Augustine said that sin, because of the "fall" of Adam and Eve, is now part of the human condition (Augustine said that we are all part of the same "lump"). Pelagianism was condemned by a church council at Ephesus in 431.

Augustine's battles and extensive writings shaped the thinking and theology of the church with regard to the doctrine of *original sin,* based on Paul's statement that "sin came into the world through one man" (Rom. 5:12); God's unmerited *grace,* which came to Augustine, as it had to Paul; *predestination,* the (controversial) doctrine that God foreordains all things, including the election of some and not others for salvation; the equality of the "persons" of the *Trinity;* and the *church* as the channel of God's grace. It is said that next to Paul, Augustine did more to shape Christian thinking and thelogy than any other human being.

THE CHURCH IN THE MIDDLE AGES (476–1453)

The Roman Empire lasted for more than twelve hundred years—from 753 B.C. to A.D. 476. During the first centuries of the Christian or Common Era, Rome ruled all of the lands bordering on the Mediterranean Sea. At the height of its power, under Emperor Trajan, the empire's borders embraced some 2 million square miles and had an estimated population of 50 million people, only a small minority of whom, however, were Roman citizens.

The Visigoths, under Alaric, entered and sacked the city of Rome in 410, and then left. Rome finally fell in the year 476—the "fall" of Rome denoting the fall of the Western Empire. The Eastern or Byzantine Empire, with its capital at Constantinople, continued for another thousand years until it fell to the Ottoman Turks in 1453. The reasons given for the fall of Rome include weak leadership, moral decay, and Rome's inability to finance and maintain an army sufficient to protect itself from ambitious, aggressive neighbors.

THE ROMAN CHURCH

The church in Rome was by far the most important church in Christendom: it was situated in the ancient imperial capital of the empire; it had the largest congregation of Christians; and its roots went back to Peter and Paul, the two greatest saints of the church, whose martyred remains it was believed were buried there. When Rome fell as a political power, the Roman church became the dominant institution in Europe, and the bishop of Rome became the leader of the church, based on the claim that Peter, the "chief of the apostles," passed on his authority as Christ's representative on earth to subsequent bishops of Rome. (John Paul II is the 264th and third longest-serving successor of Peter.) Leo the Great (440–461) was the first to argue for the primacy of the bishop of Rome over other bishops. Gregory the Great (590–604) was the first to assert that the bishop of Rome was the supreme pontificate of both the Western and Eastern churches. It was during this period that the church began calling the bishop of Rome the *pope,* from the Latin *papa,* meaning "father."

MUHAMMAD AND THE RISE OF ISLAM

In the 600s, a new force emerged on the world scene when the "prophet" Muhammad launched a new religion, *Islam,* the Arabic word for "surrender" or "submission" to the will of Allah. (We will look at Islam in some depth in chapter 8.) Following Muhammad's death in 632, Islam—using soldiers as missionaries—quickly spread across and took control of all of North Africa ("convert or die"); moved into Europe in the early 700s, with the invasion of the Moors (North African Muslims) into Spain, challenging Christianity on its own soil; and in the 1400s, under the Ottoman Turks, took control of large parts of Eastern Europe and Asia Minor. Today Islam is the world's second largest religion and Christianity's greatest competitor.

THE EAST-WEST SCHISM: ROMAN CATHOLICISM AND EASTERN ORTHODOXY

As the centuries passed, the Christian church developed two "centers": the Western Church was headquartered in Rome, the Eastern Church in Constantinople.

The Western and Eastern churches were separated by *distance:* Rome and Constantinople were one thousand miles apart; by *language:* the West spoke Latin and the East spoke Greek; and by different *authorities:* the West was monarchial and followed the pope, whereas the East was collegial and followed the ecumenical (church-wide) councils. Some important differences between the Western and Eastern churches were as follows.

- The Eastern Church did not accept the bishop of Rome as the head of the church. It viewed the governing patriarchs of Jerusalem, Antioch, Constantinople, Alexandria and Rome as equals. The patriarch or bishop of Rome was recognized as the "first among equals," because of Rome's leadership of the early church, but not supreme or sovereign.
- The Eastern Church, following the teachings of the ecumenical councils, believed that the Holy Spirit proceeded from God the Father. The Western Church taught that the Spirit proceeded from the Father *and* the Son, a clause the Western Church added to the Nicene Creed at the non-ecumenical Council of Toledo in 589. The East viewed the "and the Son" language as making the Holy Spirit subordinate to the Father and the Son, rather than equal with the Father and the Son.
- The Eastern Church venerated *icons* (holy images)—paintings, frescos, and mosaics of Jesus, Mary and the saints—that were used as teaching devices and for devotions. Many in the Western Church opposed icons because of the commandment against idols and images. (This controversy was resolved in favor of the East.)
- The Eastern Church used leavened bread for the Eucharist, whereas the Western Church used unleavened bread; and the Eastern clergy could marry (before ordination), whereas the Western clergy was celibate.

In the year 1054, a representative of Pope Leo IX excommunicated Michael Cerularius, the patriarch of Constantinople, for overstepping his authority. Cerularius returned the favor, and the church split into two halves:

Roman Catholic, meaning the Western Church owed its allegiance to Rome and that it was catholic, from the Greek word *katholikos,* meaning "general" or "universal"; and *Orthodox,* meaning "true" or "correct" belief, based on the pronouncements of the first seven ecumenical councils. Efforts were made to reconcile the Western and Eastern churches, but a tragic event put an end to this: during the Fourth Crusade (1202–1204), the crusaders, on their way to the Holy Land, passed through Constantinople and sacked, plundered and ravaged the city, which sealed the schism until well into the twentieth century.

The Eastern Orthodox Church is a federation of self-governing national churches. Three well-known Orthodox churches are the Greek Orthodox Church, the Russian Orthodox Church and the Coptic (Egyptian) Orthodox Church. According to the *World Christian Encyclopedia,* the Orthodox Church has some 215 million adherents, half of which live in the former Soviet Union. Orthodox Christians first came to the United States in 1794; today there are an estimated 5 million Orthodox in the U.S. The Orthodox Church has patriarchs in important Eastern cities like Istanbul, Alexandria and Jerusalem, and metropolitans (archbishops) and bishops, but no pope or papacy. Clergy persons are male and can marry before ordination but not after. Bishops are chosen from monastic orders and the celibate clergy.

Eastern Orthodoxy is close to Roman Catholicism in many respects— the acceptance of "tradition," the observance of seven sacraments, episcopal (bishopric) polity, and the veneration of Mary as the Mother of God. In Orthodoxy, the sacraments are called Holy Mysteries, of which Baptism and Holy Eucharist are the most important. Baptism is by triple immersion, after which the baptized child or adult is anointed with oil to seal the indwelling of the Holy Spirit. The Orthodox Old Testament is the Greek *Septuagint* and its primary confession is the Nicene Creed, without the "and the Son" clause. Orthodox worship services are elaborate and express Orthodoxy's affinity for mysticism.

THE CRUSADES (1095–1291)

The name *Crusade* comes from the Latin *crux,* meaning "cross," which the Crusaders wore on their clothing and shields. The Crusades were a two-hundred-year series of military campaigns to expel the Muslims from the

Holy Land (a "holy war" for the Holy Land) and to free Christians living under Islamic oppression. The first Crusade—there were nine major and several minor Crusades, including the Children's Crusade of Love in 1212, from which few returned (most were captured and sold into slavery)—was launched by Pope Urban II in 1095. Five thousand knights and several thousand others set out for Jerusalem, which had been under Muslim control since 638. Some went because the pope promised that doing so would wash away all past sins (the first *plenary* or "general" indulgence or pardon); others went for adventure and to visit the land where Christ had lived and died.

The first Crusade was the most successful, recapturing Jerusalem in 1099, only to lose it again in 1187. The other crusades were not successful, and many ended in disgrace and dishonor as the crusaders turned their attention from recapturing the holy places of Christendom to pillaging, rape and murder.

THOMAS AQUINAS (1225–1274)

Thomas Aquinas was the youngest son of Count Lundulf of Aquino (near Naples, Italy). A brilliant, deeply religious man, Aquinas entered the Dominican Order in 1244, to the great displeasure of his noble family, and became the greatest philosopher and theologian of the Catholic Church. (In 1880, Pope Leo XIII made Aquinas the patron saint of all Catholic schools and universities.)

Aquinas attempted to construct a synthesis between biblical or revealed theology (faith) and natural theology (reason), believing that it was possible, through reason, to come to the knowledge of God. One example was his famous Five Ways or arguments for the existence of God: movement, causation, contingency, perfection and design. Aquinas's crowning achievement was his *Summa Theologia (Summary of Theology)*, which underlies present-day Roman Catholic theology.

MONASTICISM

One response to the church's institutionalization was monasticism, a way of showing one's devotion to Jesus by living a life of prayer, study, meditation and fasting—and also celibacy, a "sign of holiness" that became, in the twelfth century, the norm for clerics and others called to the religious life.

Communal monasticism began in Egypt in the early 300s. Benedict of Nursia (Italy), who founded the *Order of St. Benedict* (OSB) in the early 500s, is the "father" of Western monasticism. His rules—The Rule of Saint Benedict—regarding community life, prayer, daily manual labor and the study of Scripture set the pattern for monks (from the Greek word *monachos,* meaning "one who lives alone") and nuns (from the Latin word *nonna,* meaning a female member of a religious community) for more than a thousand years.

RELIGIOUS ORDERS

Three of the most important Catholic orders originated during the Middle Ages. The *Order of Friars Minor* (OFM), the "Poor Brothers," was founded in 1209 by Francis of Assisi (north central Italy). At the age of twenty-three, while attending church, Francis was moved by Jesus' words in Matthew 10:7–10 to proclaim the good news, cure the sick and cleanse the lepers, without any payment. He gave what he had to the poor (and was disowned by his father for doing so) and became a "mendicant"—one who is dependent upon alms for living—and ministered to the sick, the poor and the destitute. Francis's simple faith and deep devotion have made him the most popular and revered of all the saints.

The *Dominican Order of Preachers* (OP) was founded in 1215 by Dominic of Castille (Spain). The Dominicans were the first monastic order to establish universities and seminaries to educate the clergy. The *Society of Jesus* (SJ), more commonly known as the *Jesuits,* was founded in 1534 by Ignatius of Loyola (Spain). The Jesuits led the counterattack against the Protestant Reformation; they also led the expansion of the Catholic Church into India, Latin America and the Far East. The Jesuits are the Catholic Church's largest and strongest order, with some twenty-five thousand members.

THE PROTESTANT REFORMATION

Although the Reformation occurred a long time ago—in the year 2017 we will celebrate its five-hundredth anniversary—most Catholics, and also many Protestants, are not familiar with the *protests* that led to the Reformation or the reasons for the various forms and manifestations Protestantism has taken over the years.

THE NORTH-SOUTH SCHISM: THE WESTERN CHURCH SPLITS INTO CATHOLIC AND PROTESTANT

The Protestant Reformation—the effort to *reform* the church—was the second great schism in the church. It split the Western Church into North (Germany, Scandinavia and Switzerland) and South (Italy, France and Spain), with Protestants in the majority in the Germanic north and Catholics in the Latin south. The principal protests were as follows.

- The papal system, which concentrated absolute power in the Vatican and the Roman *Curia* ("court"), the bureaus and agencies used by the pope to administer the church.
- The worldliness, immorality and corruption of many of the clergy, some of whom used their positions as avenues for personal gain. There was also widespread selling of bishopric and other clergy positions, called *simony*, after Simon the sorcerer (Acts 8:18–19), and rampant nepotism (Sixtus IV, who was pope from 1471 to 1484, made seven of his nephews cardinals).
- The addition of sacraments beyond the two clearly instituted by Jesus in the Gospels (Baptism and Holy Communion), and the church's teaching that observance of the sacraments was necessary for salvation, which obscured and weakened the belief in justification by faith *alone*.
- The church's sale of indulgences as written *pardons* to remit one's sins, and also the sins of loved ones in purgatory, the place where souls are purged of unforgiven venial (pardonable) sins so that they may enter heaven. The proceeds from the sale of indulgences were used to finance various Vatican projects, principally the building of Saint Peter's Basilica in Rome. The Reformers saw no scriptural basis for either purgatory or indulgences.
- The church's apprehension and trial of persons suspected of heresy, which began in the thirteenth century and continued for several centuries thereafter, the most violent form being the Spanish Inquisition.

Another factor in the Catholic-Protestant schism was a growth in nationalism, which challenged the dominance and authority of Rome, led by princes in Germany and elsewhere in Europe and by monarchs such as Henry VIII in England. The two giant figures of the Reformation were Martin Luther, generally regarded as the father of the Reformation, and John Calvin, who systematized Reformation theology.

MARTIN LUTHER: THE FATHER OF THE REFORMATION

Martin Luther (1483–1546) is given credit for igniting the Reformation, but the unrest that gave rise to the revolt against Rome began long before Luther arrived on the scene. John Wycliffe (1330–1384), an Oxford professor, is called the Morning Star of the Reformation. He was the first to assert that the Bible was the only authoritative guide for faith and practice, and the first to translate the Bible from Latin, the language of the educated, into English so that it could be read by the people. He also wrote and spoke out against the papacy, apostolic succession, indulgences, transubstantiation and the veneration of saints. John Hus (1370–1415) was a Bohemian religious reformer who was influenced by Wycliffe; he said that the papacy had only human, not divine, authority. The Italian Dominican Girolamo Savonarola (1452–1498) also denounced the papacy. Hus was declared a heretic and burned at the stake in 1415; Savonarola was convicted of heresy and hanged in the marketplace in Florence in 1498; and forty-four years after his death, Wycliffe was declared a heretic and his body exhumed and burned and his ashes thrown into a nearby river.

Martin Luder, who later changed his surname to Luther, was born in 1483 in the town of Eisleben in eastern Germany. Luther was baptized the day after his birth, on November 11, the feast day of Martin of Tours, a fourth-century saint for whom he is named. He was the second and eldest surviving child of Hans and Margarethe Luder. Hans was a copper smelter and businessman. In 1505, while a student of law at the University of Erfurt, Luther was caught in a thunderstorm near the small village of Stotternheim and knocked to the ground when a lightning bolt struck nearby. In a moment of terror he cried out to Saint Anne, the patron saint of miners: "Blessed, Saint Anne! Help me and I will become a monk!" (Saint Anne or

Anna was the mother of Mary, the mother of Jesus.) Two weeks later, to his father's great dismay, Luther honored his vow and entered the Augustinian monastery in Erfurt.

Luther was ordained a priest in 1507 and received a doctorate in theology in 1512. In 1513 he was appointed to the chair of biblical theology at the newly established University of Wittenberg; he also became the priest of Saint Mary's Parish in Wittenberg, a position he held until the end of his life. On October 31, 1517, Luther sent *A Disputation on the Power and Efficacy of Indulgences* to Cardinal Albrecht, the Archbishop of Mainz and Magdeburg, in whose neighboring ecclesiastical domain indulgences were being sold. (Wittenbergers were traveling to churches in Albrecht's archdioceses to purchase indulgences.) Albrecht encouraged the sale of indulgences, from which he received half the proceeds, to pay for the purchase of one of his archbishoprics.

Luther later posted the ninety-five theses (propositions) in the *Disputation* on the door of the Castle Church in Wittenberg, which made them readable by anyone walking past the church. (Luther is buried in the Castle Church.) The theses were not written to launch a new movement; Luther never intended to leave the Catholic Church. They were an invitation to discuss abuses that had built up over the years regarding the misuse of indulgences as pardons for the absolution of sins, which Luther saw as having no basis in Scripture. Some believe that if Luther's objections had been dealt with at the outset, there may have been no Reformation, but Pope Leo X needed monies from the sale of indulgences to continue the building of Saint Peter's Church. Luther's real argument was not with indulgences per se but with the pope, who authorized and sponsored their sale, which got him into trouble with Rome.

Luther believed in the forgiveness of sins by and through Christ, and this forgiveness required no payments to the church or papal pardons. The theses were printed and circulated throughout the country, resulting in popular support for Luther and his teachings—German Christians resented sending money from the sale of indulgences to support the church in Italy— and great opposition to him in Rome. The Vatican asked Luther to recant his teachings; he refused and was excommunicated (cut off from the church's sacraments). In 1521, at the Diet (an imperial assembly) of Worms, a city in western Germany, called by Charles V of Spain, the Holy Roman

Emperor, Luther defended his writings against indulgences, the papacy and other matters and delivered his famous speech: "Unless I am convinced of error by the testimony of Scripture . . . or by manifest reasoning . . . I cannot and will not recant anything. On this I take my stand."

Luther fell under the protection of Frederick the Wise, so named for his reputation for fairness and justice, the Elector of Saxony. (Frederick was one of seven princes who chose the emperors of the Holy Roman Empire.) Frederick founded the University of Wittenberg in 1502. It was his pride and joy, and Luther was its most important and famous professor. Frederick's men kidnapped Luther and hid him at Frederick's Wartburg Castle (1521–1522) to prevent his arrest by Rome. During his sanctuary at Wartburg, Luther translated the New Testament from Greek into German (the Old Testament translation was completed some years later). The *Luther Bible* had an enormous influence on the German language, more so even than the *King James Bible* had on the English language.

In 1525 Luther married Katharina von Bora, a former Cistercian nun, whom he playfully referred to as My Rib (Martin was forty-two, Katie was twenty-six). Together they raised a family of three sons, three daughters (one died in infancy, another at age thirteen) and four orphans. Luther has been Christendom's most prolific writer, with over five hundred published works to his credit, including long and short catechisms (instructions) on the Ten Commandments, the Apostles' Creed, the Lord's Prayer and the sacraments to teach Christian doctrine to pastors and the laity. Luther also loved music and wrote twenty-seven hymns, including "A Mighty Fortress Is Our God," sometimes called The Battle Hymn of the Reformation. Polls and surveys consistently rank Luther as one of the top ten most important figures in the history of Western civilization, and it is said that more books have been written about him than any person in history, except Jesus of Nazareth.

JOHN CALVIN: THE ARCHITECT OF REFORMED PROTESTANTISM

The other giant figure of the Reformation was the Frenchman John (Jean) Calvin (1509–1564), a second-generation reformer who was born in Noyon, northeast of Paris. Calvin was twenty-five years Luther's junior. He was raised a Catholic, like Luther, but had a conversion experience in his twenties (in 1533), after which he devoted his full attention to the cause of Protestantism. (Some say that Calvin turned to Protestantism because the Catholic Church excommunicated his father.) Calvin was a first-class intellectual, with a renaissance education in the law, humanities, philosophy, classical literature and the arts, and he was fluent in Latin, Hebrew and Greek. The center of Luther's theology was justification by faith; the center of Calvin's theology was the sovereignty of God. Calvin believed that the Bible was the only source of knowledge about God and his purposes and the only trustworthy guide for Christian faith and practice.

Calvin spent the last twenty years of his life in French-speaking Geneva, Switzerland, where he preached and wrote commentaries on a wide range of books in both the Old and New Testaments. Calvin's most important contribution to the Reformation was the *Institutes of the Christian Religion,* which he wrote, expanded and revised four times over the years 1536–1559 (the first version was written when Calvin was only twenty-seven years old). The *Institutes* is a complete, systematic statement of Reformation theology; it became the textbook for Calvinism as well as for most forms of non-Lutheran Protestantism. (Calvin has been called Protestantism's Thomas Aquinas.) Calvin was not as "Catholic" as Luther and went beyond Luther's more conservative reforms, especially with regard to church polity, liturgy and the Lord's Supper. During and after Calvin's life, Geneva became the center of the non-Germanic Protestant world.

REFORMATION THEOLOGY: THE WORD ALONE, CHRIST ALONE AND FAITH ALONE

The central, distinguishing differences between Reformation theology and Roman Catholicism were as follows.

- The Reformers based their teachings on the Bible and the Bible alone, called *sola Scriptura.* The Catholic Church went beyond Scripture and made church-based teachings, called Tradition, equally authoritative with the Bible.
- The Reformers translated the Bible into German, French, English and other languages so that it could be read by the people. The Catholic Bible was Latin-only and the *Magisterium,* the church's teaching office, was the final authority regarding its interpretation.

- The Reformers believed that salvation was by grace *alone* through faith *alone*. The Catholic Church held itself to be the exclusive channel through which God's salvation was made available, through the sacraments, to the people.
- The Reformers saw no scriptural basis for a priest to *dispense* God's grace. They emphasized, instead, each person's direct access to God through Jesus, based on Paul's teaching that Jesus Christ is the only "mediator between God and humankind" (1 Tim. 2:5).
- The Reformers believed in the "priesthood of all believers" (1 Peter 2:9), which eliminated divisions between clergy and the laity, which the Catholic Church maintains to the present day. The Reformers taught that all believers are called to *ministry*, not just the ordained clergy.
- The Reformers believed in the sanctity of all vocations. Luther said, "The works of monks and priests in God's sight are in no way superior to a farmer laboring in his field and a woman looking after her house."
- The Reformers rejected Catholic teachings regarding the papacy, indulgences and purgatory; the veneration of saints and the adoration of Mary; sacraments other than Baptism and the Lord's Supper; the celibacy of priests; the deuterocanonical books in the Old Testament; the use of the rosary, holy water, shrines, relics and other "sacramentals"; and the Latin Mass.

THE FOURFOLD REFORMATION: LUTHERAN, REFORMED, ANGLICAN AND RADICAL

The Reformation was not a single reformation but a series of reformations, resulting in four different forms or manifestations—Lutheranism, Calvinism or Reformed, Anglican and Radical (Baptists, Mennonites, Quakers and others). The first two are sometimes called *confessional* denominations, referring to the basic beliefs that they "confess."

Lutheranism. Lutheranism was based on the writings of Martin Luther. Luther was the great champion of *sola Scriptura* and justification by faith, but he stayed close to the Catholic Church with regard to liturgy and church practices. He was much less "Protestant" than the Reformers who came after him, such as Ulrich Zwingli and John Calvin in Switzerland (Zwingli is considered by many to be the "father" of Reformed Protestantism, though

Calvin gets most of the credit because of his *Institutes*); John Knox, the father of Scottish Presbyterianism; and Thomas Cranmer, the architect of Anglican Protestantism.

Luther's followers founded churches in Northern Germany, Sweden, Norway and other Scandinavian countries, and later throughout the world. The primary confession of the Lutheran Church is the Augsburg Confession, which is based on Luther's writings but was put in final form by Philip Melanchthon, Luther's most important colleague at Wittenberg. The Confession was presented to Emperor Charles V at the Diet of Augsburg in 1530. It was the earliest of the formal creedal statements and influenced other confessions.

Calvinism. Calvinism went further than Lutheranism and became the most influential expression of Reformation theology and practice, known today as Reformed Protestantism. Calvinism differed from Lutheranism with regard to church polity, with authority residing in presbyteries of pastors and elders rather than in bishops. Calvinists also differed with Lutherans regarding the Lord's Supper, believing it to be a mystical union with Christ rather than Luther's view that Christ is present over, under and with the bread and wine, though not in the substances themselves. Further, Calvinists wanted a simple, less liturgical form of worship: no vestments, crucifixes, stained-glass windows, candles or stone altars.

The followers of Calvin founded Reformed churches on the European continent (Dutch Reformed, German Reformed, French Huguenots) and Presbyterian churches in Scotland, England and Northern Ireland. Those who came to the New World called themselves Reformed if they came from the continent and Presbyterian if they came from the United Kingdom. The primary confessional statement of English-speaking Presbyterians is the *Westminster Catechism,* a systematic exposition of orthodox Calvinism drawn up at Westminster in 1647, which became the creedal standard for Reformed and Presbyterian churches.

The English Reformation. The English Reformation was less theological than political, breaking communion with Rome but not going as far as Luther and Calvin. The English Reformation began during the reign of Henry VIII (1509–1547). Henry divorced Catherine of Aragon (northeast Spain), the daughter of Ferdinand and Isabella, in 1533, because he wanted a male heir to assure the survival of his dynasty. Henry and Catherine had a daughter, Mary Tudor, but Henry felt that his subjects were not ready for a female monarch. Catherine was in her forties and the prospects for a son were not promising, so he divorced her, which was forbidden by Catholic canon law, following which Pope Clement VII excommunicated Henry. (Catherine's nephew, Charles V, was the Holy Roman Emperor and an ally of the pope.)

In 1534 the British Parliament passed the Act of Supremacy, which made the king of England the Supreme Head of the Church in England, also called the Anglican Church, from the Latin *Anglicanus,* the "land of the Angles" or Angleland (England). Henry was strongly Catholic in his beliefs, and the English church, during his reign, remained Catholic in many respects, though independent of Rome. Thomas Cranmer, the first archbishop of Canterbury (1533–1556), authored *The Book of Common Prayer* (1549), the official prayer book of the Church of England. Cranmer was burned at the stake in Oxford in 1556 by "Bloody Mary," the Catholic daughter of Henry and Catherine, for refusing to recant his Protestant views. The doctrinal statement of the Church of England is contained in the Thirty-Nine Articles (1571). Today there are Anglican churches in more than 150 countries, making Anglicanism second only to Catholicism as the most widespread Christian communion. In the United States the Anglican Church is called the Protestant Episcopal Church.

The Radical Reformation. The Radical Reformation went beyond Luther and Calvin. In the 1560s, English Calvinist *Puritans* wanted to "purify" the state-controlled Church of England of its Romanism—its altars, worship liturgy and priesthood. Closely associated with the Puritans were the *Separatists* and *Independents,* who withdrew from the Church of England and came to America where they founded independent congregational churches.

Other radicals were the *Mennonites,* founded by the Dutch ex-Catholic priest Menno Simons in Holland in the early 1550s, who believed in living lives of simplicity and holiness; the *Baptists,* who baptized by immersion after a believer's public profession of faith, founded by John Smyth in Amsterdam in 1609; the *Society of Friends* (named from John 15:14) or *Quakers,* who believed in pacifism and that all should "quake" before the

Word of God, founded by George Fox in 1668; and later the *Methodists,* founded in 1729 by followers of the brothers John and Charles Wesley, who were methodical about their spiritual life and believed that one should "live according to the method of life laid down in the Bible."

THE COUNCIL OF TRENT: THE CATHOLIC RESPONSE TO THE REFORMATION

When the Reformation began to spread and take root, the Catholic Church was forced to meet it head on and called a church-wide council at Trent in northern Italy, which met in three long sessions over the years 1545–47, 1551–52 and 1562–63. The Council of Trent has been called the most important Catholic council between Nicea (325) and Vatican II (1962–65). Thomas Bokenkotter, in his book *Dynamic Catholicism,* said that when the Council of Trent finished its work, "even critics had to admit that the job was well done. Trent defined the Catholic position in such clear and trenchant language that henceforth everyone knew exactly where the Catholic Church stood."

The Council of Trent prompted what historians call the Catholic Reformation or Counter Reformation, though it was less a "reformation" than a stand against Luther and his writings against the papacy and the Roman Church. Trent addressed priestly morality, simony and other matters, but its primary purpose was to reaffirm Catholic doctrines challenged by the Reformers.

Trent affirmed the church as the sole interpreter of Scripture, added several deuterocanonical books to its Old Testament canon, expanded and strengthened the pope's authority over the church, increased the church's official sacraments from two to seven, made Christ's "real presence" in the Eucharist official Catholic doctrine, and retained the Latin Bible and the Latin Mass. It also condemned and abolished certain abuses, including the sale of indulgences, the event which had ignited the Reformation. The decisions and pronouncements of the Council of Trent are referred to as the *Tridentine* teachings and doctrines, from the Latin *Tridentinus,* the ancient name of Trent.

CATHOLICISM AND PROTESTANTISM TODAY

Catholics and Protestants are in conversation today—Anglicans and Lutherans, for instance—but differences remain because of different sources of authority. For Protestants, the Bible is the sole source of authority in matters of faith and practice. Catholics have a second source of authority, Tradition, which comes from the early church Fathers, later scholars and theologians, and councils like Trent and Vatican II. Some say that Catholicism has even a third authority, the *Magisterium,* the teaching office of the Catholic Church, which interprets both Scripture and Tradition. Some important differences between Catholic and Protestant beliefs and practices are as follows:

Justification by Faith. Protestants believe in justification (or salvation) by faith *alone.* Catholics believe that faith, to be saving faith, must be accompanied by observance of the sacraments. This was the "line in the sand" between Rome and the Protestant Reformers, and as set out in the *Catechism of the Catholic Church* (1996), it still is today.

The Papacy. Catholics believe that Peter was the *vicar* of Christ and the supreme pontiff of the church, and that he passed on his vicarship in an unbroken line of "apostolic succession" to succeeding bishops of Rome. They also believe that the pope is infallible when pontificating on faith and morals. Protestants find no historical or scriptural support for either of these beliefs.

Mary. Catholics believe that Mary was conceived *immaculate,* that is, without sin. They also believe that Mary was a perpetual virgin—before, during (no rupture of Mary's hymen) and after Jesus' birth—notwithstanding references in the Gospels to Jesus' brothers and sisters. And they believe that upon her death, Mary was "assumed" (body and soul) into heaven and now sits at the right hand of Jesus. Protestants find no scriptural warrant for these beliefs.

The Lord's Supper. Catholics believe that when the priest consecrates the bread and wine in the celebration of Holy Eucharist, the "elements" are *transubstantiated* into the body and blood of Christ. They may look, smell and taste like bread and wine, but they are the *real presence*—the actual body and blood—of Christ. There is no such belief in Protestantism.

Clergy. Catholic priests are male-only and celibate. Protestant clergy persons are both male and female and need not be celibate.

Purgatory. Catholics believe that those who die with unforgiven venial sins must have their souls purged or purified before entering heaven. Protestants believe that we are saved by Jesus' all-sufficient sacrificial death, which requires no post-death purification.

Canonicity. A final difference between Catholics and Protestants has to do with their Old Testament canons. The Catholic Old Testament has forty-six books; the Protestant Old Testament has thirty-nine books. The Protestant Old Testament canon includes only those books that were accepted by the rabbis and received into the Hebrew canon (chapter 1).

CHRISTIAN MISSIONS TO ALL THE WORLD

The church has seen four important periods of mission activity throughout its history. The first occurred between the death of Jesus and the conversion of Emperor Constantine (312) when Christianity was transformed from a small quasi-Jewish sect into an international community of believers representing perhaps 10 percent of the inhabitants of the Roman Empire. The second took place in the first half of the Middle Ages with the Christianization of Europe. The third took place in the 1500s with the discovery of the Americas and the Far East. The fourth took place in the 1800s with missions into the interiors of India, Africa and China.

EXPLORATION AND COLONIZATION

The driving force behind the expansion of Christianity beyond Europe was the desire for silk, spices, coffee, tea, tobacco and other items of trade, and for precious metals (gold and silver). The kings of Catholic Spain and Portugal—the great naval explorers and early colonizers—were expected to evangelize the lands discovered by their sea captains and conquered by their soldiers. In the years following the Reformation, the Catholic Church won more converts outside of Europe—in India, Latin America and Asia—than it lost to Protestantism within Europe.

At the beginning of the nineteenth century, Protestantism barely existed outside of Europe. Protestant churches in Europe were busy fighting for survival against the Catholic Church, which had dominated Europe for a thousand years, and had limited energy and resources for foreign missions. And when England and other Protestant countries began to colonize lands of their own, they felt no urgency to evangelize the peoples they conquered, in contrast to the Catholic colonizers' mandate to do so by the Vatican. In fact, colonizers like the British East India Company did not look with favor on missionaries converting peoples they were trying to subjugate and control.

A major reason for the Catholic Church's success in overseas missions was that it had a trained "army" of missionaries—Jesuits (Ignatius considered foreign missions to be the highest form of Christian service), Franciscans, Dominicans and others—who accompanied explorers like Columbus on their overseas voyages (twelve priests accompanied Columbus on his second voyage in 1493).

The Protestant countries responded much later with volunteer societies such as the Baptist Missionary Society (1792), the London Missionary Society (1795), the Church Missionary Society (1799), the British and Foreign Bible Society (1804) and the American Board of Commissioners for Foreign Missions (1810), which sent Adoniram Judson, the first American missionary, to India and Burma in 1812. Many of the societies, like today's parachurch organizations, were lay-led, lay-staffed and lay-supported, and their independence made it possible for different denominations to work together on the mission field.

FRANCIS XAVIER AND WILLIAM CAREY

The great centuries for missionary work were the sixteenth and the nineteenth. The sixteenth century was the Catholic century; its greatest missionary was Francis Xavier, the Catholic Church's "patron" of foreign missions (the Catholic Church credits Xavier with seven hundred thousand conversions). The nineteenth century was the Protestant century; its greatest missionaries were William Carey, the "father" of modern missions, who worked in India in the early 1800s, and J. Hudson Taylor, who penetrated the interior of China in the late 1800s.

Francis Xavier. Francis Xavier was born in 1506 in northern Spain. He studied at the University of Paris with Ignatius of Loyola, a fellow countryman, who chose him, along with five others, to form the Society of Jesus (the Jesuits) in 1534. In 1537 Xavier was ordained a priest. In 1542 he went to Goa, a Portuguese city in southwest India, and then to the south of India.

In India, Xavier concentrated his efforts on young men (the next generation's leaders), teaching and having them memorize the Ten Commandments, the Apostles' Creed, the Lord's Prayer and the Rosary. In 1549 he went to Japan where he had immediate and far-reaching success. Xavier wanted to go to China, but died (in 1552) on an island outside the mainland while awaiting entry into the country.

William Carey. The Protestant missionary movement began with William Carey. He was not the first Protestant missionary, but he "marks the entry of the English-speaking world on a large scale into the missionary enterprise—and it has been the English-speaking world which has provided four-fifths of the non-Roman missionaries from the days of Carey to the present time" (Stephen Neill, *A History of Christian Missions*).

Carey was born in 1761 in Northamptonshire, England. He was converted in 1779 and became a Baptist preacher in 1783. He helped form the Baptist Missionary Society and then set out for India, arriving in Calcutta in 1793. Carey immersed himself in Indian life and thought; lived in a Danish missionary compound in Serampore (beyond the control of the British East India Company in Calcutta, which opposed Christian missions); earned money working in a dyestuff factory; and learned several Indian languages. His motto was "Attempt great things *for* God. Expect great things *from* God."

Carey, with the help of Indian nationals, supervised five complete and twenty-three partial translations of the Bible into Indian languages and dialects; wrote Indian-language dictionaries and grammars; cofounded Serampore College, the first Christian college in Asia; founded the Horticultural Society of India to promote agricultural improvements; published the first newspaper in India; and campaigned successfully against *sati*, the Hindu practice of widows cremating themselves on their husband's funeral pyres.

Church historian Ruth Tucker, in writing about Carey, said, "More than any other individual in modern history, Carey stirred the imagination of the

Christian world and showed by his own humble example what could and should be done to bring a lost world to Christ" (*From Jerusalem to Irian Jaya*). Carey never returned to England, dying in India in 1834 at age seventy-three.

EXPANSION INTO ALL THE WORLD

The following are some brief comments on the expansion of Christianity into Africa, Latin America and Asia.

Africa. Africa, at least Northern or Roman Africa, was Christianized very early (Alexandria, Cyrene, Carthage, Hippo). The name we normally associate with missions in sub-Saharan Africa is David Livingstone, who was born in Scotland in 1813. Livingstone studied theology and medicine. In 1841 he was sent by the London Missionary Society to southern Africa, where he worked as a medical missionary under Robert Moffat, the "patriarch" of African missions (he also married Moffat's daughter).

Livingstone was an avid explorer—he was the first European to "discover" Victoria Falls (in 1855), which he named for England's Queen Victoria—and was constantly on the move, pushing farther and farther into the interior of Africa where, Moffat said, "There are a thousand villages where no missionary has ever been seen and the name of Christ has never been heard." Livingstone's writings and lectures on return trips to England opened Africa to the world.

Livingstone died in Zambia in 1873, eighteen months after being *found* by Henry M. Stanley ("Dr. Livingstone, I presume"), a reporter for the *New York Herald.* (Stanley was converted by Livingstone and stayed on in Africa to do missionary work of his own.) When Livingstone died, his heart was cut out and buried in Africa and his body sent to England, where he was given a state funeral and buried in Westminster Abbey. Today Christianity is growing faster in Africa than on any other continent: in 1900 Africa was 3 percent Christian; today it is almost 50 percent Christian.

Central and South America. The expansion of Christianity to the Americas followed Columbus's discovery of the New World in 1492. Spain gained control of the West Indies in 1515 and then, in surprisingly short order, conquered the Aztec empire in Mexico in 1521 and the Inca empire in Peru in 1533. By the end of the sixteenth century, Spain controlled most of Latin America. (Portugal, as a result of a decision made by the Vatican, gained control of Brazil, now the largest Catholic country.)

The most prominent missionary in the early years of Latin America was Bartolomé de Las Casas. He was born in Spain in 1474, studied law, and in 1502 came to the New World as legal advisor to the governor of Hispaniola (today, Haiti and the Dominican Republic). Las Casas had a conversion experience and entered the Dominican order. He was the first priest ordained in the New World (in 1512) and later became the bishop of Chiapas, Mexico. He was also a historian and wrote the first biography of Christopher Columbus (his father sailed on Columbus's second voyage in 1493). Las Casas opposed the exploitation of the Indians, pleading their case, with little success, in both Spanish America and in Spain.

Two developments in Latin America in the twentieth century were the growth of Protestantism and liberation theology. South America has more Christians than any other continent (some 90 percent of the population profess Christianity), but many are Christian in name only. Protestant mission organizations are active in Latin America, many coming when other countries closed their borders to missionaries, as China did under Mao Tse-Tung in 1951. In 1900 South America was 98 percent Catholic; it is now 12 percent Protestant—and Brazil is close to 20 percent, as are several Central American countries, and Chile is close to 30 percent.

Liberation theology arose in South America in the 1960s as a protest against oppressive government regimes and exploitative capitalists. The principal spokesperson of the movement has been Gustavo Gutiérrez, a Peruvian priest and theologian, who said that theology must move beyond the study of religious truths and address the needs of the poor and the oppressed. Liberation theology started as a Catholic movement, but now includes Protestants as well. Although controversial—most liberation theology has more to do with economic and political liberation than with "theology"—it has had a profound influence on political theologies in North America (black and feminist), South Africa (antiapartheid) and Asia.

India. According to a long-standing legend, the apostle Thomas took Christianity to India in the year 52. The first efforts to establish Christian churches in India were made by the Portuguese, who went to the port city of Goa in 1498. German and Danish Lutheran missionaries went to India in the 1700s, and William Carey went at the end of the century.

Although Catholic and Protestant missionaries have been active in India for five hundred years, Indian Christians represent less than 3 percent of the population. A major reason for Christianity's lack of success in India, and also in China and Japan, is that those who live in these countries have not been willing to exchange their historic religions—Hinduism, Buddhism and Confucianism (which predate Christianity)—for a religion that repudiates most of their beliefs and many of their customs.

Japan. Francis Xavier went to Japan in 1549. The church grew, with some three hundred thousand baptized believers by the end of the century. In 1596 there was a shift in power and an active persecution of Christianity as a foreign force within the country. In 1614 Christianity was outlawed and in 1636 thousands of Japanese Christians were massacred; three years later there were no missionaries left in Japan. Mission efforts resumed in the late nineteenth century, and also after World War II, but little headway has been made into Japan's highly secularized society. Christianity, as in India, is minuscule: less than 2 percent of the population.

China. Francis Xavier wanted to establish Christianity in China, but died while awaiting an invitation to enter the country. Xavier was followed by Matthew Ricca, an Italian Jesuit priest and scholar, who was successful in establishing churches in China in the 1580s. The church grew for one hundred years, but conflicts between religious orders and a suspicion that Christianity was undermining Chinese culture led to Christianity's decline.

A new wave of growth occurred in the second half of the nineteenth century under J. Hudson Taylor, a British missionary who went to China in 1854. In 1865 Taylor founded the China Inland Mission (now, Overseas Missionary Fellowship), the first of many "faith" missions that depended on God for all financial needs. Taylor was a creative missionary who, to the embarrassment of some mission organizations, adopted the dress and manners of the Chinese he tried to convert. Taylor's focus was on evangelism— "Every hour thousands of souls are passing away into death and darkness"— and on penetrating the interior of China (under Taylor, the CIM established mission stations in each of China's eighteen provinces). Taylor, like so many other missionaries, died (in 1905) in the country he went to convert.

Christianity in China has suffered numerous setbacks in the twentieth century, most noticeably under the communists. But like the first-century church, repression fostered rather than retarded its growth. Today, with an estimated 60 million Protestants and 12 million Catholics (6 percent of China's 1.2 billion population), China has more Christians than any country in Asia.

Other Asian Countries. Two other countries of note in Asia are the Philippines, the only Christian country in Asia, and South Korea, the most Protestant country in Asia. The Philippines were discovered by Ferdinand Magellan (for Spain) in 1521; the islands were Christianized in the late 1500s. Today 90 percent of the population professes Christianity (the Catholics are the largest Christian presence). The Asian country with the largest Protestant percentage is South Korea, which is 35 percent Protestant. Most other countries in Southeast Asia are either Muslim, like Malaysia and Indonesia, or Buddhist, like Vietnam, Cambodia, Thailand and Myanmar (Burma).

CHRISTIAN MISSIONS: PAST, PRESENT AND FUTURE

The percentage of Christians in the world at the beginning of the twenty-first century was about the same as it was at the beginning of the twentieth century—about 33 percent. An obstacle that Christianity faces in expanding its presence lies in a simple statistic: half of the world's population live in countries that are not open or receptive to the gospel. In Communist countries like China and North Korea, open evangelism is prohibited. In Muslim strongholds like Bangladesh, Pakistan, Indonesia, North Africa and the Middle East, evangelism is strictly controlled. In India, Japan and the countries of Southeast Asia, the historic religions (Hinduism, Buddhism and Shintoism) are very entrenched.

But there are many reasons for hope. First, with the gospel having been planted in every part of the world, and with most people having access to some part of the Bible in their own language, there is increasing familiarity with the Christian message. Second, Christian relief and development organizations (like World Vision) are offering aid, comfort and hope to people throughout the world. Third, every year hundreds of thousands of foreigners travel and study in the West and are exposed to Christians and to Christian care-giving institutions, and it is to be hoped that when they return home they will be open (or less hostile) to Christianity. Last, there is a strong, continuing commitment to world evangelism by church denominations, missionary societies and parachurch organizations that will, hopefully, under the guidance of the Holy Spirit, one day produce the great harvest foretold in the New Testament.

CHRISTIANITY IN AMERICA

It is usually assumed that Christianity came to North America with the English Protestants. In fact, Christianity was brought to America by Spanish and French Catholic missionaries in the 1520s, nearly one hundred years before the first English settlements in Virginia and Massachusetts.

THE COMING OF CHRISTIANITY TO AMERICA

The real impetus to Protestantism coming to America was furnished by those who tried to "reform" the theology, worship and polity of the state-controlled Church of England. Being unsuccessful, they separated from the Church of England. To avoid persecution, many fled to Holland, but they were never happy there because of differences in language and culture and because they feared their children would not grow up "English."

In September of 1620 a group of separatist "pilgrims" and others (101 in all, plus a crew of 25), sponsored by London merchants, set sail aboard the *Mayflower*. They arrived in December at Plymouth, Massachusetts—named for Plymouth, England, from which they had sailed—and established Plymouth Colony, the first permanent English colony in North America. Over the first winter half of the settlers died from disease and exposure. The rest hung on, adapted themselves to their new environment and celebrated a "day of thanksgiving" in November 1621.

America's Pilgrim fathers, and the Puritans who soon followed them, led the way in establishing Christianity in the New World. As time went on, dreams of America being the "new people of God" began to collapse. One reason was the apathy of the original settlers' descendants, many of whom were more interested in establishing themselves and their families than in religion. Another reason was that many of the second-wave settlers came to

America to start a new life rather than for religious purposes (many second-wavers were unchurched). A further reason was the arrival in America of denominations with different religious views—Episcopalians in Virginia and the Carolinas, Catholics in Maryland, Dutch Reformed in New York, and English Quakers and German Lutherans in Pennsylvania.

THE GREAT AWAKENING

As America began to open up to a variety of new immigrants, and as the frontiers opened to the West, Christianity began to decline in importance. Wheaton College historian Mark Noll said that America in the early 1700s was "dominated more by tavern life than by church life."

But then something unexpected happened: a series of religious revivals called the Great Awakening. The two principal leaders ("preachers") of the revivals were Jonathan Edwards, a Congregational minister in Northampton, Massachusetts, America's first theologian, and George Whitefield, an English evangelist whose oratorical style made him one of the most popular figures in eighteenth-century America.

The Awakening lasted from the mid–1730s to the mid–1740s and had a tremendous impact on colonial America: widespread conversions to the faith—some believe as many as fifty thousand out of a population of perhaps one million; growth in church membership and attendance; an increase in personal piety (prayer, study and fasting); an increase in the number of young men entering the ministry and the building of colleges to train them, such as Princeton, Rutgers, Brown and Dartmouth.

INDEPENDENCE AND NATIONHOOD

In the latter half of the eighteenth century there was growing agitation in the American colonies for independence from Great Britain and from "taxation without representation." The American Revolutionary War, or War of Independence, began in April 1775 at Lexington, Massachusetts, when a militiaman fired the famous "shot heard 'round the world." The Declaration of Independence—the formal declaration of the independence of the colonies from Britain—was adopted by the American colonies' Continental Congress on July 4, 1776.

The war ended at Yorktown, Virginia, in September 1781. The new republic was recognized as an independent country by the Treaty of Paris in 1783. The Constitution of the United States was drafted in 1787 and ratified by the states in 1788. In April 1789, George Washington became the first president of the new United States of America.

Surprisingly, those who came to the New World to escape religious persecution made no provision for the religious freedom of others. This changed with the addition of the First Amendment to the Constitution in 1791, which read: "Congress shall make no law respecting an establishment of religion or restricting the free exercise thereof." There was to be no state church and there was to be no interference with religious worship services. Church and state were to exist as separate institutions, neither united nor integrated as in England and elsewhere in Europe.

The impact of the Revolutionary War took its toll on Christianity. And then, after nationhood was achieved, there was a second great awakening, called the Great Revival. It started in the 1790s and lasted through the first several decades of the 1800s. The dominant figure of the revival was Charles G. Finney, a lawyer-turned-evangelist who developed a "results-oriented" approach to evangelism. Finney's revivals, which were carefully prepared and promoted and had good follow-up, reinvigorated religious life in America.

INDUSTRIALIZATION AND URBANIZATION

The American Civil War—or the War Between the States—was the most devastating war in United States history: six hundred thousand killed, one million wounded and widespread destruction of land and property. The precipitating cause of the war was the secession of eleven Southern states from the Union—the North considered the Union indivisible—but the real cause was slavery, America's "original sin," so called because it went back to the founding of the Republic (there were 3.5 million slaves in 1860).

The war lasted for four years, from April 1861 to April 1865. The war was strictly an American affair; no other nation was involved. President Lincoln said that it was God's punishment for the nation's accommodation to slavery; others saw it as a sacrificial cleansing. The war ended the dream that America was God's true chosen land and light to the nations.

As a result of the war, the United States had become, by the end of the nineteenth century, the world's leading manufacturing nation, surpassing the production of both England and Germany. To get to where the jobs were, people began moving from small towns to the industrial cities, and America moved from a rural, agrarian economy to an urban, industrial giant. All of this was not without problems, however: widespread industrial abuses, tenement and slum living conditions, crime and vice in all its ugly forms, and political corruption. The church was put under heavy pressure to cope with these changes, because its strength was in the small towns, not the large cities.

One response to the shift from an agrarian to an industrialized society was the Social Gospel Movement, a name chosen to differentiate it from non-Christian social movements. Although Christian-based, it was criticized by conservative Christians for being more interested in righting the evils of society than in converting the lost. The movement, which lasted from the 1870s to the 1920s, heightened the country's awareness of abusive and unsafe labor practices and of unacceptable living conditions in overcrowded cities, which Congress passed laws to help remedy.

PENTECOSTALISM

The most significant religious movement in the last one hundred years has been Pentecostalism, which originated in the United States at the turn of the twentieth century. (The Assemblies of God, the largest Pentecostal denomination, was founded in 1914.) The principal Pentecostal distinctive is "speaking in tongues"—a language other than one known to the speaker, called *glossalalia* (*glossa* is the Greek word for "tongue," *lalia* for "talk")—which Pentecostals believe is the evidence of being "baptized in the Spirit." (The first visible sign of the Spirit—speaking in tongues—came on the first Pentecost following Jesus' death, thus the name *Pentecostals*.) In Pentecostalism, religious experience is more important than creedal confessions and theology.

Closely aligned with the Pentecostals are the charismatics—from the Greek word *charismata,* meaning "gifts"—who believe in the gifts of the Spirit but are not insistent on speaking in tongues as the only evidence of the Spirit. The charismatic movement traces its beginnings to 1960 when Dennis Bennett, rector of St. Mark's Episcopal Church in Van Nuys, California, announced to his congregation that he had experienced "the baptism of the Holy Spirit," which led to his forced resignation.

An important distinction between Pentecostals and charismatics is that charismatics belong to "mainline" denominational and independent churches rather than Pentecostal churches. Another difference is that most charismatics do not embrace Pentecostalism's anti-intellectualism and its pre-millennial dispensationalism.

Pentecostalism is growing throughout the world. It is very strong in Africa, and also in Latin America where it is the largest Protestant movement. According to church demographer David Barrett, Pentecostals and charismatics together, in January 2000, numbered 524 million (25 percent of Christians worldwide). A major reason for the explosive growth of the Pentecostal-charismatic movement is the desire for a more experiential faith, one that goes beyond church tradition, doctrine and liturgy. Another reason is the belief that gifts of the Spirit are as available today as they were in the first century. A further reason is the desire of many for the Holy Spirit to deepen and enliven their faith and to give them "words of knowledge" concerning their lives and the lives of others.

MODERNISM AND FUNDAMENTALISM

The twentieth century witnessed an American schism between Protestant liberals and conservatives. European liberal Protestantism, which substituted reason and human experience for the Bible as the primary authority for life, came to the United States in the late 1800s. In the first decade of the 1900s it burst onto center stage in debates between *modernists,* Protestant liberals who wanted to "modernize" the Bible and Christianity—that is, reconcile Christianity with modern science—and *fundamentalists,* conservatives who argued for "the fundamentals of the faith," the most important being the verbal inerrancy of Scripture and Jesus' virgin birth, substitutionary atonement, bodily resurrection and imminent return.

The conflict culminated in the Scopes Trial in Dayton, Tennessee, in 1925. The American Civil Liberties Union (ACLU) persuaded John Scopes, a high school biology teacher, to teach evolution to test the constitutionality of Tennessee's antievolution law. Clarence Darrow, an agnostic and America's leading trial lawyer, represented the ACLU. William Jennings Bryan, a conservative Protestant and thrice the unsuccessful Democratic candidate for the presidency, represented the World Christian Fundamentalist Association. Bryan agreed to testify as an expert on the Bible and was brutally cross-examined by Darrow regarding the early chapters of Genesis. Bryan's answers were sometimes clever—"It is better to know the Rock of Ages than the age of the rocks"—but rarely convincing. The liberals (modernists) won the debate, at least in the mind of the public. The fundamentalists suffered ridicule and became defensive, which split many Protestant denominations into conservative and liberal wings.

EVANGELICALISM

The early 1940s saw the emergence of a new group, called *evangelicals,* a coalition of conservative Christians who wanted to distance themselves from fundamentalism and its narrowness and anti-intellectualism; its social taboos against smoking, movies, dancing, card-playing and the like; and its separatist philosophy. Evangelicals began to accept some findings of science (regarding Creation, for example) and some aspects of biblical scholarship (regarding biblical criticism, for example) and began to play an active role in society.

Evangelicalism is not a denomination like Lutheranism. It is a generic term that embraces the teachings of apostolic Christianity and includes adherents of both mainline and independent Protestant churches. Some of these teachings and beliefs are the infallibility and authority of Scripture, the triune Godhead, the necessity of spiritual rebirth and having a personal relationship with Jesus, and the Great Commission.

The Institute for the Study of American Evangelicals estimates there are upwards of 100 million evangelicals in the United States. Some well-known evangelical organizations are the Navigators (founded in 1933), the Wycliffe Bible Translators (1934), Young Life (1938), Intervarsity Christian Fellowship (1941), Youth for Christ (1945), Billy Graham Evangelistic Association (1950), World Vision (1950), Campus Crusade for Christ (1951), Youth With A Mission (1960) and Prison Fellowship (1976).

IMPORTANT DATES AND EVENTS IN CHRISTIAN HISTORY

The following are dates of important events in the history of the Christian church from the first century to the end of the twentieth.

30 The Death of Jesus (April 7)
30 Pentecost (May 27): The "Birthday" of the Church
33 The Conversion of Saul (Paul) on the Road to Damascus
46 Paul's First Missionary Journey
57 Paul's Letter to the Roman Church: Paul's Magnum Opus
64 Nero's Burning of Rome and Persecution of Christians
65 The Martyrdom of Peter and Paul in Rome
70 Roman Army Destroys Jerusalem (First Jewish War: 66–70)
70 The Gospel According to Mark: The First Gospel
200 Trinitarian Baptismal Creed: Forerunner of the Apostles' Creed
230 Earliest Known Christian Churches Built
270 Anthony Begins Life as a Hermit: Beginning of Monasticism
312 The Conversion of the Roman Emperor Constantine
313 The Edict of Milan: The Beginning of Religious Toleration
325 The Council of Nicea: The Divinity of Christ
367 Athanasius' *Easter Letter*: Earliest List of Books in the New Testament Canon
380 Christianity Becomes the Official Religion of the Roman Empire
386 The Conversion of Saint Augustine in Milan
405 Jerome Completes His Translation of the *Vulgate*
410 The Fall of Rome: The Beginning of the Dark Ages
451 The Council of Chalcedon: The Dual Nature of Christ
540 Benedict of Nursia Writes "The Rule of Saint Benedict"
800 Charlemagne Crowned Holy Roman Emperor
1054 Split of the Church Into West (Catholic) and East (Orthodox)
1095 Pope Urban II Launches First Crusade Against Islam
1208 Francis of Assisi's "Renunciation" (of wealth)
1273 Aquinas's *Summa Theologica*: Summary of Catholic Theology
1382 The Wycliffe Bible: The First Bible Translated Into English
1456 The Gutenberg Bible: The First Bible to Be Printed
1478 The Spanish Inquisition (King Ferdinand and Queen Isabella)
1492 Columbus Crosses Atlantic: Christianity Comes to the New World
1517 Luther's Ninety-five Theses: The Protestant Reformation
1534 The Act of Supremacy: England Separates From Rome
1534 Ignatius Establishes the Jesuits: Catholicism's Largest Order

1536 John Calvin's *Institutes of the Christian Religion*
1542 Francis Xavier Begins Missionary Work in South India
1545 The Council of Trent: The Catholic Reformation
1549 Archbishop Thomas Cranmer's *The Book of Common Prayer*
1559 John Knox Returns to Scotland to Lead Scottish Reformation
1609 Anglican-Turned-Separatist John Smyth Baptizes First "Baptists"
1611 The King James "Authorized Version" of the Bible
1620 *The Mayflower Pact:* "A Colony for the Glory of God"
1647 Westminster Catechism: "To Glorify God and Enjoy Him Forever"
1648 George Fox Founds the Society of Friends (the "Quakers")
1678 Publication of John Bunyan's *The Pilgrim's Progress*
1734 The Great Awakening in the Colonies (Edwards and Whitefield)
1738 The Conversion of John Wesley: Start of Wesleyan Revivalism
1780 Robert Raikes Starts Sunday School Movement in England
1793 William Carey Sails to India: Protestant Missionary Movement
1807 William Wilberforce Leads Parliament to Abolish the Slave Trade
1812 Adoniram Judson Sails to India: America's First Missionary
1825 Charles Finney and the Urban Revival Movement
1841 David Livingstone Begins Missionary Work in Southern Africa
1844 The YMCA Is Founded in London by George Williams
1854 J. Hudson Taylor Begins Missionary Work in China
1859 Darwin's *The Origin of Species* Challenges the Biblical Story
1860 The China Inland Mission: The First "Faith" Mission
1865 William Booth Establishes The Salvation Army in London
1886 Student Volunteer Movement Takes the Gospel to the World
1906 The Azusa Street Revival: The "Birthday" of Pentecostalism
1910 *The Fundamentals:* The Beginning of "Fundamentalism"
1919 Karl Barth's Commentary on Romans: The Birth of Neo-Orthodoxy
1921 First Christian Radio Broadcast: Station KDKA in Pittsburgh
1934 Cameron Townsend Launches the Wycliffe Bible Translators
1942 National Association of Evangelicals: The Dawn of Evangelicalism
1945 Dietrich Bonhoeffer Hanged by Nazis in German Prison Camp
1947 Discovery of Dead Sea Scrolls: The Oldest Old Testament Manuscripts
1948 First World Council of Churches: 47 Countries Represented
1949 Billy Graham's First Crusade: 210 Million Attendees to Date
1962 Second Vatican Council: Beginning of Catholic "Modernism"
1963 Martin Luther King Jr.: "I Have a Dream"
1971 Gustavo Gutiérrez: *The Theology of Liberation*
1974 Lausanne (Switzerland) Council on World Evangelization
1978 Pope John Paul II: First Non-Italian Pope since 1523
1991 Dissolution of USSR: Reinstatement of Religious Freedoms
2000 Amsterdam 2000: *Amsterdam Declaration on Evangelism*

CHAPTER 7

CHRISTIAN BELIEFS

We believe in one God, the Father, the Almighty, maker of heaven and earth, of all that is, seen and unseen. We believe in one Lord, Jesus Christ, the only Son of God, eternally begotten of the Father, God from God, light from light, true God from true God, begotten, not made, and of one Being with the Father, through him all things were made. For us and for our salvation he came down from heaven, was incarnate of the Holy Spirit and the Virgin Mary and became truly human. For our sake he was crucified under Pontius Pilate; he suffered death and was buried. On the third day he rose again in accordance with the Scriptures; he ascended into heaven and is seated at the right hand of the Father. He will come again in glory to judge the living and the dead, and his kingdom will have no end. We believe in the Holy Spirit, the Lord, the giver of life, who proceeds from the Father [and the Son], who with the Father and the Son is worshiped and glorified, who has spoken through the prophets. We believe in one holy catholic and apostolic Church. We acknowledge one baptism for the forgiveness of sins. We look for the resurrection of the dead, and the life of the world to come. Amen.

THE NICENE CREED

Translation by the ecumenical English Language Liturgical Commission. The words "and the Son," added later in the West, are included in brackets.

A SUMMARY OF CHRISTIAN DOCTRINES AND BELIEFS

What do Christians believe? Most introductions to the Bible don't address this. They study the books of the Bible, but frequently do not cover the doctrines and beliefs derived from the Bible. We need to have a clear understanding of Christian doctrines and beliefs, as well as which beliefs are primary and nonnegotiable and which are not. The early church had to address this issue as well and came up with confessions and creeds like the Apostles' Creed and the Nicene Creed.

In this chapter we will look at the knowledge, nature and triunity of God; the creation of the universe and of life on planet Earth; humankind's alienation from God; the saving death and bodily resurrection of Jesus; the person and work of the Holy Spirit; the church and its sacraments; and the end times or final things—the return of Jesus, the final judgment, the intermediate state and the life hereafter. The better we understand and can articulate our beliefs, the more confident we will be in sharing our faith.

CHRISTIAN THEOLOGY

The word *theology* comes from the Greek words *theos,* meaning "God," and *ology,* meaning the science or knowledge of something. So theology is the study of God, just as biology is the study of living organisms. The classic definition of theology, dating back to Anselm in the eleventh century, is "faith seeking understanding"—faith asking questions, faith probing for answers. Does God exist or are we just imagining the whole thing? What is sin and where did sin come from and how does Jesus' death save us from our sins? In what sense are the Scriptures the Word of God and in what sense are they the words of the authors who wrote them? The task of theology is to ask such questions and to answer them in a complete, rigorous and systematic way.

GOD OUR FATHER, ALL-MIGHTY AND ALL-LOVING

Does God exist? This is the first theological question—the *ultimate* theological question. The Christian answer, which is a statement of faith ("I believe in . . .") rather than something that can be scientifically proven, is a resounding YES.

THE KNOWLEDGE OF GOD

The first task of theology has to do with the knowledge of God: How do we *know* that God exists? The knowledge of God comes to us in four ways. First, God is made known in *creation* (Rom. 1:20). The world cannot be explained or accounted for in terms of itself: something cannot come from nothing. Reasoning back from what we observe, we come to a Creator or Designer or Author of creation. Second, God is made known in *providence*—his "provide-ence" for his people. Read again the Karl Barth quotation at the beginning of chapter 2 regarding God's providence in the life and history of the people of Israel, which cannot be seen in the life or history of any other people.

Third, God is made known in human *conscience,* that aspect of the human psyche that distinguishes humans created in the image and likeness of God from all other creatures. Conscience enables humans to discern what is morally right and wrong, and urges us to do the right and not the wrong. Fourth, God is made known in *Jesus,* the one Paul calls "the image of the invisible God" (Col. 1:15), the one in whom, Søren Kierkegaard said, "the infinite became finite."

The first three ways of knowing God are called *general* (or natural) revelation because they have been revealed generally to all people everywhere since the beginning of time. The fourth way is called *special* revelation because it relates to specific revelations of God to the patriarchs and prophets of Israel and in the life, death and resurrection of Jesus, which are recorded and attested to in the Old and New Testaments.

THE NATURE OF GOD

A story is told about Augustine coming upon a boy on the shore of the Mediterranean filling buckets of water and pouring them into a hole in the sand. Augustine asked the boy what he was doing. The boy said, "I'm emptying the Mediterranean Sea into this hole." Augustine laughed and said, "You'll never fit the Mediterranean into that small hole. You're wasting your time." The boy looked up and said, "And you're wasting your time writing a book about God. You'll never fit God into a book."

How are we to visualize and understand God, who is pure *spirit* (John 4:24)? One way is to think about God in anthropomorphic terms, as if he were a human, as in Michelangelo's painting of God and Adam on the ceiling of the Sistine Chapel. Another way is to talk about God's *attributes*, those qualities that are intrinsic to him by virtue of his being God. The following are some attributes of God.

God Is Eternal. Time began with God and will end with God. There was no time when God "was not." God is "from everlasting to everlasting" (Ps. 90:2 and 103:17).

God Is Almighty. God is *omnipotent*, meaning all-powerful; he is able to do whatever he wills to do (Ps. 135:5–6). God is *omnipresent*, meaning everywhere present at one and the same time; he is one from whom no one can hide (Ps. 139:7–12). God is *omniscient*, meaning that he is all-knowing, with complete and perfect knowledge of things past, present and future (Heb. 4:13); he knows those who love him and those who do not.

God Is Creator. God created the universe and life in all its varied forms, and he created out of nothing—*creatio ex nihilo*—rather than molding what already was. If God had created "out of matter," matter would have been coeternal with God. Before God created, there was nothing except God.

God Is Transcendent and Immanent. God is *transcendent*—beyond and external to all that is, as in the creation of the universe. God is also *immanent*—present and active in creation, as he was in the Exodus and at Mount Sinai and in Jesus. God is the one in whom "we live and move and have our being" (Acts 17:28).

God Is Personal. God is a *person* (Mark 12:26–27), not an object or an *it*, who created us in his image and likeness so that we could have a relationship with him. Among God's personal attributes are love, kindness, mercy and compassion. God is like a parent who cares for and guides us; whose words and promises can be relied upon; who comes to us in times of pain, suffering and need.

THE TRINITY OF GOD

Christianity has a number of mysteries—how God became incarnate in Jesus of Nazareth, how Jesus' death saves us from our sins, how Jesus is present in the celebration of the Lord's Supper—that are beyond human comprehension and understanding. Another mystery is the Trinity.

The Trinity is the *triunity* or three-ness of God—the doctrine that God comes to us as God the *Father,* the transcendent, "wholly other" Creator of the universe; as God the *Son,* Jesus Christ, who came to reveal God, to redeem us from our sins and to reconcile us with the Father and with one another; and as God the *Holy Spirit,* the indwelling Spirit who calls us to faith and regenerates and sanctifies us. The triunity of God is like *sound:* God is the source or speaker (Isa. 55:11), Jesus is the Word spoken (Heb. 1:2) and the Holy Spirit is the way God continues to speak (John 16:13).

How are we to understand God the *Son?* When Jesus was on earth he prayed to his Father, and said that his Father was greater than he, and he died and was buried (how could God *die?*). When Jesus came to earth, he subordinated himself to his Father's will and purposes. Paul writes to the Philippians that when Jesus was on the earth he "emptied himself . . . and became obedient to the point of death—even death on a cross" (Phil. 2: 7–8). Jesus, as God's obedient Son, died so that we, through his saving death, might be reconciled with God. As to whether the incarnate God can "die," the answer is yes as to his human nature but no as to his divine nature.

In thinking about the triunity of God, we need to hold together the *unity* of the Godhead and its *three-ness.* Analogies, though always imperfect, are sometimes helpful in explaining difficult concepts. The following analogies show how something or someone can be both one and three at the same time. An example from nature is that of *water:* if water in a test tube is frozen at one end and heated at the other, the water in the test tube has three different "forms"—it is solid ice at one end, vapor or gas at the other and liquid in the middle. Another example from nature is the *sun:* it comes to us each day in three different "modes"—as light, as heat and as energy. Still another example from nature is the rainbow: each of the colors is separate and distinct from one another—but all are part of the same "bow." An example from life is that of a *married person with a child:* such a person is, at one and the same time, three different "persons"—someone's son or daughter, a spouse's husband or wife and a child's father or mother.

OTHER "GOD-ISMS"

Monotheism, from the Greek *monos* ("one") and *theos* ("god"), is the belief in a single deity or god. *Theism* is the belief in the ultimate reality of

God, and for Christians in a *personal* God. *Atheism* is the belief that there is no god (the prefix *a* means "no," so *a-theism* means "no-god"). *Agnosticism* is the belief that it is not possible to know whether God exists (*gnosis* is the Greek word for knowledge, so *a-gnosis* means "no knowledge").

Polytheism (*poly* means "many") is the belief that there are many gods, as in Hinduism. *Pantheism* (*pan* means "all") is the belief that everything is god, or that god is in everything, a view the New Age movement calls "monism." *Deism* (from the Latin *deus,* meaning "god") is the belief that God created the universe but is no longer involved with life on planet Earth. *Animism* is the belief that all natural phenomena (humans, animals, plants, stones) have souls.

THE DOCTRINE OF CREATION

The doctrine of Creation, Martin Luther said, "is the foundation of the whole of Scripture." It is one of the pillars on which our faith rests. If we have doubts regarding the doctrine of Creation—for instance, if we believe that life was not created but came into being and evolved "upward" by chance—then our faith, like the house built on sand, rests on a weak foundation. Unfortunately, the current tendency in much of North America and Europe is to explain the universe and life in natural rather than supernatural terms.

SCIENCE AND RELIGION

Science clearly dominates the Western way of thinking, not only about the world but also about life in general, including religion. Before looking at the doctrine of creation, we need to understand how science arrives at its conclusions. First, it measures and records phenomena (observed facts and occurrences). Second, it hypothesizes about the meaning of its observations and findings. Third, it tests its hypotheses until a particular hypothesis is proven either true or false.

There is no conflict here between science and religion. The conflict comes when science postulates about the truth of things that cannot be proven, such as the origin of the universe and the origin of life. Why do many scientists insist on *naturalistic* explanations for these origins? Because their "closed system" worldviews will not allow them to consider the possibility of *super*natural explanations.

THE CREATION OF THE UNIVERSE

The Christian doctrine of Creation is a statement of faith (Heb. 11:3), beyond which we may only theorize. The most popular scientific theory is the Big Bang, the belief that 15 billion or so years ago a super-stupendous explosion gave birth to the universe, which is still expanding, even today, at tremendous speeds. (The expansion of the universe was discovered by Edwin Hubble in the mid–1920s, which gave rise to the Big Bang hypothesis.)

This still leaves a question: What caused the Big Bang? Was it a random accident of nature or was it *willed* into being by a purposeful Creator? According to the Bible, "In the beginning . . . God created the heavens and the earth" (Gen. 1:1).

Is there any *evidence* for the biblical view that God created the heavens and the earth? Everyone acknowledges the universe's consistency and precision, and as the existence of a watch implies a watchmaker, so the universe implies the mind of an intelligent Agent or Designer. This is much easier to believe than creation by *pure chance*. That is, it is much easier to believe in the universal principle of cause and effect, with God as the Prime Mover or Creator, than to believe the cosmos came into being as a result of an uncaused event. Something cannot come from nothing.

If there was a Creator, how did he *create*? We are not told, other than that he created by his Word ("God said . . . and it was so"). The Genesis Creation accounts are not scientific statements about the processes of creation; they are faith statements about the one who is behind creation, the one who brought everything into being.

THE CREATION OF LIFE

The first Genesis Creation account states that vegetation, animal life and human life were created by God. But how did each, especially human life, come into being? According to the Bible, "God said, 'Let the earth bring forth living creatures . . . Let us make humankind in our image'" (Gen. 1:24, 26).

Is there any *evidence* for the biblical view that God created life on planet Earth? Some say that living matter, even man and woman, came into being by chance after the earth cooled down following the Big Bang. But how could inanimate matter give birth to animate, purposeful life, such as human life? Life can only come from preexisting life. And how could the two thousand or so enzymes (proteins within cells) required for human life have come together in the right sequence by chance? A distinguished British scientist, Sir Frederick Hoyle, estimated the probability of this happening as "about the same as the chance of throwing an uninterrupted sequence of 50,000 sixes with unbiased dice" (*The Intelligent Universe*).

What about Darwinism? Genetic mutations can be seen in the animal kingdom, and also among humans. But Darwin's theories of the origin of life and evolution by natural means have been shown by Lehigh University biochemist Michael Behe to have very little scientific support (*Darwin's Black Box*). Research on DNA in the 1950s unlocked the secrets of the cell, the building blocks of life. We now know, which of course Darwin did not, that cells consist of interconnected molecular systems. According to Behe, all of the systems must function for the cell to function, and complex, interacting subcellular structures cannot have originated and evolved as Darwin hypothesized.

A more reasonable explanation of the origin of life is that of "intelligent design." As with the universe, stories of the creation of life are not *how* stories but *why* stories: God created us in his "image and likeness" so that we could have a relationship with him and be in fellowship with him and care for and be stewards of his creation.

Sin: The Human Predicament

Man and woman are God's special creation, the crown of his creation, but the first "parents" of the human race fell into sin. And because the human race is interconnected—as a species, everyone is literally related to everyone else—we, as their heirs, are in a broken relationship with God.

The Doctrine of Sin

Sin is a theological concept. It is disobeying the divine law or will of God. One definition of sin is the Greek word *hamartia*, which means "missing the mark." We miss the mark when we step over the line, and also when we do not step up to the line. What is the *mark* or *line*? In a word, it is *love*. We sin when we do not love God with our whole heart—when we disobey his will and his commandments (1 John 5:3a)—and when we do not show love, kindness and compassion to others.

The Christian doctrine of sin has two elements. First, we are born sinful, sons and daughters of Adam and Eve. Theologian Peter Kreeft says that sin is to the soul what disease is to the body. Our indwelt sinfulness—our sinful disease—gives rise to sinful acts, sometimes called "actual" sins or "daily" sins. Second, Christians believe that Christ died that we might not perish in our sins, which distinguishes Christianity from all other religions, none of which believes that human beings are innately sinful. Because of our indwelt sinfulness, we are estranged from God, we are not in fellowship with God.

The world does not like the word *sin* and rarely uses it, as psychiatrist Karl Menninger observed in his book, *Whatever Happened to Sin?* Looking at the world around us—crime and violence, terrorism and war, drugs and other substance addictions, spousal abuse and child molestation, greed and corruption in government and business, suicide bombings in the Middle East and school and sniper shootings in the United States—it is hard to deny the all-pervasiveness of sin. The English writer G. K. Chesterton, in his spiritual autobiography, *Orthodoxy,* said that sin is one Christian doctrine no one can dispute. Chesterton said all you have to do is read the daily newspaper. Today we would say all you have to do is watch the evening news on television.

ORIGINAL SIN

The origin of sin and evil is second only to the origin of life as the greatest of all enigmas: Where did sin come from? How is it that human beings become evil people? Most religions, in an effort to come to grips with this question, have a doctrine of sin. Some believe that sin comes from uncontrolled carnal cravings. Others believe that we are born neutral and are pushed one way or the other by good and evil forces. Christianity believes that sin is part of the human condition.

But when and how did sin and evil enter the human race? The Bible teaches that the first humans disobeyed God, so the origin of sin—the fall into sin—goes back to the progenitors of the human family. How is sin passed on? This is a mystery. It used to be thought that sin was passed on by procreation, like a defective gene. This view no longer has much support. One thing we know, though, is that humankind is sinful, and this goes all the way back to the beginning of time. Sin is part of the human condition, however this happened. But this does not mean that we are not responsible for our individual sins and trepasses. There is no "The devil made me do it" escape clause in Christian theology.

THE FALL IN THE GARDEN

How are we to understand the story of Adam and Eve: God *forming* humans and *planting* a garden? A "tree of knowledge"? A talking serpent? Some believe that stories must be historical to be true and read Genesis 3 as an actual historical account of sin entering the world through the disobedience of Adam and Eve, which Paul elaborates on in Romans ("Sin came into the world through one man," 5:12). Others believe that stories themselves contain truths, as with Jesus' parables—there was no actual, historcial *Good Samaritan,* for instance—and read the fall of Adam and Eve as a "story" that expresses an indisputable truth: men and women are sinful, fallen creatures and have been since the dawn of human history.

The question, though, is not *how* sin entered the world, but the recognition of the *universality* of sin—not how we got ourselves into this mess, but how do we get out, because "the wages of sin is death" (Rom. 6:23). The Christian answer is Jesus Christ, the One who defeated the *power* of sin in his victory over death (1 Cor. 15:55–57), the One who came to give *new life* to all who confess their sins and follow him as Lord and Savior.

JESUS CHRIST: LORD AND SAVIOR

The fundamental question of every religion is the question of the Philippian jailer in the book of Acts: "What must I do to be saved?" (Acts 16:30), meaning, What must I do to be rightly related to God? The Christian answer is, "Believe on the Lord Jesus" (Acts 16:31).

THE PERSON AND NATURE OF CHRIST

The early church debated the person and nature of Christ. Arius of Alexandria contended that Jesus was less than or different from God, because Jesus was created (born), thus had a beginning, and because Jesus said, "The Father is greater than I" (John 14:28). Arius said that Jesus was *similar* to God but not the *same* as God. Athanasius, also of Alexandria, insisted that Jesus was one with God from all eternity. Jesus said, "I am in the Father and the Father is in me" (John 14:10–11) and "The Father and I are one" (John 10:30). Athanasius said that if Jesus were not God, he could not be our Savior, which was Arius's downfall. The Arian-Athanasian controversy was resolved at the Councils of Nicea (325) and Constantinople (381), which stated that Jesus is "very God of very God, begotten not made, of one substance with the Father." (Arius refused to sign the Nicene Creed and was excommunicated and sent into exile.)

Arguments also arose about Jesus' nature. Was Jesus part God and part human? And if there were "parts," were they equal or different, and were they separate or mixed? The nature of Jesus was resolved at the Council of Chalcedon (451), which declared that Jesus was one person with two natures, one divine ("conceived by the Holy Spirit") and one human ("born of the Virgin Mary"), and that these "natures" were neither separate nor mixed. This came to be known as the Chalcedon Definition.

So Jesus was fully *human*—human so that we can identify with him ("one like us"), and also fully *divine,* because only God can save us. As to his *humanity,* Jesus was born of a woman, was tested in the wilderness, ate with friends and sinners and went to weddings, preached to the crowds and debated the Pharisees, was often weary and sorrowful and at times even angry, and he suffered, died and was buried. As to his *divinity,* Jesus was conceived by the Holy Spirit (thus by God himself), performed miracles, which pointed to his divinity, had foreknowledge, as in knowing what others were thinking (Mark 2:6–8), and he claimed "oneness" with God and personal attributes of God, such as forgiving sin (Mark 2:5).

JESUS' VIRGIN BIRTH

The miraculous conception of Jesus in the womb of the Virgin Mary underlies the church's teaching that Jesus was conceived apart from a human father—that is, supernaturally, by God himself. The birth narratives, of course, do not *prove* that Jesus was God incarnate (God "in the flesh"). Rather, they *announce* that from the moment of his conception, Jesus was both human and divine. How did this occur—or to ask Mary's question: "How can this be, since I am a virgin?" (Luke 1:34). Matthew and Luke tell us in their birth narratives that it occurred through the agency or power of the Holy Spirit.

Today the Virgin Birth is a stumbling block for non-Christians, and even for many Christians. British scholar Keith Ward said the strongest argument for the veracity of the Matthean and Lukan birth narratives is that it is very hard to see why they would have been invented when their claim—that a child conceived out of wedlock (Luke 2:5) was the genetic, anointed, messianic descendant of King David—would have been so offensive to Jewish ears.

To deny that Jesus was conceived by God is to deny that he was God incarnate, which is to deny his "savior-ness." We are not saved by fellow humans, no matter how wonderful and worthy they may be, but by God and by God alone.

JESUS' SAVING DEATH

As to the *work* of Jesus, he came to reveal God, but his principal work was his saving death to heal our broken relationship with God. The Swiss scholar Karl Barth, the most influential Protestant theologian in the twentieth century, said the most important word in the New Testament is the Greek word *huper,* which means "on behalf of." Jesus died for us—for our inability to save ourselves—which is the greatest of all ironies: the one who came to offer new life to others had to give his own life to do so.

Theologians refer to Jesus' death as the *Atonement,* meaning that Jesus died to "atone" for our sins. To understand the doctrine of Atonement, we need to go back to the Old Testament. In ancient Israel, priests sacrificed *animals* to cover the sins of the people (Lev. 1–7); the prophet Isaiah said that one is coming who will bear the sins of the people in his own *body* (Isa. 53). Jesus said that he had come to fulfill the prophecy of Isaiah (Luke 22:37) as the sin-bearer who would die a sacrificial death for the sins of the world (see Heb. 10:1–18).

When two people have a serious disagreement, they become estranged. If the person in the wrong does not seek forgiveness or is not forgiven, the estrangement continues, sometimes forever. Because we do not love God with our whole heart, we are estranged from God. How can we be reconciled with God? By accepting his saving gift of forgiveness, namely, Jesus' death for us. Jesus' atoning death is the way to our *at-one-ment* with God.

But how does Jesus' death in the first century save us from our sins in the twenty-first century—our sin of separation from God and our daily trespasses? The apostle Paul said that we are saved "through faith . . . for faith" (Rom. 1:17). We are saved *through* the faithful act of Jesus dying for us on the cross . . . and by our faith and trust that his saving death was, is and will be salvific (sufficient for salvation) *for* us.

JESUS' RESURRECTION

There were messianic movements before and after Jesus. They all collapsed with the deaths of their founders. Why did the "Jesus movement" survive—not only survive, but *flourish,* with large, active communities of believers all over the Mediterranean world? The reason was the proclamation that God had raised Jesus from the dead. What convinced these early Christians that Jesus had been raised and was now alive?

The empty tomb. Most scholars believe that Jesus died on April 7, 30. Fifty days later, on the feast of Pentecost, his followers began preaching that he had risen from the dead. If the Jewish leaders had produced Jesus' body, which in the dry Palestinian climate would not have decomposed, it would have put an end to his followers' claim that he had been raised and was now, again, alive. The German theologian Paul Althaus said, "The claim that Jesus had been raised could not have been maintained for a single day, for a single hour, if the emptiness of the tomb had not been established as a fact for all concerned."

The written testimony to Jesus' resurrection. The New Testament records twelve appearances of the risen Christ in the Gospels, the book of Acts and Paul's first letter to the Corinthians. No one would have taken the time or gone to the expense of writing and copying manuscripts about an executed Jewish peasant from rural, backwater Galilee if he had remained in the grave.

The witness of the disciples. When Jesus died, his disciples were afraid for their lives—too afraid even to fulfill their duty as his closest friends to bury him, so Joseph of Arimathea had to do so. Soon thereafter, however, on the first Pentecost, they began preaching on the streets of Jerusalem, and later throughout the Roman Empire, that Jesus had been raised from the dead—and many were martyred for doing so, both in Jerusalem (like Stephen and James) and in Rome (like Peter and Paul). The Christian apologist Paul Little said, "People will die for what they *believe* to be true, but no one willingly dies for what he or she *knows* to be false."

The honesty of the Gospel accounts. The accounts of Jesus' post-resurrection appearances are reported as fact, as something that actually happened, not as wish-fulfillment stories. Further, in the first century, women (and minors, convicts and slaves) were not considered credible witnesses, yet all four gospels report that the empty tomb was discovered by "the women" (see Mark 16:1–8). If the writers had fabricated their narratives to make them more believable, they would have had men, not women, as the first witnesses to Jesus' resurrection, as Paul does in writing to the Greco-Roman church in Corinth, where no women are mentioned in his sixfold list of witnesses to Jesus' resurrection (1 Cor. 15:5–8).

The conversion of Saul of Tarsus. The apostle Paul met the risen Christ on the road to Damascus and changed overnight from the bitterest foe of Christianity—who stood by while Stephen was stoned in Jerusalem, and then left for Damascus to bring Christians back to Jerusalem for trial—to its greatest church-planting missionary and champion.

When Lord Nelson defeated the French fleet in the Battle of the Nile in 1798, he told the British Admiralty that *victory* was not a big enough word to describe what had taken place. When we talk about Jesus' victory over death on Easter morning—a victory for all believers for all eternity—*victory* is not a big enough word to describe what took place.

SALVATION: BY GRACE THROUGH FAITH

Frederick Buechner reminds us that "the Gospel is bad news before it is good news." It is the news that we stand as sinners before a holy, just and righteous God. But it is "also the news that we are loved anyway, cherished, bleeding to be sure, but also bled for."

JUSTIFICATION BY FAITH

The twentieth-century novelist Dorothy Sayers said no one would deny that there is a wide and deep cleavage in Christendom, "but it does not run between Catholics and Protestants, it runs between those who believe that salvation is of God and those who believe that salvation is of man." Christianity is unique among the world's religions in believing that we are saved "by grace . . . through faith" (Eph. 2:8).

The first part of the equation is God's gift of *grace* (Jesus' death "for us"), which is free. There is nothing that we can do to earn our salvation, nothing that will oblige God to save us. But for God's offer of salvation to be effective, it must be accepted. If you are told that you need a surgical operation to live—say, a heart bypass—you have to have the surgery. If you don't, you will die. So it is with God's offer of salvation: if we don't accept his offer—Jesus Christ—we will be lost for all eternity. This is the second part of the equation. We are saved *through faith* in Jesus Christ. This means believing, trusting and confessing Jesus and living under his lordship. (We like thinking of Jesus as our Savior. It is submitting to his lordship that we have trouble with.) So we are "saved" by accepting God's offer of salvation.

What are we saved *from* and *for*? We are saved *from* "our sins" (1 Cor. 15:3), a theme that is repeated throughout the New Testament. What does "our sins" mean? First and foremost, it means ignoring or dishonoring God. Second, it means disobeying God's "shall nots" regarding adultery, stealing, lying and the other commandments in the Decalogue (see chapter 10). Third, it means falling prey to "deadly sins" like greed, hate, apathy toward others and lust (see chapter 9). Jesus gave his life that we might be forgiven of "our sins"—our failure to acknowledge and honor God, and our actual everyday sins. What are we saved *for*? For eternal fellowship with the triune God and with all other believers.

WILL EVERYONE BE SAVED?

Today many believe that everyone will be saved, a view called "universal salvation" or "universalism." According to the New Testament, however, there will be two final outcomes: some will be saved and others will not. Perhaps the clearest statement concerning the two outcomes is John 3:16, often referred to as the "gospel in a nutshell": whoever believes in the one whom God has sent will not *perish* (one outcome) but will have *eternal life* (the other outcome).

THE DOCTRINE OF ASSURANCE

Another confusion regarding salvation is the possibility of losing one's salvation. If one truly believes in Christ—that is, places his or her total trust in Jesus and confesses him and lives under his lordship—there is every reason to be confident of one's salvation. Jesus said that everyone who believes in him will be saved (John 6:40) and that none who are his will be lost (John 10:27–29). Paul told the Philippians that "the one who began a good work among you will bring it to completion by the day of Jesus Christ" (1:6).

If we truly believe that through Jesus we can be restored to a right and righteous relationship with God, our salvation is secure. If we had to work out our salvation, it would rest on *our* achievement rather than the finished work of Christ on the cross.

THE HOLY SPIRIT: THE PERFECTER OF OUR FAITH

The Holy Spirit—or Holy "Ghost," from the Old English *gast,* meaning "spirit"—is the Third Person of the Trinity. In the Old Testament, the Spirit (without the adjective *Holy*) was active in creation (Gen. 1:2), in the lives of the judges (throughout the book of Judges), in the lives of the kings ("and the spirit of the Lord came mightily upon David," 1 Sam. 16:13), and in the lives of the prophets ("The spirit of the Lord God is upon me," Isa. 61:1). In the New Testament, the Holy Spirit was the creative agent in the conception of Jesus ("The Holy Spirit will come upon you," Luke 1:35), was present at Jesus' baptism ("And the Holy Spirit descended upon him," Luke 3:22), and was active in the lives of the apostles ("All of them were filled with the Holy Spirit," Acts 2:4). One symbol of the Holy Spirit is the dove, the likeness of which descended on Jesus at his baptism (Luke 3:22).

THE PERSON AND WORK OF THE HOLY SPIRIT

The Holy Spirit is the Third Person in the Godhead, thus a person, not some vague, impersonal "force." As to the *work* of the Holy Spirit, one function is to grant specific "gifts" to believers, some twenty of which are listed in the New Testament, among them ministry, evangelism, teaching, hospitality, generosity, prophecy, discernment, tongues and healing (see 1 Cor. 12:8–10 and Rom. 12:6–8). Paul's lists of gifts are not meant to be understood as all-inclusive, because each time he mentions gifts he adds to the lists of gifts in his previous letters. According to the New Testament, every believer has been given at least one gift of the Spirit (1 Cor. 12:7 and 1 Peter 4:10).

REGENERATION

Repentance is the first step in conversion ("repent and believe the good news," Mark 1:15). It is something that we do, though Christians disagree about how we come to faith. Some say that belief is a conscious human choice and act (Rev. 3:20, for instance); others say the ability to "repent and believe" comes from a God-given prevenient or anticipatory gift of grace (Eph. 2:8). Regeneration is something that God does through the power of the Holy Spirit, the power that enables us to be "born again" or "born from above," as in Jesus' discourse with Nicodemus (John 3). Being regenerated does not mean that we are no longer tempted to sin; the tendency to sin lives on. The apostle Paul wrote, "I do not do what I want, but I do the very thing I hate" (Rom. 7:15). Being regenerated means that we are no longer controlled by sin or are "slaves" to sin.

SANCTIFICATION

Sanctification comes from the word *sanctify,* meaning "to make holy." It denotes the continuing work of the Holy Spirit that enables believers to grow in purity. Again, as with regeneration, sanctification does not mean that one no longer sins. The battles of the flesh continue, but through the sanctifying power of the Holy Spirit the believer grows in obedience to God and in righteousness and in holiness.

THE RECEIPT OF THE HOLY SPIRIT

There is confusion and disagreement regarding *how* and *when* one receives the Holy Spirit. Is the Spirit received at baptism? Or with some form of anointing, such as the laying on of hands (as with Paul in Acts 9:17)? Or upon accepting or confessing Jesus? The more sacramental denominations—those that place a high value on the sacraments—have long held that one receives the Holy Spirit at baptism (Acts 2:38). Some nonsacramental denominations believe that a necessary precedent to receiving the Holy Spirit is the public confession of Jesus as Lord and Savior.

There are also differing beliefs about second or post-water baptism experiences, which Pentecostals call "the baptism of the Holy Spirit." Pentecostals claim that one evidence of being filled with the Spirit is the manifestation of one or more miraculous or dramatic gifts of the Spirit, such as speaking in tongues. Others believe that there is only one Spirit, and when we receive the Spirit we receive him in all his fullness and completeness. American theologian Millard Erickson says that being filled with the Spirit is not so much a matter of our possessing more of the *Spirit* as it is the Spirit possessing more of *us*.

THE CHURCH: MARKS AND SACRAMENTS

In the New Testament, the word *church* does not refer to a denomination or building but to believers who gather together to worship Jesus as Lord and Savior. The Christian church traces its beginnings back to the first Pentecost, following Jesus' death and resurrection. Some have asked, Did Jesus intend to found a church? The answer is yes: he referred to himself as the Good Shepherd, which implies a community of believers to care for (John 10:11); he talked to the disciples about building "my *church*" (Matt. 16:18); and he told the disciples what to do if a "member of the *church*" sins (Matt. 18:15–17). In Paul's letters, the church is called "the body of Christ," of which Jesus is the head, and "the bride of Christ," of which he is the groom.

An argument occasionally heard from nominal Christians (Christians "in name only") is that they worship God in the world: I see God in creation. While God desires and encourages this, enjoying God's creation while hiking in the mountains or fishing or playing golf is not a substitute for worshiping God in community—coming together to give praise to his name, to hear his Word, to pray both individually and corporately, to partake in the sacraments and to be in fellowship with other believers.

THE MARKS OF THE CHURCH

The Nicene Creed confesses the church as one, holy, catholic and apostolic—four characteristics that define what the church is called to be.

One. There are several thousand denominations, but there is only "one body . . . one Spirit . . . one Lord . . . one God and Father of all" (Eph. 4: 4–6). Being *one,* however, does not mean that the church must everywhere be uniform, which allows for differences in history, language, church governance and forms of worship. One of the tragedies of the church is the effort spent fighting "within the family" over doctrine, sacraments, missions and other matters when there are still so many outside the church in need of salvation.

Holy. The word *holy* is often translated religious, pious or sacred. With regard to the church, it means being separate, distinct and set apart for ministry in and to the world.

Catholic. The word *catholic* does not mean Roman Catholic; it comes from a Greek word meaning "universal." The church of God is the whole church, the ecumenical church, the worldwide church, created for all people everywhere that they might be one human family under the lordship of Christ.

Apostolic. Apostolic means the church founded by the apostles; the church's agreement with the apostles' witness to Jesus; and the church's apostolic mission to make him known "to the ends of the earth."

THE CHURCH'S SACRAMENTS

The word *sacrament* comes from the Latin *sacramentum,* meaning "sacred oath," referring to sacred oaths that Roman soldiers took to the emperor. The North African theologian Tertullian applied the word to baptism as a rite in which adult baptismal candidates pledge their lives to Christ. The Belgian Dominican theologian Edward Schillebeeckx said, "Just as we encounter God in the tangible person of Jesus, so we encounter Jesus in the tangible sacraments."

Sacramental churches believe that sacraments bestow grace or are "channels of grace." (Nonsacramental churches prefer the word *ordinance* to sacrament, meaning that Christ "ordained" these acts.) The church has long recognized two major sacraments, *Baptism* and *Holy Communion,* sometimes called the "Gospel Sacraments." They were instituted by Jesus when he told his disciples, "Go therefore and make disciples of all nations, *baptizing* them . . ." (Matt. 28:19), and at the Last Supper, in breaking the bread and extending the cup, when he said, "*Do this* in remembrance of me" (Luke 22:19).

In addition to the two major sacraments, Catholic and Orthodox churches recognize five other sacraments: *Confirmation,* the confirming of vows made by one's parents or sponsors at baptism, which admits those confirmed ("confirmands") to full membership in the church. *Reconciliation* or *Penance* (previously called Confession), the forgiveness of post-baptismal sins. *Matrimony,* the covenanting of two people to each other in the sight of God. *Holy Orders* or *Ordination,* the consecration of those set apart for Christian ministry. And *Anointing the Sick,* formerly called *Extreme* (from *in extremis,* meaning "near death") *Unction* (meaning "anointing"). The name Extreme Unction was changed to Anointing the Sick in 1972 and broadened to include those who were seriously ill, not just those who were at or near death's door. Sacramental churches believe that sacramental grace is directly proportionate to the faith of the recipient. For instance, if one comes to the Lord's Table with no faith, the sacrament of Holy Communion has no power.

Baptism. Baptism is a sacrament by which a person is incorporated into the fellowship of the church. It has been practiced since the first century, as we read in the book of Acts: "Repent and be baptized . . . in the name of Jesus Christ" (2:38). (The Quakers and The Salvation Army are the only major denominations that do not baptize—in fact, they don't recognize any of the sacraments.) Though baptism has a long history, there are widespread differences in its understanding and practice, called by one writer "the water that divides." The following are some examples.

First, *infants* have been baptized into the church since apostolic times possibly corresponding to infant circumcision in Judaism. In some Protestant denominations, infants are *dedicated* rather than baptized; baptism for such persons is delayed until they are able to make a conscious decision for Christ. Further, some require a public confession of faith before a candidate is baptized, called *believer's* baptism, based on Acts 2:38. Many object to this because it narrows rather than widens the New Covenant. Second, the word *baptize* means to "immerse," which was the form of baptism in the early church and still is today in Baptist, Pentecostal, Brethren and many other churches. In most mainline denominations, however, baptism is by *affusion* (pouring) or *aspersion* (sprinkling). Third, for some, particularly Catholics, baptism *washes away* original sin; for others, it is an act or *sign* of inclusion in God's covenant of grace.

Holy Communion. The second major sacrament is Holy Communion, meaning "common union." In some sacramental denominations it is called the Eucharist, meaning "thanksgiving" for Jesus' atoning sacrifice. In the Catholic Church it is called the Mass, from the Latin *missio,* denoting an early practice of dismissing catechumens—adult converts who had not yet been baptized into the church—prior to the celebration of the Eucharist. Today the word *Mass* refers to the Catholic worship service, the central feature of which is the Eucharist. In the early church it was called the Lord's Supper and was celebrated within the context of a fellowship meal among believers (see 1 Cor. 11:17–34).

With regard to the sacrament itself, there are several different understandings. Roman Catholics believe that Christ is *literally* present in the consecrated bread and wine. Others believe that Christ is *spiritually* present in the celebration and partaking of the bread and wine, but not in the "elements" themselves. Still others—Congregationalists, Baptists, Pentecostals and Mennonites, for instance—believe that Christ is only *symbolically* present, recalling Jesus' words at the Last Supper: "Do this in *remembrance* of me" (Luke 22:19, emphasis added).

THE CHURCH: POLITY, CLERGY TITLES AND CALENDAR

CHURCH STRUCTURE AND GOVERNANCE

There are two billion Christians in the world, divided, according to the *World Christian Encyclopedia,* roughly 50–40–10 percent between Catholics,

Protestants and Orthodox (in the United States the division is 26–71–3).
Catholicism is a papal monarchy; Orthodoxy is a federation of self-governing national churches; Protestantism is a "loose association" of mainline
denominations and independent churches holding similar beliefs. Denominations themselves are often further divided. The *Handbook of Denominations in the United States,* for instance, lists twenty-five Baptist denominations, each with a different, distinguishing name: American Baptist, Black
Baptist, Conservative Baptist, Free Will Baptist, General Baptist, National
Baptist, Reformed Baptist, Separatist Baptist, Southern Baptist, United Baptist, and so forth.

There are three different forms of church governance or polity, as follows.

Episcopal, from a Greek word meaning "overseer," with bishops having
authority over ecclesiastical districts, synods or conferences. This is a "top-
down" form of authority, and the earliest form of church polity. It is used
by Roman Catholic and Eastern Orthodox churches, and within Protestantism by the Episcopal Church, each of which lays claim to a form of apostolic
succession (chapter 6). The United Methodist Church and the Evangelical
Lutheran Church in America, and also some independent churches, have
bishops, but their "office" or position is different and neither claim apostolic
succession.

Presbyterian, from a Greek word meaning "elder," is a representative
form of polity, with power vested in presbyteries made up of clergypersons
and governing elders of churches within a district or region, as in Reformed
and Presbyterian churches.

Independent or Free, with each church body or congregation being self-
governing. Baptist, Brethren, Covenant, Disciples of Christ, Evangelical
Free, Mennonite, Pentecostal and the United Church of Christ are examples
of independent churches. This is the most democratic form of government,
with authority residing in the laity rather than in bishops, synods and presbyteries.

CLERICAL TITLES

The church has different titles for those called to the ordained ministry.
A *priest* is a clergyperson in a Roman Catholic, Orthodox or Episcopal

church who has authority to administer the sacraments. *Minister* comes from a Latin word meaning "servant"—in its religious context, one consecrated and set aside to serve others—a general term or title for members of the clergy. *Reverend* comes from the Latin *reverendus,* meaning one "worthy of respect," a common courtesy title for clergypersons. *Pastor* comes from the Latin *passere,* meaning "to pasture," as a shepherd caring for sheep. *Rector* comes from the Latin *réctor,* meaning "director," one in charge of an Episcopal church or parish. A *Vicar* is one who acts *vica*riously for a rector. A *Curate* is one who assists a rector or vicar in the care (or cure) of the souls of a parish. *Chaplains* minister in chapels in hospitals, schools, prisons, on military bases and in other nonchurch settings. *Deacons* (from a Greek word meaning "attendant") are either clerics ranking below priests in Catholic, Orthodox and Episcopal churches or laypersons who assist the clergy in other churches.

THE CHURCH'S LITURGICAL CALENDAR

The church's liturgical calendar has three cycles. The Christmas cycle includes the "seasons" of Advent, Christmas and Epiphany; the Easter cycle includes the seasons of Lent, Easter and Pentecost; the post-Pentecost cycle starts on Trinity Sunday and runs through to Advent. Some denominations refer to the times between the Christmas and Easter cycles, and during the post-Pentecost cycle, as Ordinary Time, meaning "nonfestive" time.

Advent. The liturgical year begins with Advent, a word that means "coming"—Jesus' first coming in Bethlehem, his coming among us now in Word and in sacrament, and his promised second coming at the end of the age. The first of the four Advent Sundays is the Sunday nearest to November 30.

Christmas is the second most important celebration in the Christian year (after Easter). The word *Christmas* comes from the Old English *Christes messe,* meaning "Christ's Mass." As mentioned in chapter 3, Christmas has been celebrated in Western churches on December 25 since 336, but there is no indication in the Gospels, or in any ancient sources, as to the actual day of Jesus' birth, which is no great concern because we don't even know for certain the year of his birth (chapter 3). The big celebratory events in the early church were Jesus' death and resurrection (Good Friday and Easter), not his birth.

The word *merry* in "Merry Christmas" comes from an Old English word meaning "blessed." The association of Santa Claus with Christmas comes from Saint Nicholas of Myra—*Claus* is an abbreviation for *Nicholas*—the patron saint of children who, according to legend, rewarded good children by putting presents in their shoes while they were asleep. (Nicholas was one of the bishops at the Council of Nicea in 325.)

Epiphany commemorates several *manifestations* of Jesus as the Son of God, the most important being his presentation to the wise men or "magi" who came to Bethlehem. We don't know who the wise men were. Some believe they were Jews who stayed behind in Babylon after the Exile and came to Bethlehem when they heard about the birth of the Messiah. We usually think in terms of *three* wise men, but the Gospels do not tell us how many there were. The number three comes from the three gifts (gold, frankincense and myrrh) mentioned in Matthew 2:11. Epiphany is celebrated on January 6.

Lent is a forty-day period from Ash Wednesday to Holy Saturday—six days each week from Monday through Saturday, plus the four days from Ash Wednesday to the first Saturday—which dates back to the 600s. The word *Lent* comes from the Old English word *lencten,* meaning "spring." The forty days of Lent recall Jesus' forty days in the wilderness. It is a time of spiritual preparation for Christ's death and resurrection and for the gift of the Holy Spirit. The name *Ash Wednesday* comes from the smudge of ashes placed on the foreheads of parishioners to remind them of their need for repentance (a popular Scripture reading on Ash Wednesday is Psalm 51) and as a symbol of their mortality (Gen. 3:19).

Good Friday is the day Christ died so that we might be forgiven of our sins. It is a solemn day of prayer and fasting. Many churches have services from twelve noon to three o'clock commemorating Jesus' last three hours on the cross, with meditations on his Seven Last Words or utterances—three from Luke (23:34; 23:43; 23:46), three from John (19:26–27; 19:28; 19:30) and one that appears in both Mark and Matthew (Mark 15:34 and Matt. 27:46).

Easter is the oldest of the celebratory days in the Christian year, the day on which we say, "Christ is risen! He is risen indeed!" The word *Easter* comes from *Eostre,* the name of the Anglo-Saxon goddess of fertility. (As

Christianity grew, it took over pagan names, like Eostre and Sunday, and holidays, like the winter solstice.)

Pentecost is a celebration of the coming of the Holy Spirit on those waiting in Jerusalem after Jesus' ascension (Acts 2:1–13). Pentecost Sunday is often an occasion for baptism, and in some denominations is called *Whitsunday* because those being baptized are dressed in white.

The Season After Pentecost or Ordinary Time begins on the Sunday following Pentecost (Trinity Sunday) and continues on to Advent. The lectionary readings from the Gospels on the Sundays between Pentecost and Advent focus on the life, ministry and teachings of Jesus.

THE END TIMES OR FINAL THINGS

Theological reflection on the close or end of the age, or on the last things, is called *eschatology*, from the Greek word *eschaton,* meaning "last" or "end." The Christian view of history is that there will be an "end time," or a "new time," when all things will be made new. The Christian view is hopeful and optimistic, as opposed to the ancient Greek view that history is cyclical, like the seasons of the year, or the Eastern view that history is an illusion, or the secular view that history is a series of unconnected events without meaning—"just one thing after another going nowhere." The New Testament view is that history is headed toward a final consummation, at which time Christ will return, the dead will be raised, all will be judged, and those who have believed will live in God's final, perfected kingdom.

JESUS' RETURN OR SECOND COMING

Christianity is a religion of *hope*—the hope that Jesus will return and raise up all who have believed. Jesus' return is something that he promised— "I will come again" (John 14:3); that others prophesied—"Christ . . . will appear a second time" (Heb. 9:28); and that all of the creeds confess—"He will come again" (the Apostles' Creed). Three questions are *why, how* and *when* Jesus will return.

First, as to *why* Jesus will return, the New Testament tells us that he is coming back to *defeat,* once and for all time, the forces of evil (1 Cor. 15:23–25); to *judge* the living and the dead (Acts 10:42); and to *grant* everlasting life to all who have believed (John 6:40).

Second, as to *how* Jesus will return, the New Testament is more con-cerned with the belief that he is coming than in the manner of his return. It does, however, give us three poetic images of his return. First, Jesus is coming back *personally:* "This Jesus . . . will come in the same way as you saw him go into heaven" (Acts 1:11). Second, his coming will be *visible:* "Every eye will see him" (Rev 1:7). Third, his return will be *victorious* and *glorious:* He will come "on the clouds of heaven with power and great glory" (Matt. 24:30), that is, supernaturally.

Third, as to *when* Jesus will return, the answer is that *no one knows,* for not even Jesus knew: "But about that day or hour no one knows . . . only the Father" (Mark 13:32). Nevertheless, some think the Bible indicates when Jesus will return and that this knowledge can be gleaned by "decod-ing" symbolic language in books such as Revelation.

The problem with trying to calculate Jesus' return has to do with the concept of *time.* For us, time is quantitative and chronological; for God, time is qualitative—things happen in the *right* time, as in Jesus' coming in the "fullness of time" (chapter 3). Efforts to calculate when Jesus will return are, by definition, doomed to failure. The only thing we are told is that Jesus' return will come as a surprise—"like a thief in the night" (1 Thess. 5:2)—so we should, as the Boy Scouts say, "Always be prepared."

RESURRECTION, JUDGMENT AND ETERNITY

With regard to the coming resurrection, the final judgment and the life to come, the following may be said.

The General Resurrection. As to those who will be raised, Jesus said, "The hour is coming when all who are in their graves will hear [my voice] and will come out—those who have done good . . . and those who have done evil" (John 5:28–29). At the close of history, Scripture tells us, there will be a *general* resurrection.

The Final Judgment. When God brings down the final curtain, all will appear before the judgment seat (2 Cor. 5:10; Rom. 14:10). The defining questions are: To whom are we accountable? And for what? We are account-able to Jesus, the one who will be our "judge" (Acts 10:42; John 5:22). What a comfort it is to know that the one who will judge us at the end is the one who died for us at the beginning. As to *how* we will be judged, the answer is that we will be held accountable for what has been revealed to us, which is not the same for all people. Those who have never heard the gospel will not be judged as if they had.

As to what the *judgment* will be, for those who have believed in Jesus, it will be eternal life; for those who have not, it will be everlasting punishment (Matt. 25:46). Some, however, argue that subjecting those who have never *heard* the good news to eternal torment and suffering is inconsistent with a God of love and mercy. How, they ask, could those who through no fault of their own don't know Jesus—children who die in infancy, persons who are mentally retarded, those who live in remote areas of the world—be punished in hell for not believing in him?

Resurrection and the Intermediate State. The Irish-born British playwright George Bernard Shaw said, "Death is the ultimate statistic: one out of one dies." What happens at death, and between death and the final resurrection? Regarding death, Christians hold two different views. Some believe that we perish completely and then are resurrected. Others believe that the *soul* separates from the body at death and lives on until the body is resurrected. The latter view takes support from Jesus' word to the so-called penitent thief: "Today you will be with me in Paradise" (Luke 23:43). Catholics believe that the souls of those who die with unforgiven venial sins to go Purgatory.

The period between death and the final general resurrection is referred to as the Intermediate State, about which the Bible tells us, one writer wrote, "little more than a whisper." Theologians who hold that the soul continues to live on assume that it goes to some heavenly place, perhaps the "Paradise" mentioned in Luke 23:43 and by Paul (2 Cor. 12:2–4), a place that is permanent and eternal but incomplete until Jesus returns and raises up all who have believed. Then, so the argument continues, the soul takes up residence in a new, resurrected body.

The Life Hereafter. Theologian J. I. Packer says, "Heaven is shorthand for the Christian's final hope." Where is heaven? Is it a place or a state of being? Heaven is where the triune God "dwells"—the *new* Jerusalem—akin to this earth but a new and transformed earth. It is also the dwelling place of the angels and of all the redeemed.

What will life in heaven be like? For one thing, we will have new, imperishable bodies, free from disease and decay (see 1 Cor. 15:35–58). Will we recognize and know those whom we love? The Apostles' Creed confesses "the communion of saints," the common bond of all believers in and through the Holy Spirit. American theologian R. C. Sproul, in his book *Now, That's a Good Question!,* understands this to mean that we will be in fellowship with everyone who is in Christ.

What more can we say about heaven? Only that "no eye has seen, nor ear heard, nor the human heart conceived, what God has prepared for those who love him" (1 Cor. 2:9). To say more is impossible because, as Louis Jacobs has observed, "For human beings in this world to try to grasp the nature of the hereafter is like a man born blind trying to grasp the nature of color."

ANGELS, SATAN AND DEMONS

The modern world dismisses angels, Satan and demons as superstition and views those who believe in them as naïve, but the Bible has much to say about them.

ANGELS

Angels are mentioned in more than half of the books of the Bible, and three angels are named in different writings—Michael, the archangel or highest angel (Dan. 10:13; Jude 9; Rev. 12:7), Gabriel (Dan. 8:16; Luke 1:19, 26) and Raphael (in the apocryphal book Tobit).

What are "angels"? And what is their function? Angels are not physical beings but spirit beings. And though they are created beings, they are immortal beings (Luke 20:36). And though often described in masculine terms, they are not sexual beings. Their function is to act as messengers of God—the word *angel* comes from a Greek term meaning "messenger"—as when angels brought messages to Zechariah in the temple (Luke 1:11–20) and to Joseph and Mary about the coming birth of Jesus (Matt. 1:20–25 and Luke 1:26–38) and to the women at Jesus' tomb (Matt. 28:2–7; John 20:12–13).

The purpose of angels is to encourage and minister to the needs of God's people and to oppose the work of Satan and his demons. Are angels still active? There is no scriptural warrant for believing they were active only in biblical times, and the book of Revelation suggests they will be active at the end of the age. Are there such things as "guardian angels," which protect and preserve a believer's well-being? Matthew 18:10 ("their angels") and Acts 12:15 ("his angel") suggests the possibility of an angel for each believer, but there is not much more than this to go on.

SATAN

Satan is mentioned in the Old Testament, but he is much more prominent in the New Testament, where he is mentioned by almost every writer. Who is Satan? He may have been an angel (Lucifer) who was thrust out of heaven and became the archenemy of God (see Luke 10:18).

Satan is not a "thing" but an active spirit being with an intellect and a will. His mission is to oppose God (the word *Satan* comes from a Hebrew verb meaning "to oppose") by attacking the people of God—tempting them, as he did Jesus in the wilderness; confusing their minds, thereby leading them into disbelief; and urging them to follow him and his evil ways. C. S. Lewis said that some people take the devil too seriously, while others don't take him seriously enough.

DEMONS

As angels are God's "agents," so demons are Satan's agents—evil spirit beings that are hostile to God and to the people of God. They are often referred to in the New Testament as "unclean spirits" (for example, Mark 1:24–27; 5:2; 9:25). Most of the references to demons appear in the Gospels; they are not prominent in the Old Testament or in the letters, epistles and other writings in the New Testament. Although some theologians and psychologists dismiss the idea of demons and demon-possession, the latter is a worldwide phenomenon.

CHAPTER 8

OTHER
RELIGIONS

There have been great teachers and leaders of souls . . . but
none of them claimed to do or did what Jesus has done.
Through Moses came a law to be obeyed; Muhammad was a
prophet of a truth about God; Gautama [Buddha] offered men
the secret of salvation which must be secured by their own
efforts. Christ brings us to God and God to us in an immediacy
of relation, in an intimacy of communion, in a sufficiency and
efficacy of divine grace through human faith which is a new
creation in our inmost, highest life. . . . This cannot, of course,
be demonstrated by intellectual arguments to those who have
not had the experience of what Christ has done; but for those
who have had that experience, there need be no other
evidence.

A. E. GARVIE
Anthology of Jesus

Other Religions and Beliefs

Do all religions lead to God? If not, how does Christianity differ from other religions? This chapter will attempt to answer these questions. First, we will look at three world religions that have come to the West—Hinduism, Buddhism and Islam—and then touch briefly on five others. Second, we will look at two aggressive cults that parade under the banner of Christianity but deny the central truth claims of the Christian faith—the Mormons and the Jehovah's Witnesses—and then comment briefly on Christian Science, the Unification Church, the Church of Scientology, Eckankar and several others. Third, we will look at the popular, growing New Age Movement. Last, we will look at two ways the church has dealt with religious pluralism: exclusivism and inclusivism.

Other World Religions

Today there is a great influx of people to the United States. Some come to start a new life; others come to be reunited with relatives who came before them; still others come to study in American colleges and universities. When they come, they bring with them religious beliefs that most Americans know very little about. The purpose of this chapter is to provide some background on other religions to show how they differ from Christianity. This will allow us, in sharing our faith, to start with the other person's beliefs rather than our own, which is essential to effective evangelism.

Hinduism: The Religion of India

Many people in the West—in fact, throughout the world—are fascinated with Eastern religions. Millions are involved in some form of Eastern mysticism, and according to a 1990 CNN poll, 35 percent of adult Americans believe in reincarnation. The essential differences between Eastern religions and Christianity are set out below.

First, Christians believe in a God who has made himself known (in Jesus Christ) rather than a God who is impersonal and not knowable. Second,

Christians believe in humankind's innate sinfulness and separation from God (there is no sense of original or indwelt sin in Eastern religion). Third, Christians believe in the forgiveness of sins so that we may be "at one" with God rather than having to endure endless reincarnations. Last, Christians believe that salvation comes from above (God's grace) rather than from below (liberating oneself from the wheel of birth, death and rebirth).

ORIGINS AND PRACTICES

Hinduism claims to be the oldest religion in the world, dating back to the second millennium B.C. As a developed belief system, however, it followed rather than preceded Judaism. (Early Hinduism, as expressed in Brahmanism, dates back to 1200 B.C., shortly after the Exodus.) Hinduism is the religion of India—85 percent of all Indians are Hindus—and it is more concentrated geographically than Christianity, which has spread throughout the world. The number of Hindus is estimated to be in excess of 800 million, making Hinduism, after Christianity and Islam, the third largest religion in the world.

The word *Hindu* comes from the Sanskrit word *Indus*—"people of the land of Indus"—referring to those who lived in the Indus Valley (now Pakistan). The principal Hindu scriptures are the *Vedas* ("wise sayings") and the *Upanishads* ("sitting near" one's teacher). A later book, the *Bhagavad Gita* (the "Song of the Lord"), composed around A.D. 100, has been called "Hinduism's favorite bible."

Hinduism, in contrast to most other religions, had no "founding father." It has temples but no established corporate worship, no institutional form and no "sabbath." Hindus believe the most important place of worship is in the home, where they maintain small shrines with a representation of their family god. Hinduism claims to have great tolerance for other faiths, but this is not true, at least not in India.

CASTES AND COWS

Something that is confusing to many people is India's caste system, a hereditary system of social stratification that dates back to the 1500s B.C. when the Aryans (Indo-Europeans) invaded India. Hindus believe the caste system is part of the cosmic law of cause and effect, part of the "ladder of life," part of the explanation of why things are the way they are.

There are four primary castes and thousands of subcastes, which are hereditary and for life—one cannot move from one caste to another—and determine a person's social status and vocation. The four principal castes are comprised of priests, scholars and teachers (the Brahmins); nobles, rulers and soldiers; artisans, merchants and farmers (Gandhi's caste); and, at the bottom, peasants, servants and manual laborers. Some see the hierarchy of the castes metaphorically, like the human body: the priests and teachers are the head, the rulers and warriors are the arms, the merchants and laborers are the thighs, and the servants and serfs are the feet.

One who has been expelled from or abandoned his or her caste is called an "outcaste." Those considered ritually unclean are called "untouchables," of which there are some 100 million in India today. The occupational barriers of the caste system are breaking down due to economic pressures— "untouchability" was declared illegal in 1949—but social dimensions still persist and are important in the villages and in such areas of life as table fellowship and marriage.

Another thing that is little understood is the sanctity of the cow, which cannot be killed and consumes grain needed to feed India's masses. The veneration of the cow comes from Vedic literature and from the Hindu belief that the cow is the living symbol of Mother Earth and of the divine blessings she bestows upon humankind. Reverence for the cow symbolizes reverence for all animals, which is one reason why Hindus are vegetarians; another reason is the belief that animals contain reincarnated souls.

BRAHMAN, ATMAN AND REINCARNATION

Hindus believe that the human soul, called *atman,* is eternal, and that it is linked with the universal soul or spirit, called *Brahman,* which sustains the universe. Hindus believe that one's state in life is the result of one's *karma,* from a Sankrit word meaning "actions" or "deeds." Bad actions lead to the reincarnation of the atman into lower orders (animals, plants and insects) and good actions into higher orders (higher castes). This process is called *samsara,* and may occur many, many times. The goal or purpose of life is to release one's atman or soul from the endless repetition of rebirths and merge with Brahman, like a drop of water falling into an ocean. The absorption of the atman into Brahman is called *moksha,* at which point the soul enters into a state of supreme blessedness.

The paths to enlightenment or moksha are *knowledge*—which comes from studying with gurus or teachers and reading sacred scriptures; *contemplation*—disciplines and psychophysical exercises that concentrate one's attention on the atman; *devotion*—singing hymns of praise, offering sacrifices and making pilgrimages to sacred places such as Varanasi, Hinduism's holiest city, located in north central India on the banks of the sacred Ganges River (Hindus bathe in "Mother Ganges" to wash away bad karma); and *works*—the acting out of one's duties to society.

Hindus believe that there are many gods, each of which has a different function. The three principal deities—the Hindu "trinity"—are *Brahma* (or *Brahman,* the neuter form of Brahma), the Creator; *Vishnu,* the Preserver; and *Shiva,* the Destroyer. In Hindu mythology, gods have descended to earth as *avatars* (divine "manifestations"). The most important avatars are those of Vishnu, the most popular being Rama and Krishna. Modern Hinduism believes that avatars have also manifested themselves in humans, such as Ramakrishna, a highly esteemed nineteenth-century Hindu mystic.

THE HARE KRISHNA MOVEMENT

Hare Krishna—*Hare* meaning "Lord" and *Krishna* being the avatar of Vishnu—is a form of Hinduism found in the United States, Europe and Latin America. The official name for the community is The International Society for Krishna Consciousness (ISKCON). One attains Krishna "consciousness" by chanting the Hare Krishna mantra and meditating on "Lord" Krishna.

The movement was founded in the United States in 1965 by "His Divine Grace" Swami Prabhupada, who claimed to be a "representative" of Krishna (Prabhupada died in 1977). ISKCON follows Hinduism in most respects—its primary scriptures are the *Bhagavad Gita* and it believes in both karma and reincarnation—but it does not believe in a plurality or pantheon of gods or in the caste system. It has temples and communes in many cities, and its followers distribute evangelistic literature on street corners and elsewhere.

Many Hare Krishnas live in structured communities, with rules regarding food and drink (no meat, fish, eggs or alcohol), dress, devotions (devotees chant mantras on a string of 108 prayer beads sixteen times each day) and celibacy (married couples are allowed to have sex only once a month). Adherents hope that their devotion to Lord Krishna will one day enable them to escape the wheel of death and rebirth.

HINDUISM VERSUS CHRISTIANITY

Three important differences between Christianity and Hinduism are as follows. First, Christianity believes in a single, sovereign, personal God; Hinduism believes in a universal soul and in thousands of "gods." Second, Christianity believes that salvation comes by grace through faith; Hinduism believes that salvation (from *samsara*, the wheel of rebirths) comes through knowledge, devotion and good works. Third, Christianity believes that Christ's saving death is offered to everyone, no matter what caste he or she is born into, and that it is offered now—in this life and with assurance—rather than in a future reincarnated life.

BUDDHISM: THE MIDDLE WAY

Buddhism began as a reform movement within Hinduism. It was successful in various parts of India for hundreds of years, and then died out. Buddhism is beginning to grow outside Asia as immigrants from Vietnam, Cambodia and other Southeast Asian countries come in increasing numbers to the West.

BUDDHA

Buddhism was founded by Siddhartha Gautama, who was born in what is now Nepal, in 566 B.C. His father was the ruler of a small kingdom who shielded Gautama from the cruelties and sufferings of life. According to legend, when Gautama finally ventured out into the world, the only happy man he saw was a serene and peaceful hermit. At the age of twenty-nine he left his wife and child (the Great Renunciation) and embarked on a quest for peace and serenity. This came to him six years later while sitting under the famous *bodhi* tree (the tree of knowledge or enlightenment), probably a fig tree, in north central India.

According to Gautama, the cause of suffering is desiring or craving things that are worldly and temporal. The way to peace and serenity is the Middle Way—the way or path of moderation between pleasure and denial, between self-indulgence and asceticism.

THE FORMATION OF BUDDHISM

Gautama became known as *Buddha,* a Sanskrit word meaning one who has found or attained enlightenment. He gathered disciples around him, founded monasteries, and went about preaching and teaching his newfound enlightenment until his death in 486 B.C. at the age of eighty. After his death, his followers wrote down his teachings. Over time he came to be highly venerated (as a deity by some) and statues and temples were built in his honor.

Like many religions, Buddhism has different traditions. *Theravada,* the Doctrine of the Elders, is very conservative. It teaches that to find enlightenment one must devote his or her life to the *way* of Buddha, the highest form of which is monasticism. *Mahayana,* the Great Vehicle, believes that enlightenment is possible with the help of *bodhisattvas,* saintly personages who postpone final enlightenment in order to help others. Mahayana Buddhists practice love and compassion and devote themselves to the *teachings* of Buddha. Mahayana is more liberal and popular and the larger of the two traditions.

Today there are an estimated 360 million Buddhists, principally in countries like Myanmar (Burma), Thailand, Laos, Cambodia, Vietnam, China and Japan, making Buddhism the fourth largest religion in the world.

THE EIGHTFOLD PATH

There are several major differences between Buddhism and Hinduism. Unlike Hinduism, Buddhism does not believe in a universal being or spirit, or that men and women have souls, or in the caste system, and it believes that there is something one can do to escape the misery and suffering of this life rather than waiting for a future life.

What can one do? Adopt the Four Noble Truths of the Middle Way, the fourth of which is the Noble Eightfold Path of right thoughts, right aspirations, right behavior, right speech, right livelihood, right effort, right mindfulness and right contemplation. The Eightfold Path leads to *nirvana*—from a Sanskrit word meaning "to blow out" the flame of desire, the cause of suffering—and to the absorption of the self into the infinite.

ZEN BUDDHISM

A popular form of Buddhism in the West is Zen Buddhism, which came to the fore after World War II. In the United States there are some one hundred Zen temples and centers and nearly one million adherents. The word *Zen* comes from a Sanskrit word meaning "meditation." Zen Buddhism developed in China in the 500s A.D.; it later expanded to Japan, where it was highly esteemed as a path to self-discipline.

Zen adherents practice meditation according to strict rules in order to achieve enlightenment (called *satori*) more quickly than through traditional Buddhism, thus escaping the wheel of reincarnation. Zen Buddhism expresses itself in a variety of ways: judo, calligraphy, poetry, the *ikebana* art of flower arrangement, and the seemingly formless sand and rock garden— each of which has religious significance.

BUDDHISM VERSUS CHRISTIANITY

Three distinguishing differences between Christianity and Buddhism are as follows. First, Christianity believes in a God who created the world and who revealed himself in Jesus of Nazareth; Buddhism does not believe in a Creator God or higher being. Second, Christians practice the two "love commandments" (God and neighbor); Buddhists practice the Eightfold Path (right thoughts, behavior, speech, efforts, etc.). Third, Christians look forward to a resurrected life with the triune God and all other believers; Buddhists look forward to escaping the bondage of *samsara* (rebirths) and to the absorption of the finite (self) into the infinite, like a passing cloud that dissolves and disappears.

FIVE OTHER EASTERN RELIGIONS

The following are brief introductions to five smaller world religions. They are included because in our increasingly pluralistic world we occasionally encounter adherents of these religions.

CONFUCIANISM

Confucianism is more a system of ethics than a religion. It is based on the teachings of K'ung Fu-tzu ("Kung the Master"), whose name was Latinized to Confucius by Christian missionaries. He was born and lived in China from 551 to 479 B.C.

Confucius was concerned with right relationships, especially within the family (husband-wife, parent-child, sibling-to-sibling), and with the virtues of respect, compassion, benevolence, wisdom, trustworthiness and propriety. His view of humankind was optimistic, and his commonsense sayings and writings were collected and revered after his death. Beginning with the Han dynasty in 206 B.C., Confucianism became the official "religion" of China and remained such, more or less, until the revolution in 1911 under Sun Yat-sen, the "father" of modern China.

TAOISM

Taoism (pronounced "*dow*ism") is another Chinese religion. Unlike Confucianism, it is not concerned with the virtues of life but with nature. Taoism dates back to Lao Tzu or Lao Tse ("Old Master" or "Old Philosopher"), its founder, who lived from 604 to 517 B.C., though some doubt such a person ever existed. The word *tao* means "way"—the way to achieve harmony with the universe.

The three "jewels" of Taoism are compassion, moderation and humility. When these three are practiced, and there is equilibrium between the *yang* (positive, active, masculine) and the *yin* (negative, passive, feminine), there is harmony between humankind and the universe, which in Taoism is the goal of life. Taoism is not a major religion (most adherents live in Taiwan), but there is a growing interest in Tao writings, such as *Tao Te Ching* ("The Way of Power").

SHINTOISM

Shintoism—from the words *shen* (gods) and *tao* (way)—is the "divine way" or the "way of the gods." It is the religion of Japan. Shinto's principal "affirmations" have to do with nature, family, tradition and personal cleanliness and purity. In 1890 Shinto became the state religion, called State Shinto, which demanded loyalty to Japan and to the emperor, who was thought to be a descendant of *Amaterasu,* the sun goddess, and thus divine. (State Shinto was abolished at the end of World War II.)

Adherents worship one of many spirits or *kami,* a Japanese word meaning "above" or "superior." Worship takes place at thousands of public shrines, at miniature in-home shrines, and recently at shrines outside Japan. Shintoism has a greater resemblance to ancient mythology than to religion, at least in the Western sense of the word: it has no concept of a true, omnipotent, living God; no written scriptures; no dogmas or doctrines to be believed and followed; no belief in the need for salvation or redemption; and no institutional form of worship.

SIKHISM

Sikhism was founded by Guru Nanak around 1500. Nanak lived in Punjab, in northern India, where Hindus and Muslims were in close contact with one another. Sikhism began as a reform movement within Hinduism (Nanak was born a Hindu) and is considered a middle way or path between Hinduism and Islam. It is monotheistic and teaches submission to God, like Islam, but also accepts the law of karma and reincarnation and is close to Hinduism in religious life and ritual.

The term *sikh* comes from a Sanskrit word meaning "disciple," one who follows the gurus or teachers. Nanak was the first guru. He was succeeded by nine others who guided the development of Sikhism (the last guru died in 1708). Sikhism is now guided by a collection of sacred writings called the *Adi Granth* ("Original Book").

Though Sikhism is small (20 million followers) and highly concentrated (the vast majority live in Punjab in northwest India), it is very influential and has found its way to North America, where there are now more than one million adherents. Male Sikhs take the last name *Singh* ("lion") and women the name *Kaur* ("princess"). Strict, observant Sikhs do not cut their hair (they wear turbans to cover their hair), and they wear steel bracelets on their right wrists. Sikhs believe that God, called *Sat Nam* ("True Name"), is the true, ultimate, eternal guru, and that by meditating on and repeating his name one's sins will be removed. The goal or hope of Sikh adherents is to be absorbed into "God."

BAHA'ISM

Baha'i is a recent world religion, dating to the middle 1800s. It arose out of the teachings of two religious personages in what is now Iran: Mirza Ali Muhammed, the *Bab* ("Gate"), and Mirza Husayn Ali, the *Baha'u'llah* ("Glory of God"), who believed that he was the divine manifestation of God. The name *Baha'i* comes from its founder, Baha'u'llah. Baha'is have been persecuted in Muslim countries because of Baha'ism's claim that Muhammad was not the *final* prophet.

Baha'ism claims to be the fulfillment of all other religions. Some underlying principles of Baha'i are the oneness and equality of all people; the unity of all religions ("as rivers merge in the ocean"); the idea that truth is relative, not absolute; the harmony of science and religion; and the need for universal education, world peace and an international tribunal.

Baha'i's headquarters are in Haifa, Israel. It claims to have 5 million followers, though this seems doubtful. The center of Baha'ism in the United States is the Baha'i House of Worship in Wilmette, Illinois, a nine-sided (nine is the Baha'i symbol of unity) tower featuring nine "manifestations" that God has raised up over the centuries—Moses, Buddha, Zoroaster, Confucius, Krishna, Jesus, Muhammad, Bab and Baha'u'llah.

ISLAM: CHRISTIANITY'S GREATEST COMPETITOR

The third great monotheistic religion (along with Judaism and Christianity) is Islam, an Arabic word meaning "submission" to the will of *Allah,* the Islamic name for God, derived from Arabic words *al* (the) and *ilah* (deity). Islam is not a small Middle Eastern religion, as some think, but a large (1.2 billion adherents), worldwide, rapidly growing, well-financed missionary faith. There are an estimated 5 million Muslims in the United States,

60 percent of whom are immigrants and 40 percent converts (mostly African-Americans).

We often think of Muslims as Arabs (those who speak and write Arabic), but the countries with the largest Muslim populations are not Arabic. Indonesia is the largest Muslim country, followed by Pakistan, India, Bangladesh, Turkey (the largest Islamic country in Europe), Iran (which is Persian, not Arab), Egypt (the only Arabic country in the top ten Islamic nations), Afghanistan, Nigeria and China.

History shows that religious conflicts are resolved either by the conversion of one side to the other or by war. It will be difficult for the West to convert fervently believing Muslims, for whom Islam is a way of life, to faith in Christ, which has led some to observe that the next Cold War will be between Islam and Christianity.

Islam is a faith without priests or sacraments. Muslims worship in *mosques* ("place of prostration"), which are not churches but buildings where the faithful—usually only men, at least in the main hall—gather to pray as a group. The prayers are led by an *imam* ("he who stands before"), a person with religious training who, on Friday, Islam's day of formal worship, delivers a sermon. Friday seems to have been chosen to distinguish Islam from Judaism and Christianity.

Most mosques have a minaret, a tower from which the faithful are called to prayer; a fountain for washing one's hands, face, mouth and feet; a niche in the wall indicating the direction of Mecca, which Muslims face when they pray (Muslims in the United States face east when they pray); and if a mosque is large enough, education rooms for teaching Arabic, the Koran and Islamic law.

THE PROPHET MUHAMMAD

The founder of Islam was Ubu'l-Kassim, who became known as Muhammad, an Arabic word meaning the "Praised One." He was born in the year 570 in Mecca, an ancient city in present-day Saudi Arabia. He was orphaned at the age of six and raised first by his grandfather and then by an uncle. When he was twenty-five, he married a wealthy widow, Khadija, some fifteen years his senior. Muhammad and Khadija had three sons, who died in infancy, and four daughters; the youngest and his favorite was

Fatima, who married Muhammad's cousin, Ali. After Khadija's death, Muhammad married a number of women, some say as many as fifteen, which is strange if true because, according to the Koran, Muslim men are allowed no more than four wives.

When Muhammad was forty years of age (in 610), he claimed to have had visions of the angel Gabriel while meditating in a cave on Mount Hira, north of Mecca. Gabriel told Muhammad that he was to be Allah's "messenger" and he promised to dictate to him the word of God. Many in Mecca strongly opposed Muhammad's monotheism (Arabia was polytheistic) and his preaching against the worship of idols.

In the year 622, Muhammad fled to Medina (250 miles north of Mecca)—the *Hijra* ("going forth") or *flight*—which marks *year one* in the Islamic calendar. (In the Islamic calendar, dates are noted as A.H., meaning After Hijra.) In Medina, Muhammad established himself as a religious and political leader. Medina became the City of the Prophet (Muhammad is buried in Medina); its inhabitants included both Christians and Jews, who undoubtedly influenced Muhammad's thought and theology.

In the year 630, Muhammad and his followers fought against and took control of Mecca, which became their holy city. Muhammad died in 632 at the age of sixty-one. He did not consider himself to be divine but, rather, the one chosen by God to be his final *prophet*. There are twenty-five "prophets" in Islam. Nineteen come from the Old Testament; two from the New, Jesus and John the Baptist; three are pre-Muhammadan Arabic prophets; and last and most important, Muhammad, the "seal" of the prophets. During his lifetime, Muhammad welded an independent, polytheistic nomadic people into a united monotheistic nation whose military zeal carried Islam from the Arabian peninsula to the Atlantic Ocean (Morocco) within one hundred years of his death.

THE KORAN

In Islamic theology, God did not reveal himself in the form of a person, Jesus, but in words, which are recorded in the *Qur'an* or *Koran* (the "recitation"). According to Islam, the contents of the Koran were revealed to Muhammad over a period of twenty-three years (from 610 to 632), in Mecca and Medina, in manageable segments so that each "revelation" could be memorized exactly as received. Muhammad is believed to have been illiterate and conveyed his visions to his followers and associates.

Shortly after Muhammad's death, his former secretary, Zayd ibn Thabit, collected and wrote down the orally conveyed remembrances of Muhammad's visions. Zayd's text was later organized into a book by Uthman ibn Affan, the third caliph, around the year 650. There were different versions of the Uthmanic text until the tenth century, due to different readings and dialects. In 1924 an Egyptian edition of the Koran became the "official" text throughout the Islamic world.

The Koran has 114 *suras* or chapters, arranged, after the first and most important chapter, called *al-Fatihah* ("the Opening"), roughly in order of descending length rather than chronologically as "received," which makes the Koranic story in places hard to follow (Gabriel's first revelation to Muhammad, for instance, is recorded in sura 96). Anyone reading the Koran will immediately notice that it is filled with stories of Adam, Noah, Abraham, Jacob, Moses, David, Mary, Jesus and others that appear in the Old and New Testaments, though in some cases the stories have been rewritten. For instance, Jesus was born under a palm tree, not in a manger, and he was able to talk from the cradle. The Koran is slightly smaller than the New Testament.

The New Testament and the Koran have two significant differences. First, no one was in the cave to hear and observe what the angel Gabriel allegedly conveyed to Muhammad, in contrast to multiple attestations to Jesus' words in the Gospels. Second, there is only one *official* copy of the Koran, in contrast to thousands of partial and complete New Testament manuscripts and hundreds of Bible versions and translations.

SOME ISLAMIC BELIEFS

Most Christians know very little about Islam. The following are some similarities and important differences.

Abraham and Jerusalem. Judaism, Christianity and Islam are historical, revelatory, monotheistic religions that look back to Abraham as their founding father. Islam believes that Abraham was a Muslim, because Muslims submit to the will of Allah and Abraham was the first to do so, leaving his family to follow God's call to go to the land of Canaan. Also, Islam claims that Ishmael, who was born fourteen years before Isaac, was the "promised son," and that it was Ishmael, not Isaac, whom God told Abraham to offer as a sacrifice.

All three religions revere Jerusalem as a holy city, Islam because it is the place from which Muhammad made his famous "night journey" into heaven (in 620) on a winged horselike creature, accompanied by the angel Gabriel. Muhammad claimed that he traveled all the way to the seventh heaven, where Allah resides. Some Muslims understand this to be a vision, others as an actual journey. The Dome of the Rock—the rock from which Muhammad ascended, whose splendid gold dome we see in photographs of Jerusalem—was built on the site of Solomon's temple to memorialize Muhammad's flight.

Scriptures. Jews, Christians and Muslims are "People of the Book." Islam believes that the Koran is God's final word. It acknowledges four books as holy: the Torah, the book of Moses; the Psalms, the book of David; the Gospels, the biographies (not good news) of Jesus; and most important of all, the Koran. Islam teaches that God *dictated* the words of the Koran through Gabriel to Muhammad rather than transmitting them through inspired prophets and apostles. Muslims believe that there is an exact copy of the Koran in Arabic in heaven.

Jesus. Islam reveres Jesus—*Isa* in Arabic—as a great prophet, second only to Muhammad. (In Islam, Jesus was the herald or forerunner of Muhammad.) It believes in Jesus' virgin birth and in his miracles and that before he died he was "assumed" into heaven and now resides with God. But Islam does not consider Jesus to be divine, because it would be unfitting for the sovereign, transcendent God of the universe to become incarnate in a human being. Muslims say that calling Jesus the Son of God implies that God had sexual relations with Mary. (In Islam, Jesus is called the Son of Mary.) Surprisingly, Jesus is mentioned ninety-seven times in the Koran, and Muhammad only twenty-five times.

Also, Islam does not believe that Jesus was crucified, because God would not allow one of his prophets to die such a disgraceful, humiliating death. According to the Koran, someone who resembled Jesus, possibly Judas Iscariot or Simon of Cyrene, was killed in his place. Because Muslims deny Jesus' death on the cross, they also deny his resurrection.

The biggest difference between Islam and Christianity, as with Judaism, has to do with Jesus. Christians believe that Jesus Christ, God's incarnate Son, who gave his "life as a ransom for many" (Mark 10:45), was the consummation of God's plan of redemption. Muslims believe that six hundred years after Jesus died, God revealed his final law and purposes to Muhammad. There is no way to reconcile these two positions: either Jesus was the capstone in God's plan of salvation, or he wasn't.

Sin. Islam teaches that men and women are fundamentally good, not fallen. Some Muslims believe that Muhammad, though human, was sinless. The Fall in the Garden of Eden was caused by Satan, after which Adam repented and was pardoned by God. (In the Koran, Satan tempted Adam rather than Eve.) There is no concept of innate or indwelt sin in Islam.

Good Works. Islam is a salvation-by-works religion. It teaches that on the last day—the Day of Reckoning—every person will appear before God (not Jesus) to be judged by his or her good and bad deeds and works. Those faithful to the *Shari'a* ("path to follow"), Islam's sacred law, whose good deeds outweigh their bad deeds, go to an oasis-like *paradise* (the Koranic word for heaven) of indescribable sensual pleasure; sinners go to a hell of eternal and indescribable punishment.

ISLAM VERSUS CHRISTIANITY

There are several important differences between Islam and Christianity. First, in Islam God (Allah) is transcendent and removed; in Christianity God is likewise transcendent, but also immanent and personal, and it is possible, through Jesus, to have a relationship with God. Second, Christianity believes in a triune Godhead; Islam, like Judaism, does not believe that God is triune.

Third, Christianity believes that the human race is innately sinful and in need of salvation; Islam believes that humankind is weak and in need of guidance, but not fallen. Fourth, Christianity believes in salvation by grace through faith in Jesus Christ (Eph. 2:8–10); Islam has no concept of "saving grace" or of a "savior." Because there is no savior, Muslims must *earn* their salvation.

Fifth, Christians can be assured of salvation in this life (Rom. 10:9–10); Muslims have to wait until the final Day of Reckoning. Last, Islam believes

Jesus to be a prophet like, but less than, Muhammad; Christianity believes Jesus to be the incarnate, resurrected, ever-living Son of God.

Another difference is that Islam is all-encompassing, covering in addition to religious ritual—at least in most Muslim countries (Islam is the majority religion in some sixty countries)—such matters as marriage and inheritance, civil and criminal law, gambling, abstinence from pork and alcohol, and *purdah,* the veiling of women (for modesty purposes), which has been abandoned in many parts of the world. There is no theological distinction in Islamic countries between sacred and secular: the law of Islam is the law of the land.

THE FIVE PILLARS

The "pillars" that undergird Islamic religious life for observant Muslims are laid down in the *Hadith,* a collection of sayings that was assembled after Muhammad's death. The pillars are as follows:

The profession "There is no God but Allah, and Muhammad is his prophet." Islam's understanding of God is very different than that of Christianity. Allah is mysterious; he is not knowable, nor is he personal or approachable; he is not a God of love (there are ninety-nine words for God in the Koran, but *love* is not one of them); he is never referred to as "Father"; and he is clearly not Trinitarian.

Prayer to Allah five times a day—upon rising, midday, midafternoon, after sunset and upon retiring. Muslims believe that the fivefold prayer practice was revealed to Muhammad when he came into the presence of Allah on his "night journey." When Muslims pray, they often prostrate themselves in a position of humility with their foreheads on the ground. The words of the prayers come from the short first chapter of the Koran and follow established formulas.

Almsgiving, the sharing of one's wealth, out of gratitude for God's favor to support the sick and the needy. The amount of giving varies, but the practice is one-fortieth (2.5 percent) of a person's income or wealth (there is some confusion about this). Almsgiving is strictly enforced in some Muslim countries (as a tax) and completely voluntary in others.

Fasting from food and drink, for those old enough and in good health, from sunup to sundown during the month of Ramadan (the ninth month in Islam's lunar calendar), the month it is claimed that Gabriel first appeared to Muhammad.

A pilgrimage (*hajj*) to Mecca during one's lifetime, if possible, to worship at the Great Mosque, visit the *Ka'ba* or *Kaaba* ("cube") and kiss the famous Black Stone, the most venerated object in Islam. Muslims believe that the stone was carried to earth by the angel Gabriel and given to Abraham who, along with his son Ishmael, built the Kaaba. Muslims believe the stone was originally white but humankind's evil turned it black.

Some fundamentalist Muslims believe in a sixth pillar, *Jihad,* a word meaning "spiritual struggle" (though often translated "holy war"), which requires obedience to Allah and the furtherance of the cause of Islam. The Koran promises that those who die a martyr's death fighting for Allah are assured of a place in paradise.

SUNNIS AND SHI'ITES

Islam is divided into two major groups, the Sunnis and the Shi'ites. The Sunnis, with 85 percent of Islam's adherents, are the "mainstream," but the Shi'ites—the visible, vocal fundamentalists—are the more conspicuous. The groups differ over the question of the true or rightful line of Muhammadan succession, because Muhammad did not leave or appoint a successor.

The Sunnis follow the *Sunna* ("way" or "custom") of Muhammad, as recorded in the *Hadith,* and appoint as their leaders *caliphs* ("successors" or "representatives") from the Kuraish tribe, to which Muhammad belonged. The Shi'ites ("party" or "partisans") are followers of Ali, Muhammad's cousin and son-in-law (Ali married Muhammad's daughter, Fatima), the fourth Caliph. They believe that Ali represents the true line of succession, which continues today in spiritual leaders like the *ayatollahs* ("sign of God") in Iran. The Shi'ites follow the Koran and the teachings of their imams. The Sunnis observe other writings as well and also the oral tradition.

BLACK MUSLIMS

The Nation of Islam, an African-American expression of Islam, was founded by Wallace Fard in 1931 in Detroit. Fard claimed to be the reincarnation of Allah. He was succeeded by Elijah Muhammad, who claimed to be Fard's "messenger." From 1934 until his death in 1975, Muhammad ruled over and built the NOI into a large, nationwide black religious movement.

During the 1950s and early 1960s, the NOI's principal spokesperson and evangelist was Malcolm X, the son of a radical Baptist minister in Omaha, Nebraska, whose surname was Little. The letter X, the mathematical symbol for something unknown, meant that Malcolm did not know his African surname. Malcolm X joined the NOI in 1952 and became the "Saint Paul" of the movement until he split with Elijah Muhammad in 1963. Two years later, in 1965, Malcolm was shot and killed in a public auditorium in New York City.

Following Elijah Muhammad's death in 1975, the NOI split into two groups. The minority followed the charismatic and controversial Louis Farrakhan, who had been a disciple of Malcolm X, and continued the NOI's black nationalism and black separatism. The majority followed Elijah Muhammad's son, W. Deen Muhammad, who founded The World Community of Al-Islam in the West, which is far more orthodox, and also interracial.

There are an estimated 2 million Black Muslims in the United States. The vast majority are in organizations like Al-Islam in the West and the Islamic Society of North America, which is an umbrella organization for local mosques and associations. One reason for the popularity of the non-NOI Muslim groups is their less rigid lifestyle. Another reason is that Malcolm X, after he split with Elijah Muhammad, visited Mecca, where he saw Arabs, Africans and Caucasians worshiping together and publicly embraced and espoused orthodox Islam.

The NOI had its greatest impact during the Malcolm X years. Malcolm was a culture hero who preached black consciousness (he gave birth to the change from Negro to Black), black pride and black power. During this period, the NOI became known as the Black Muslims. Malcolm and the NOI preached that Christianity was a white religion, whereas Islam was the black person's natural religion—some of the slaves who came from Africa were Muslims—though their focus often had more to do with "blackness" than with religion. The NOI had little connection with worldwide Islam, and its Bible was the Christian Bible, on which its members had been raised, rather than the Koran.

The focus of Muslim groups like The Community of Al-Islam in the West is on religion rather than separatism. They are trying to bring the Black Muslim movement into the mainstream of Islam by emphasizing historic Islamic doctrines and practices like the Five Pillars. The Black Muslim movement stresses self-esteem, personal morality, sobriety and family unity and is having a positive impact in urban African-American communities across the country.

CHRISTIAN AND NON-CHRISTIAN CULTS

A strong challenge to the Christian church over the last one hundred and seventy-five years has been the emergence of religious movements that refer to God, Jesus and the Bible, but deny the central truth claims of biblical Christianity. These groups are hereafter referred to as "Christian cults," two examples being the Mormons and the Jehovah's Witnesses. Those who make no pretense to being Christian are referred to as "non-Christian cults," two examples being the Church of Scientology and Eckankar.

WHAT IS A *CULT*?

Before looking at Christian and non-Christian cults, we need to define the word *cult*. Some find the term offensive, preferring, instead, to call non-Christian and fringe-Christian groups "alternative religions" or "new religious movements." The term *cult* is a descriptive term, not a pejorative one. Christian cults are groups that claim to be Christian but reject orthodox Christianity. Historian Ruth Tucker, in her book *Another Gospel*, defines a cult as a religious group whose prophet/founder claims to have received a special revelation from God—often set forth in his or her "inspired" writings—to proclaim a message not found in the Bible. Tucker says that most cults have authoritarian leadership structures, are legalistic in lifestyle, are exclusivistic in outlook, and have a persecution mentality. Tucker's definition fits, for the most part, the eight cults highlighted in this section.

WHY DO PEOPLE JOIN CULTS?

Those who have studied cults, and who have "deprogrammed" people who have come out of cults, claim that people join them because they have become disillusioned with—or have needs that are not being met by—traditional churches. These needs include the need for love, often due to family breakups; the need of some to commit their lives to a charismatic leader such as Jim Jones (the Peoples' Temple), David Koresh (the Branch Davidians) and Marshall Applewhite (Heaven's Gate); and the need of some, with low self-esteem, to be dominated. Sharing Christian beliefs with members of cults is difficult because they are convinced of the "truth" of their cult and because they are usually well grounded in their cult's beliefs.

Studying and knowing something about religious cults is important for at least three reasons. First, Christians need to combat counterfeit movements that misrepresent Christianity. Second, Christians need to be sensitive to reasons why people join cults so they can meet their needs and keep them within the Christian community. Third, Christians need to know the theology of cults so that they can guide family members and friends away from error and toward the truth.

COMMON BELIEFS OF "CHRISTIAN" CULTS

The following are common beliefs of cults regarding truth claims that Christians hold dear. For more information, see *Dictionary of Cults, Sects, Religions and the Occult* by Mather and Nichols.

Scripture. Cults deny the Bible's authority in matters of faith and life, claiming it to be faulty, incomplete and written for another era. To correct this, founders of cults wrote their own books, among them Joseph Smith's *The Book of Mormon,* Mary Baker Eddy's *Science and Health,* Charles Russell's *Studies in Scripture* and Sun Myung Moon's *The Divine Principle.*

God. Cults worship a god other than the biblical or Christian God, and each denies the Trinity (Christian cults are Unitarian rather than Trinitarian).

Jesus. Cults deny the divinity of Jesus, regarding him as only human, and none regards him as a "savior."

Salvation. Cults do not believe in justification by faith. They believe, instead, in salvation by "works," especially proselytization.

UNDERSTANDING CULTS

Cults are found in every culture. To understand how they develop and how they twist Scripture, we will look at two cults that most Christians are familiar with—the Mormons and the Jehovah's Witnesses—which are worldwide and aggressively evangelize both non-Christians and nominal Christians. We will also look at Christian Science, the Unity School of Christianity, the Unification Church, the Church of Scientology, The Way International and Eckankar.

THE CHURCH OF JESUS CHRIST OF LATTER-DAY SAINTS

The Church of Jesus Christ of Latter-day Saints (LDS) has been called the most successful and distinctive religion ever born on American soil. The LDS is not a Christian denomination, like Lutheranism or Presbyterianism. Rather, it claims to be the restoration of the true church by Joseph Smith Jr., the fourth of ten children born to Joseph and Lucy Smith in Sharon, Vermont, in 1805.

The LDS is the largest Christian cult, with an estimated 11 million adherents in some one hundred countries, including 5 million in the United States. The Mormons—a nickname derived from the LDS's most important "scripture," *The Book of Mormon*—are the fifth largest church body in the United States, behind Catholics, Baptists, Methodists and Lutherans. The LDS is very mission-minded, with some 60 thousand missionaries in the United States and overseas. Most are college-age males who give two years of their lives to mission work; their goal is six converts per year.

Despite its strange beliefs, the LDS espouses several wonderful qualities: the priority of the family, abstinence from tobacco and alcohol, the importance of education and hard work, patriotism (the LDS believes that the U.S. Constitution was divinely inspired) and free enterprise.

JOSEPH SMITH

Mormonism stands or falls on Joseph Smith, so we need to start with his story. According to Smith's *The Book of Mormon*, members of the tribe of Manasseh, one of the twelve tribes of Israel, sailed to America during the Diaspora (c. 600 B.C.) and formed two separate nations: the Nephites, to whom Jesus preached the gospel following his resurrection, and the Lamanites, who became the ancestors of the American Indians. The two nations fought a catastrophic war in upstate New York in A.D. 385 in which 2 million people were said to have been killed, though archaeological research has unearthed no artifacts to support this claim.

A Nephite prophet named Mormon wrote the history of his people, *The Book of Mormon*, on golden plates and buried them in a hill in Palmyra, New York (near Rochester). In 1823 the angel Moroni, Mormon's son and the last Nephite survivor, visited Joseph Smith when he was seventeen and told him of the plates. Four years later, in 1827, Smith said that he translated the plates from Egyptian into English with the aid of spectacles made of Urim and Thummim (Ex. 28:30), after which the plates were taken to "heaven" by Moroni, never to be seen again. The LDS considers *The Book of Mormon* to be the final word of God and the equal of the Bible. Although the book ends with the year 421, it contains several thousand words, some verbatim, from the *King James Bible,* which was translated twelve hundred years later.

According to Mormon teaching, John the Baptist returned in May 1829 and ordained Smith to the Aaronic priesthood, and a month later Peter, James and John conferred upon him the Melchizedekian priesthood. In 1830 Smith founded the Church of Jesus Christ of Latter-day Saints at Fayette, New York. (*Latter-day* refers to the time before Jesus returns; *saints* are members of LDS churches or "wards," as they are called.)

The Mormons were persecuted for their beliefs and moved west to Ohio, then to Missouri, and finally to Commerce (renamed Nauvoo), Illinois, on the Mississippi River, where they received a charter in 1840 to establish their own community. Smith became the mayor of Nauvoo and the head of the local militia. In 1843 Smith had a vision that it would be desirable to have more than one wife in order to produce saints for the church, and he took to himself some forty additional "wives." (Mormon polygamy was abandoned in 1890, when it became clear that its continued practice would prevent Utah's entry into the Union.)

In February 1844 Smith sought to give public voice to his views and announced his candidacy for the presidency of the United States. In June of that year he was arrested for smashing the printing presses of a local newspaper that was publishing articles denouncing Mormon polygamy. Smith was arrested and jailed in nearby Carthage. Before he could be brought to trial, he was killed by an angry mob (at the age of thirty-nine).

After Smith's death, the Mormon Church divided. Some followed his first wife to Independence, Missouri, to establish the Reorganized Church of Jesus Christ of Latter-day Saints. The majority followed Brigham Young—the "Saint Paul" of Mormonism—to the Salt Lake Basin in Utah, the new "promised land," arriving there in July 1847.

MORMON BELIEFS

Mormon beliefs are based on three writings—*The Book of Mormon, Doctrine and Covenants* and *The Pearl of Great Price*—and the teachings of Joseph Smith and Brigham Young.

God. Mormons believe that God was a personage who lived on the planet Kolob somewhere in the universe. He died and went to the celestial heaven, after which he became God of our earth. Mormons believe that God was once a man, with flesh and bones, and is now a tangible being (not a spirit); that there are many gods (polytheism), the "Christian" God being the deity who rules over our earth; that God is not eternal but had a father ("a father must have been someone else's son"); and that God was married and had several wives (thus a polygamist), because calling God "father" implies a "mother."

Jesus. Mormons believe that Jesus is "firstborn" in terms of status as the eldest son of God. Brigham Young taught that Jesus was the child of the God-man of the planet earth, who sexually impregnated Mary (the only person to be "physically" fathered by God). An older Mormon teaching, which some Mormons still believe, is that Jesus was married at the wedding in Cana and had several wives, among whom were the sisters Mary and Martha, and had children.

Salvation. Mormons do not believe in original sin or that men and women are fallen. They believe, rather, that men and women can become gods: "As man is, God once was; as God is, so man can become." In Mormonism, salvation comes through obedience to the laws and ordinances of the Mormon church.

Other Beliefs. Mormons believe that Adam had many wives; that Adam and Eve committed no original sin; that the Garden of Eden was located in Missouri; that Abraham, Isaac and Jacob are now "gods"; that Zion is North

America, not Israel; and that the Ten Lost Tribes of Israel will be ingathered and restored in America.

JEHOVAH'S WITNESSES

Jehovah's Witnesses is the second largest made-in-America religion, with 8 million members, 20 percent of whom live in the United States (the JW's headquarters are in Brooklyn). Jehovah's Witnesses, like Mormons, are very authoritarian. They meet in modest buildings called Kingdom Halls (Mormons meet in "temples"); are millenarian in theology (waiting for the end of the world); publish two magazines, *Awake!* and *Watchtower;* believe that Christianity is an apostate religion and that they alone are the sole bearers of God's truth; and have a number of strange beliefs regarding government and holidays. Similar to Mormons, Witnesses read Acts 20:20 as requiring its members to do door-to-door proselytizing. To be a member in good standing, Witnesses must devote ten hours each month to proselytizing.

CHARLES RUSSELL

Jehovah's Witnesses was founded by Charles Taze Russell, who was born in Allegheny, Pennsylvania, in 1852, and raised a Presbyterian. In 1872, at the age of twenty, he established a Bible study; he later wrote *Studies in Scripture,* the authority underlying Jehovah's Witnesses' theology and doctrines. In 1879 Russell published the forerunner of the *Watchtower.* In 1886 he formed The Zion Watchtower Bible and Tract Society; in 1931 the name was changed to Jehovah's Witnesses, the name coming from Isaiah 43:10: "You are my witnesses, says the Lord."

Russell believed in the imminent end of the world and predicted that the final Battle of Armageddon would take place in 1914. Russell was succeeded by "Judge" J. F. Rutherford, a legal advisor to the JWs. In 1916, Rutherford predicted the world would end in 1925. (The last JW date for the end of the world was 1975.)

JEHOVAH'S WITNESSES' BELIEFS

Jehovah's Witnesses' theology is based on its own in-house version of the Bible, *The New World Translation of the Holy Scriptures* (1961), and on its very literal interpretation of its Bible. The following are some Jehovah's Witnesses beliefs:

God. Witnesses do not believe that God is triune, and they do not believe the name *God* is biblical; preferring, instead, the name Jehovah—an artificial name that is clearly not biblical (see discussion of YHWH, from which the name Jehovah derives, in chapter 2).

Jesus. Witnesses believe that Jesus was Michael the archangel, a "spirit-person" who laid down his spirit-nature when he became a man; that Jesus was crucified on a stake rather than on a cross; that his death was a ransom paid to Satan rather than "for us," and does not bring salvation to those who believe or accept it as such; and that his resurrection was spiritual rather than physical.

Other Beliefs. Witnesses believe that the world was created in 46,000 B.C. (7,000 years for each of the six days of creation plus 4,000 years from the time of Abraham to the present); that only 144,000 people will go to heaven (Rev. 7:4 and 14:1–5); that the Antichrist is the Christian clergy; that the Beast referred to in the book of Revelation is the United Nations; and that Satan controls both Catholic and Protestant churches.

Witnesses oppose "earthly kingdoms" and do not participate in government (they do not even vote), serve in the armed forces, salute or pledge allegiance to the flag, or sing the national anthem. Nor do they celebrate Christmas or Easter ("pagan holidays") or their own or anyone else's birthday.

CHRISTIAN SCIENCE

Another made-in-America religion is Christian Science. It was founded by Mary Baker (maiden name) Eddy (her third husband). Mary was born in Bow, New Hampshire, in 1821, and raised a Congregationalist; she lived to be ninety years old.

In 1866 Eddy fell on an icy sidewalk and injured her back. Bedridden, she read the account of Jesus healing the paralytic in Matthew 9:1–8. She got up from her bed and claimed that she was healed. In 1875 Eddy published *Science and Health,* the "textbook" of Christian Science, which underlies Christian Science theology. (It is not clear what is *scientific* about Christian

Science.) The early appeal of Eddy's mind-over-matter theology was to people who felt that nineteenth-century medical science had no answers for their illnesses and diseases. In 1879 "Mother Mary," as she was known by her followers, founded the First Church of Christ, Scientist, in Boston; all other churches are branches of the Mother Church in Boston.

Christian Science has little in common with historic Christianity: it does not believe in the Trinity, the Virgin Birth, original sin, or heaven and hell. It is a philosophical system that believes in the superiority of spirit over matter and that God is the divine mind or principle of the universe. Because everything is spiritual, according to Christian Science, evil, sickness and even death are illusory and unreal because they are physical, that is, "material."

Jesus was the one who revealed God as a spiritual principle—the "Way-shower"—but he did not die for the world's sins because death is an illusion. Christian Science is in decline, with an aging membership and only two thousand or so churches in the United States and around the world, each of which is expected to provide a Reading Room for proselytization purposes. Christian Science's highly respected newspaper, *The Christian Science Monitor*, was started by Mary Baker Eddy in 1908.

UNITY SCHOOL OF CHRISTIANITY

Unity School of Christianity was the first major religion established by a husband and wife team—Charles and Myrtle Fillmore. Charles was born in a log cabin on an Indian reservation in Minnesota in 1854; Myrtle was born into a Methodist family in New England in 1845. The Fillmores were sickly (both suffered from tuberculosis) and became Christian Scientists, which influenced their thinking and theology. In 1889 they established the Unity School of Christianity ("school" rather than "church," though there are now churches).

The term *Unity* refers to the oneness or unity of each individual with God (Jesus is the "inner Christ" who resides in every individual). Although Unity *looks* like Christianity, its beliefs are far from orthodox. In fact, Unity is closer to Eastern philosophical monism than to Christianity. It has no agreed-upon scriptures (it understands the Bible to be an allegory); it believes that God is a principle (of love), not a "person"; and that Jesus was human only, not divine. In addition, it believes in reincarnation (Charles Fillmore believed that he was a reincarnation of the apostle Paul) and that one is "saved" when he or she breaks free from the cycle of birth and rebirth.

Unity's headquarters are in Unity Village, a suburb outside Kansas City, Missouri. Unity's popular *Daily Word* is distributed in more than one hundred and fifty countries.

RECENT RELIGIOUS MOVEMENTS

The second half of the twentieth century saw the rise of a number of new religious movements. In the following sections we will look at four of these—Sun Myung Moon's Unification Church, L. Ron Hubbard's Church of Scientology, Paul Wierville's The Way International and Paul Twitchell's Eckankar.

THE UNIFICATION CHURCH

The Unification Church was founded by Sun Myung Moon in 1954. It is one of the most aggressive cults formed after World War II. The Moonies' greatest success has been on college campuses among youth separated from their families. The Moonies claim to have 2 million members; their actual membership is believed to be one or two hundred thousand (the vast majority live in Korea).

Moon was born in what is now North Korea in 1920 and raised in a Presbyterian family. He claims that on Easter Sunday in 1936, when he was sixteen years old, he had a vision in which Jesus told him to complete the mission he had begun some two thousand years earlier. He also claims to have been visited by Abraham, Moses, John the Baptist, Paul, Buddha, Confucius and Muhammad.

In 1954 Moon founded the Holy Spirit Association for the Unification of World Christianity, more commonly known as the Unification Church. In 1972, Moon came to the United States; he now lives in Tarrytown, New York. The Unification Church's world headquarters are in Washington, D.C.

According to Moon, the archangel Lucifer (Satan) resented God's love for Adam and Eve, with whom God wanted to form a "trinity" to build his kingdom on earth. Lucifer seduced Eve (thus Cain was the son of Lucifer and Eve), who received certain "elements" from him. Eve in turn seduced

Adam, and these elements were passed down from generation to generation.

God sought to redeem humankind through Noah, Abraham, Moses and others, but all failed. Finally, he chose Jesus, the son of Zechariah and Mary, to begin a new, pure, sinless race (the second Adam). But Jesus was murdered by evil forces before he could marry the second Eve and begin the process. (Moon regards the Cross as a symbol of the defeat of Christianity.)

Moon is now the third Adam, and he and his fourth wife and their twelve children, each of whom was born "sinless" (recent scandals among Moon's children have been very embarrassing), are to be the forerunners of the new perfect race—God's kingdom of heaven on earth. The primary sacrament of the Unification Church is the "holy wedding," the marriage of suitable mates, which is blessed by Father Moon.

CHURCH OF SCIENTOLOGY

The Church of Scientology was founded in the 1950s by L. Ron Hubbard, a science fiction writer and journalist who, in 1949, boasted, "If a man wants to make a million dollars, the best way would be to start his own religion."

Scientology, the religion invented by Hubbard, is based on his book *Dianetics: The Modern Science of Mental Health.* According to Hubbard, humans are imprisoned by painful past memories and experiences, called *engrams,* which need to come to the surface so that they can be released and "cleared." How is this accomplished? Through Dianetics and with the help of Scientology counselors (or "auditors"). When the engrams have been cleared, individuals can realize their inborn divine potential.

Hubbard established the Church of Scientology in Washington, D.C., in 1955; its headquarters are now in Los Angeles. Scientology believes that there are many gods (polytheism); that Jesus was a human whose mind was *cleared;* that there is no such thing as original sin or heaven or hell; and that salvation comes by clearing the mind so the soul can be released from the karmic cycle of reincarnation.

THE WAY INTERNATIONAL

The Way International was founded by Victor Paul Wierville in 1958, after he claimed a direct revelation from God. The Way (from Acts 9:2) is an insidious, mind-control cult that uses Christian language and accepts a number of Christian doctrines. Wierville graduated from Princeton Theological Seminary and was a United Church of Christ pastor.

The Way denies the Trinity and the divinity of Jesus and claims that much of the Bible, including the Gospels, is of no use or value. Further, it believes that the Gospels belong in the Old Testament, not the New, because the church began with Paul, not Jesus. The Way's "Bible" is Wierville's book *The Power for Abundant Living.* The Way emphasizes spiritual gifts, such as speaking in tongues, which the Way teaches, as assurances of salvation. The Way's headquarters are in New Knoxville, Ohio.

ECKANKAR

Eckankar, the Religion of the Light and Sound of God, was founded by Paul Twitchell in 1965. Twitchell embraced Eastern religion and was a staff member of the Church of Scientology. He claims to have learned the principles of Eckankar from a five-hundred-year-old Himalayan Eck master who traced his lineage back to the beginning of life on earth.

Eckankar believes that God is in all things (pantheism) and in the law of karma and reincarnation. A central focus of Eckankar is out-of-body "soul travel"—the body does not *have* a soul, it *is* soul—through several "astral" (heavenly) planes to *Sugmad,* the everlasting Eck or spirit. When one "comes home" to *Sugmad,* the wheel of rebirth ends. Soul travel or projection is achieved with guidance from living Eck masters and through meditation, singing the mantra HU (pronounced "hue," a love song to God), dreams, trancing, hypnosis and other spiritual exercises. Eckankar's headquarters and temple are located in Chanhassen, a suburb of Minneapolis, Minnesota.

THE NEW AGE MOVEMENT: BLENDING EAST AND WEST

The New Age Movement (NAM) is difficult to define, but we have come full circle back to a form of Hinduism. The New Age believes that God and humankind are actually one, a concept it calls *monism* (one-ism), and like Hinduism, in the impersonal law of karma and in the transmigration of human souls or spirits.

WHAT IS THE NEW AGE MOVEMENT?

In contrast to the religions in this chapter, the New Age Movement has no founder, no scriptures or dogmas (the New Age is a patchwork of many different beliefs), no organization and no form of worship (there is no *one thing* to "worship"). The New Age is not a cult, nor is it satanic; it is a worldwide phenomenon whose adherents believe that the present age is coming to an end, soon to be replaced by a new age or era—the mythical Age of Aquarius, the age of new beginnings.

The underlying worldview of the New Age is the belief in the oneness and interconnectedness of humanity, nature (Mother Earth) and the divine. Adherents embrace spirituality, ecology, women's rights and holistic healing, and they believe that yoga, meditation and channeling are ways of getting in touch with the divine.

The New Age was not well known until Hollywood actress Shirley MacLaine, the "prophetess" of the New Age, went public in the 1980s. It has now come of age, with media publicity, books (even separate sections for them in bookstores) and talk-show coverage. Though loosely structured, the New Age Movement has an estimated 12 million adherents.

The New Age believes that everything is of one "essence"—which has staggering implications: if *all* is God, and God is *all,* then men and women, who are part of the "all," are also God. (Christianity believes that we are created in God's image, not his essence.)

The goal of New Agers is to release their suppressed, hidden, higher selves so they can connect with the divine force or power of the universe. (The New Age "god" is not a personal God; it is a cosmic force or consciousness.) How is this possible? By altering one's consciousness through visualization techniques and hypnosis; by channeling—getting in touch with "spirit entities" to receive their "wisdom"—often aided by psychics and crystals; through yoga, meditation and other relaxation techniques; and by chanting mantras and listening to mood-altering music.

HOW DID THE NEW AGE ORIGINATE?

New Age thinking has been around for a long time; its roots go back to the Theosophical Society, founded in 1875. It came to the fore in the United States in the counterculture of the 1960s, a period when youth and others began to question and challenge societal norms and values.

Today's interest is coming from three different directions. First, there is a rebellion against the cold, detached, impersonal materialism of science and technology. Second, there is a hunger for something deeper, more meaningful, more spiritual, which many claim is not being satisfied by organized religion. Third, there is a growing belief in monism and mysticism—the belief that the spirits of humans and the divine are one and that it is possible to experience the transcendent divine in a personal way.

THE NEW AGE VERSUS CHRISTIANITY

New Age thinking holds that all religions are the same and that Jesus, Buddha, Krishna, Muhammad and the founders of other religions all taught the same thing—how to be at one with God. From a Christian point of view, the New Age Movement is a great heresy: if all is *one,* then God is not the eternal, transcendent Creator of the universe; and if humans are "gods," then Jesus is not the only begotten Son of God; and if we are all "gods" or part of God, then Jesus' death on the cross accomplished nothing. According to the New Age, there is no need for Jesus. What is needed, instead, is direction so that all may realize their unlimited potential by connecting with the supernatural soul of the universe—and repeated reincarnations may be required until this is achieved.

DO ALL RELIGIONS LEAD TO GOD?

In today's world of religious pluralism, Christians are in constant contact with people of different faiths. The question is often asked, Do all religions lead to God? The answer is that other religions and beliefs may lead to "a" god but not to the triune, personal, knowable God of Christianity. Hinduism, Buddhism, Islam, Mormonism, Christian Science and the other religions and beliefs in this chapter all confess a god (or gods) different than the God of Christianity.

According to Bruce Winter, the director of Tyndale House (Cambridge, England), the difference between Christianity and all other religions is the difference between *doing* and *done.* In all other religions, salvation comes through "doing" something. In Christianity, everything necessary for salvation has already been "done" by Jesus on the Cross; all we have to do is accept the *done-ness*.

Regarding the salvation of nonbelievers, there are two different positions—*exclusivism* and *inclusivism*—the boundaries of which often overlap.

EXCLUSIVISM

Exclusivism asserts that God has provided a particular way of salvation for humankind, and that way is Jesus Christ. Exclusivism has good biblical support (Mark 10:45; Luke 19:10; John 6:40); is theologically sound (Jesus as the *apex* of God's plan of salvation); and has a long tradition in the church—in fact, it was the dominant position up to the end of the nineteenth century.

But there are some who object to this position. First, there are biblical verses on the other side, for example, 1 Timothy 2:3–4 (God's desire that everyone be saved). Second, there is biblical evidence that God works in other ways, as in the stories of Melchizedek, the Ninevites (in the book of Jonah) and Cornelius (in the book of Acts), none of whom was part of the called or chosen people of God. Third, humankind was made in the "image and likeness" of God, so he must have made some provision for those who have never heard the gospel.

The exclusivist position has two streams. *Strict* conservatives believe that Christ is "the only way" to salvation. Those who do not claim the name of Christ, including those who have never heard the name of Christ—those referred to by Fuller Seminary missiologist Charles Kraft as "informationally B.C."—are condemned, which according to some is an overly severe position.

Lenient conservatives believe that persons will be judged by the "light" they have been given, which is not the same for all people. Those in this camp believe that we are not saved by knowledge but "by grace through faith," as with Abraham, who *knew* very little but believed in and trusted God (chapter 2), and it was "reckoned . . . to him as righteousness" (Gen. 15:6).

INCLUSIVISM

Inclusivism argues for the love and mercy of God, who "desires everyone to be saved" (1 Tim. 2:4). Inclusivists say the problem with exclusivism is that it excludes the majority of the human race. Inclusivists believe that God makes himself known in and through general revelation—a revelation to all people everywhere since the beginning of time (Rom. 1:19–20); that he "has not left himself without a witness" (Acts 14:17); and that he accepts anyone "who fears him and does what is right" (Acts 10:34–35).

The problem with inclusivism is that it is a start down the path to universalism—the belief that eventually all will be saved, which is not biblically supportable. Also, it relaxes the urgency of missions: why bother to witness and evangelize if God is already working in the hearts of those who have not heard the gospel?

Some who defend the inclusivist position say that other religions are preparing people for Christ, as Judaism prepared the people of Israel for God's final revelation in Jesus. There is very little evidence, however, that this happened in the past or that it is happening today. Another difficulty with the inclusivist position is that in order to be broadly inclusive it shifts the center of faith from Christ to God, which makes Christianity one of several ways—rather than *the way*—God has provided for humankind to come to the knowledge of the truth and be saved (Acts 4:12).

The final decision about who will and will not be saved, of course, is with God. What Christians know for certain is that Jesus is "the way, and the truth, and the life" (John 14:6)—the true way to abundant life in the kingdom of God on earth, and the way to everlasting life in the kingdom of God to come. This is a great comfort in today's world of religious pluralism, especially when one considers those trapped in religions that believe in reincarnation (Hinduism, Buddhism, Unity, Scientology, Eckankar, the New Age) and in works-righteousness (Islam, Mormonism, Jehovah's Witnesses). What a blessing it is to know that we are saved by the grace of God and the finished work of Christ!

CHAPTER 9

GROWING IN AND SHARING CHRIST

There is a legend about Jesus in heaven shortly after his time on earth. The angels were talking with him, and Gabriel said, "Master, you suffered terribly down there. Do the people know how you loved them and what you did for them?" "No," said Jesus, "not yet. A few people in Palestine know." "What have you done," said Gabriel, "to let everyone know?" Jesus said, "I have asked Peter and James and John and a few others to make it the business of their lives to tell others about me, and the others still others, and yet others, until the farthest person on the widest circle knows what I have done." Gabriel looked very doubtful. "Yes," he said, "but what if Peter and James and John grow tired? What if the people who come after them forget? What if way down in the twenty-first century people just don't tell others about you? Haven't you made any other plans?" Jesus answered, "No, I haven't made any other plans. I am counting on them."

SOURCE UNKNOWN

GROWING IN CHRIST AND SHARING CHRIST

As Christians, we are called to be transformed by the renewing of our minds and to be ambassadors for Christ. In this chapter we will look at three challenges to the Christian faith—the existence of God, the omnipresence of evil, and Jesus as "the way" of salvation. Second, we will look at growing our faith through prayer—the life and practice of prayer, different forms of prayer, including the Lord's Prayer, and answers (and non-answers) to prayer. Third, we will look at growing our faith through the discipline of study. Fourth, we will note some things that can weaken and even destroy our faith, namely, the Seven Deadly Sins. Last, we will look at sharing our faith, starting with Jesus' question to his disciples at Caesarea Philippi—"Who do people say that I am?"—and then look at some do's and don'ts to keep in mind in sharing our faith.

CHRISTIAN APOLOGETICS

Are there good and sufficient reasons for believing in Christianity—in the existence of God, in the incarnation of God in Jesus, in Jesus' promise of eternal life—or is Christianity just wishful thinking? The intellectual defense of Christian beliefs is called *apologetics,* which does not mean making an "apology," as the term might suggest, but providing reasoned answers "to anyone who demands from you an accounting for the hope that is in you" (1 Peter 3:15).

Some Christians do not believe that it is necessary to have reasons for faith; for them, faith is enough. Others believe that there must be solid, convincing reasons for faith. Still others believe that Christianity embraces both components: faith and reason. The following is a brief overview of these three views.

FIDEISM

Fideism (faith-ism) is faith in faith, or believing *in spite of* the evidence, not because of it. Those holding this view say that if we let the camel of reason into the tent, there may be positions that we cannot defend, which might weaken or compromise our faith. The problem with this position is that Christianity makes truth claims: that Jesus is divine, that Jesus died for our sins, that Jesus rose from the dead. Faith is important, but we need to know that there are good reasons for believing Christianity to be true, which is the job of apologetics.

RATIONALISM

On the other side are those who believe that we need strong, persuasive arguments for our beliefs. But not *every* truth claim can be defended with rigorous, convincing proofs: for instance, that God created the universe out of nothing, that God became incarnate in Jesus, that God is triune. Attempts to provide unassailable evidence for such beliefs is "mission impossible." Reasons for believing are essential, but they rarely alone compel or bring a nonbeliever to faith.

FAITH PLUS REASON

The task of apologetics is not to produce empirical proofs for the truth of Christianity, but to demonstrate that there are compelling reasons for believing Christianity to be true, evidence that would lead one to conclude that it is more reasonable to believe in the truth of Christianity than not to believe. In the end, though, it is often the heart that responds, not the mind. The French mathematician and physicist Blaise Pascal said, regarding the Christian faith, "The heart has its reasons of which reason knows nothing."

SKEPTICISM AND TRUTH

An example of people being skeptical about truth claims that cannot be confirmed or verified is illustrated in a story told by James Boswell, the famous biographer. Boswell visited David Hume, the Scottish philosopher and skeptic, in the summer of 1776, when Hume was on his deathbed. Boswell was curious to know if Hume, now facing death, had changed his mind regarding the possibility of life beyond the grave. Hume said to Boswell, "Yes, it's possible. It is also possible that if I toss this piece of coal into the flames of that fire that it will not burn. Possible, but there is no basis for believing it—not by reason, not by sense perception, not by experience" (T. Z. Lavine, *From Socrates to Sartre*).

Skeptics only accept propositions that can be proven scientifically, but religious beliefs cannot be proven "scientifically"—that is, no one can empirically prove or disprove God, or how the cosmos came into existence, or whether there is another life beyond this life. Christianity is a worldview, and scientific measures cannot prove or disprove worldviews. What can be shown is that Christianity is a *more reasonable* worldview than other worldviews (see discussion of the Christian worldview in chapter 10).

CHALLENGES TO CHRISTIANITY

What are the principal challenges to Christianity? First, there is a growing belief, at least in the rationalistic West, that the universe is a closed system, which rules out the possibility of a supernatural God who created and sustains the universe. Second, if there is a God, and he is all-powerful and all-loving, as Christians claim, why is there evil and suffering in the world? Third, in today's world of religious pluralism, how can Christianity be "the only way" to God? We will look at each of these objections individually.

A fourth objection has to do with miracles, which we looked at in chapter 4. The two big miracles are the Incarnation, which C. S. Lewis called *The Grand Miracle* ("Every other miracle prepares for this or exhibits this or results from this"), and the Resurrection, about which much has already been said. Nonbelievers reject the Incarnation and the Resurrection because neither can be understood in human terms. But lots of things cannot be understood in human terms. Take the mind, for example. No one can explain how the wiring in the brain enables us to dream, reason, create works of art, remember the past and enjoy vivid colors and fragrant aromas. Just because we can't explain *how* Jesus was conceived and resurrected does not mean that these two "miracles" did not happen.

THE EXISTENCE OF GOD

It is said that there are two "tracks" to God: one by way of *nature,* the other by way of *revelation*—the "works" of God in creation and the "words" of God in the Bible. Natural Theology believes that it is possible to affirm the existence of God through the "light of natural reason." That is, we have been endowed with rational faculties and can infer, by reflecting on the heavenly bodies, with their unbelievable movement and precision, and on the incredible variety and beauty of the life on planet Earth, that there is an Author or Designer or Creator. The cosmos and the species did not give rise to themselves.

The other way that we know God is through Scripture, which is called Revealed Theology. If there is a Creator, it seems natural that he would want to reveal his nature and his love for us and his will for our lives. How did God do this? By calling prophets and apostles to speak and record his Word so that one day all the world would know him. The center of this revelation—God's most important, perfect and complete revelation—is Jesus of Nazareth. It is said that Natural Theology tells us of God's *creating* will and Revealed Theology of his *saving* will.

There is also a third way that we know God: through the "inner witness" of the Holy Spirit. There are things that we *know* are true even though we cannot prove them. Right now, for example, I am working at my word processor and I am hungry and thinking about lunch, but I cannot "prove" that this is what I am thinking, or even that I am hungry. We "know" when God has touched us or called us, and we often know when he has touched others because of changes that we see in their lives. The fact that much of this is subjective and cannot be proven does not make it false or untrue. When we experience God's *touch* in our lives, it is as true as any other form of "knowledge."

Nevertheless, some continue to doubt. They say that it is not possible to believe in something that cannot be seen. But scientists believe in protons and electrons (subatomic particles), and no one has ever seen a proton or an electron. Others say, if there is a God, why doesn't he do a better job of convincing us? The answer may be that he wants us to love him on the basis of faith. He draws us and beckons us, hoping that we will come to him and believe in him through faith.

EVIL AND SUFFERING

How can the omnipotent God of the universe, who loves his creation, allow evil and suffering to exist? Some would say that God is not all-powerful; others might say that he is indifferent or unconcerned about his creation.

Peeping through the horns of the dilemma, however, is an explanation: God created us as *free-will* human beings, with the freedom to make choices. If we were programmed like robots, we could not love God of our own volition. For us to freely love him, God had to "let go." And when we are free to make choices, we often choose, as did Adam and Eve, to go our own way rather than God's way, which sometimes results in personal pain and suffering, and also in the suffering of others.

Nonetheless, there are no completely satisfactory answers to suffering, especially unmerited or undeserved suffering. What we do know is that God suffered in Jesus' death on the cross, so he is not oblivious or indifferent to suffering. And he is omniscient, so he knows of *our* suffering. This is comforting—some would say small comfort—when a loved one dies of a sudden heart attack or in an automobile accident or from an untreatable disease.

The good news for Christians is that suffering is not the end of the story. Joni Eareckson Tada was injured in a diving accident in 1967, when she was a teenager, leaving her paralyzed from the neck down. Joni said the thing that helped her the most during her hopelessness and depression was to know that "one day I would have a body that worked, hands that would hug, feet that would run . . . much like the body Jesus had after his resurrection. . . . It gave me a great deal of comfort to know that I had not been left alone . . . that [God would give me] a new body beyond the grave." In the words of the apostle Paul: "God has prepared [something wonderful and beautiful] for those who love him" (1 Cor. 2:9).

JESUS AS "THE *ONLY* WAY" TO SALVATION

Another reason people object to Christianity is that it makes *absolute* claims. The world prefers consensus, not absolutes. Absolutes exclude people who do not agree with the absolutes, such as Jesus being the once-for-all-time way of salvation. Some call this the Scandal of Particularity: God came in a particular person, at a particular place, at a particular time to redeem the world. Particularity, though, is part of the biblical story. Everything began with Adam, who disobeyed God. So God started over again with Noah, and then with Abraham, and then settled on the House of David, and finally came in the person of Jesus.

Other religions also have truth claims—such as Buddhism's "way of Buddha" and Islam's "Shari'a" or law of life. All religious truths and claims cannot be correct. If Christianity *is* true, it is true for everyone—for the whole human race—and Christians are called to make this truth known "to the ends of the earth" (Acts 1:8).

GROWING IN CHRIST THROUGH PRAYER

How can we grow and strengthen our faith? How can we make our faith a vibrant, living faith? Quaker thinker and writer Elton Trueblood said, "The three areas that must be cultivated if any faith is to be a living faith are the inner life of devotion, the intellectual life of rational thought, and the outer life of human service" (*A Place to Stand*).

THE LIFE OF PRAYER

Polls indicate that a majority of Christians are dissatisfied with their prayer life, and this includes both pastors and seminary students. One reason is that we find it difficult to be "quiet" before God, to sit and "wait upon the Lord." We do not realize that God is omnipresent—that he is everywhere present, like radio waves everywhere around us. All we have to do is switch on our antennas.

Success in prayer comes from being faithful and obedient. The key is *discipline.* When prayer becomes a habit—and a habit to which we look forward—it moves from being a chore to a joy. How can it be otherwise? The God of the universe created us in his "image and likeness" so that we could communicate and be in fellowship with him.

The Westminster Catechism of 1647 asks: What is the chief end of man? The answer: To glorify God and to enjoy him forever. We glorify God when we come to him in prayer; we enjoy God when we "bask in his presence," as a child on the lap of a parent. Brother Lawrence, a seventeenth-century Carmelite brother, believed that it is possible to "practice the presence of God," a phrase that became the title of a book containing his writings that was published after his death.

FORMS OF PRAYER

There are many different approaches to prayer. The following are three commonly used forms or methods of prayer:

Vocal Prayer. Vocal prayers are *spoken* prayers. An outline for verbal prayer that some Christians have found helpful is contained in the acronym (a word formed from the first letters of other words) ACTS, which stands for the *Adoration* of God, the *Confession* of sins and transgressions against God and others, *Thanksgiving* for God's gifts and promises, and *Supplications* (petitions or requests) to God for special needs. God does not care about the beauty or correctness of our words, only that we come to him with a prayerful heart.

Meditative Prayer. Meditation is praying with the *mind,* usually based on a passage from Scripture. In meditation, the pray-*er* does not study the words he or she is reading but meditates on the words. Dietrich Bonhoeffer said, "Just as you do not analyze the words of someone you love, but accept them as they are said to you, so it is with meditation." The key, Bonhoeffer said, "is to ponder God's Word in your heart, as Mary did." In meditation, the pray-*er* internalizes the words or passage. They become, Richard Foster says in his book *Prayer,* "a living word addressed to us . . . a call to repentance, to change, to obedience. . . . In meditative prayer, God addresses us personally."

Contemplative Prayer. Contemplation is the most advanced level of prayer. Vocal prayer is praying with words; meditative prayer is praying with the mind; contemplative prayer is praying with the heart. Contemplation is hungering for a "felt experience" of God; for hearing God's "still, small voice within"; for union and intimacy with God. How does this happen? By quieting down—called "centering," clearing the mind of all thoughts and distractions—so that we can *listen* to God, who is always and everywhere present, speak to our heart.

THE LORD'S PRAYER

The disciples asked Jesus to teach them how to pray. His response—"Pray then in this way" (Matt. 6:9)—is the Lord's Prayer, which is found in both Matthew (6:9–13) and Luke (11:2–4). Though the prayer is called the

"Lord's Prayer," it is not Jesus' personal prayer because, among other things, it petitions God to "forgive us our sins" and Jesus was sinless. The Lord's Prayer is the best outline for prayer that we have. It is widely used in corporate worship as a congregational prayer, and by some Christians for meditative prayer.

The Lord's Prayer has two parts. The first part contains three *thee* petitions or supplications to God (name, kingdom and will); the second part contains three *we* petitions for ourselves (sustenance, forgiveness and the strength to resist temptation). It takes only fifteen seconds to *say* the prayer, but several minutes to *pray* the prayer, that is, to reflect and meditate on each petition in the prayer.

Introduction. "Our Father in heaven" is the prayer's "address." Calling God our *Father*—as we are "bold to say"—means that God is personal, that he loves us in a special way, like the father of the Prodigal Son, who rejoiced when his son came to his senses and returned home.

Name. The first petition regarding God is "hallowed be your name." The Bible identifies one's name with one's nature or character. This petition is that God's name—his very essence—be hallowed, honored and reverenced, for he is the sovereign, supreme God of the universe.

Kingdom. "Your kingdom come." In the New Testament, the kingdom of God means the rule or reign of God. In Jesus, the kingdom of God was *already* but *not yet* (chapter 4). In this petition we pray for God's "not yet" kingdom to come in all its fullness, with love, mercy and justice; for Jesus to return in glory and power; and that we may be living witnesses to this hope.

Will. "Your will be done, on earth as it is in heaven." In this petition we pray that God's will be done—his will that we love him and others—and that we might be used by him to draw others into his kingdom.

Bread. "Give us this day our daily bread." The Scottish commentator William Barclay said the three "we" petitions can be thought of as present, past and future. We pray for *today*—for our daily bread; for *yesterday*—for words, thoughts, deeds and omissions that need to be forgiven; and for *tomorrow*—for the temptations that are sure to come. The term *daily bread* includes, in addition to food and drink, clothing, shelter, medical care and other necessities of life.

Forgiveness. "And forgive us our debts [our moral debts to God; in Luke, our "sins"], as we also have forgiven our debtors." This petition is for God's forgiveness when we have failed to love him with our whole heart and our neighbors as ourselves; when we have "missed the mark"; when we have failed to be all that we were meant to be.

We do not confess our trespasses to tell God something that he does not already know. We confess them so that they may be forgiven—and we are forgiven only if we *have* forgiven, which Jesus confirms in the two verses following the prayer: "If you do not forgive others, neither will your Father forgive" (Matt. 6:15).

Temptation. "And do not bring us to the time of trial, but rescue us from the evil one." The sixth petition has to do with temptation, which is not sin per se: we all are tempted. It is *yielding* to temptation that is sin. In this petition, we pray that God will be present when we are tempted with a course of action contrary to his will (see 1 Cor. 10:13).

How do we avoid falling prey to temptation? By avoiding occasions of temptation; by asking the Holy Spirit to guard us from the evil one; and when faced with temptation, by praying Psalm 51:1–12, David's prayer for "a clean heart."

Conclusion. The Lord's Prayer often concludes with the words, "For thine is the kingdom, and the power, and the glory, forever and ever." These words are not in the Matthean or Lukan versions of the prayer. They are the doxology ("praise to God") to the prayer.

THE PRACTICE OF PRAYER

The following are some suggestions regarding the practice of prayer. First, dedicate a certain *time* each day to being alone with God, perhaps first thing in the morning when your mind is not yet thinking of all the tasks you must do that day. Second, find a quiet *place,* with few distractions, to be together with God. Get comfortable, maybe light a candle to remind you of Christ's presence, and sit quietly and center on God. Third, keep a *spiritual diary* to record thoughts and reflections that come to you during these times. Last, though prayer is an attitude, not a formula, *structure* is sometimes helpful. Martin Luther's prayer outline was the Ten Commandments. A popular current outline is found in Bruce Wilkinson's book *The Prayer of*

Jabez (1 Chron. 4:10). Another outline is the acronym PRAY.

P stands for *Praise*. We give praise to God for his goodness and blessings, for our faith and the assurance of salvation, for our family and those we love and who love us, and for our health and well-being.

R stands for *Reflect*. We read a few verses from Scripture or from a daily devotional (below) or from one of the psalms, and reflect on the words as they come into our mind. As mentioned earlier, the Bible is God's "telephone line" to us. We need to ask: What is God saying in these readings? What do they mean for me and for my life?

A stands for *Ask*. Jesus said, "Ask, and it will be given you" (Matt. 7:7). What are we to ask for? First, for forgiveness for our sins of commission and omission—in the words of *The Book of Common Prayer*, for "doing those things we should not have done and not doing those things we should have done." Second, for our daily needs and for strength to overcome the temptations of the world. Third, for those who need intercessory ("on behalf of") prayer—perhaps someone whose marriage is in trouble or who has suffered a personal tragedy or is out of work—and also for victims of poverty and persecution. Jesus tells us that we who abide in him by faith are to ask for these things in his name (John 16:23–24).

Y stands for *Yearn*. We are to "yearn" for God, to hunger and desire for intimacy with God, to be "at-one" with God. How do we draw close to God? By focusing on Jesus, the "human face" of God, the "image of the invisible God" (Col. 1:15), "the way" to God. Our prayer should be that day by day we "see him more *clearly*, love him more *dearly*, and follow him more *nearly*."

We are all amateurs at praying; we need help along the way. One "help" is to invoke the presence of the Holy Spirit to guide our time and thoughts, as Paul advises in his letter to the Ephesians (6:18). Another help is to acquire a book of daily devotions. The following are some suggestions. *Our Daily Bread* is an easy-to-use devotional that follows the church year (to order, write to RBC Ministries, Box 2222, Grand Rapids, MI 49501). *My Utmost for His Highest* by Oswald Chambers is the bestselling devotional of all time. *A Guide to Prayer* by Reuben Job and Norman Shawchuck is a book "for every pilgrim who yearns for God." Each of these books has readings for each day of the year.

ANSWERS TO PRAYER

What about *answers* to prayer requests and petitions? Some answers are direct and immediate—for instance, the removal of a temptation or the coming to faith of a loved one or a healing. Sometimes answers are delayed and require persistence in prayer. And sometimes the answer is no, as in Paul's prayer to remove the "thorn" in his flesh (2 Cor. 12:7–10). God hears all prayers; we do not know why he *seems* to answer some and not others. Some say the real issue, though, is not too few answers to prayer, but too few prayers.

FASTING

The Old and New Testaments are filled with stories about godly men and women who fasted. The longest recorded fast was Jesus' forty days in the wilderness, during which he "ate nothing" (Luke 4:2). Following his teaching on prayer in the Sermon on the Mount, Jesus said, "Whenever you fast . . . when you fast . . . your fasting" (Matt. 6:16–18). From this it seems clear that Jesus intended his disciples to fast after he left them.

Fasting—abstaining from food but not from water—was widely practiced in the early church, and "fast days" became obligatory in the Middle Ages. The ancient Greeks fasted, and also the American Indians (for religious purposes); Muslims fast during the month of Ramadan, Jews fast on *Yom Kippur* and Catholics fast on Ash Wednesday and every Friday in Lent.

Unfortunately, most Protestants have abandoned fasting, perhaps because the Reformers rejected "things Catholic." Fasting is an important spiritual discipline—something done for spiritual purposes—the conscious control of the carnal side of our nature in order that we might "feast," instead, on God. Richard Foster, in his book *Celebration of Discipline,* has some helpful guidelines on the practice of fasting.

GROWING IN CHRIST THROUGH STUDY

Prayer is the inward or interior life of Christian growth. Next, we need to make the Jesus of our heart the Jesus of our mind, and then allow our faith to issue forth in works of service. Study will help us "give an answer" to those who ask about the hope we have in Jesus (1 Peter 3:15, NIV). Service will let others see how this hope expresses itself in the good works spoken of by Paul in his letter to the Ephesians (2:10), and by James (2:14–26).

THE LIFE AND DISCIPLINE OF STUDY

God wants us to grow in knowledge, to be "transformed by the renewing of your minds" (Rom. 12:2), to deepen our understanding of his love for us and his will for our lives. To be sure that all people everywhere on earth would know him, God inspired the writing of a witness to his saving acts, and he preserved this witness so that one day all might "come to the knowledge of the truth" and be saved.

Most of us are readers—of newspapers and magazines, business and professional periodicals, novels and nonfiction—but few of us have taken the time to read the most important book ever written, the Bible, God's "divine library" (Jerome). One suggestion would be to purchase *The One Year Bible* (Tyndale), which has daily readings from the Old and New Testaments in both the *New International Version* (NIV) and the *New Living Translation* (NLT) that take the reader through the entire Bible in one year. Another suggestion would be *Meet the Bible* by Philip Yancey and Brenda Quinn, a panorama of 365 readings and reflections that highlight the central stories and events in the Old and New Testaments.

With regard to the process and discipline of study, the following are some general suggestions:

First, get a study Bible in a modern translation (see chapter 1). Start with small, digestible doses of Scripture, perhaps a healing, a parable or a discourse. Read the verses slowly and carefully, perhaps two or three times. Then ask two questions. First, what was the *meaning* or point of the passage or verses to those to whom it was addressed (you may need a Bible commentary, like those recommended in chapter 1, to do this), and also to us today? Second, how might I *apply* this passage or teaching in my own life? Keep a journal of your answers as a personal road map for following Jesus.

Second, be consistent. Get into the habit of reading the Bible every day, perhaps as an extension of your daily quiet time or as the last thing you do before going to bed. Attempting to read through the Bible in large "chunks" usually results in *skimming* the Bible—like a newspaper or magazine—rather than *reading* the Bible.

Third, be systematic. Stay with something and see it through to the end, rather than jumping from one book of the Bible to another. The best place to begin is with one of the Gospels, perhaps with Luke because of the orderliness and completeness of his story. Read Luke's gospel at one sitting to get the plot and story line in mind. It will take only a couple of hours, about the same time as a two-hour special on television. Then work through Luke section by section.

Many Bibles divide the text into individual *pericopes* (self-contained literary units), like the birth of Jesus, the healing of the paralytic, the feeding of the five thousand, the Transfiguration and the Last Supper. Several editions of the Bible have divided Luke's gospel into more than one hundred pericopes. If you read a pericope in Luke each day, Dr. Luke will keep you busy for several months.

Last, memorize meaningful verses, perhaps a verse a week. This will help you locate important verses in the Bible (Where was that verse again?) and, when and if appropriate, help you to share your faith.

Study is a lifelong pursuit or process; no one ever "graduates." There is always more to learn, more to grasp, more to understand. One advantage of studying with a group, or being part of a formal Bible study program with discussion materials, is that people see and hear the Scriptures in the context of other peoples' life experiences, which is helpful in seeing different meanings in the text.

BUILDING A STUDY LIBRARY

In addition to the study of the Bible, one should read books on the life and teachings of Jesus, the history of the church, Christian doctrine and beliefs, and how to live "Christianly" in the world. Those who are serious should start a small Christian library. Begin with a good introduction to the Bible, perhaps John Drane's *Introducing the Old Testament* and *Introducing the New Testament.*

Then get a Bible dictionary and a one-volume Bible commentary (see chapter 1); some reference books such as *The Oxford Companion to the Bible* and Lion Publishing's *Introduction to the History of Christianity;* books on doctrine like Paul Little's *Know What You Believe* and Millard Erickson's *Introducing Christian Doctrine;* and a book on Christian living, maybe one of John Ortberg's books. You then might want to add some solid Christian authors such as C. S. Lewis (*Mere Christianity*) and John R. W. Stott (*Authentic Christianity*).

THE LIFE OF SERVICE

Christians are the *best* argument for Christianity—and also the *worst.* We are at our worst when we fail to reflect the one we profess as Lord and Savior in our daily lives. If we expect others to consider the person, claims and promises of Jesus, we need to be the further incarnation of his message and teachings.

How should we do this? By living lives of purity, coming alongside the marginalized, visiting the incarcerated, standing up for human rights, championing social justice, speaking out against immorality, cleaning up the environment and doing acts of goodness and kindness. In chapter 10 we will look at some biblical guidelines to follow in living out our faith in the world.

OBSTACLES TO GROWTH: THE SEVEN DEADLY SINS

The church in the Middle Ages developed two lists of "sevens," another biblical number: God rested on the seventh day; seven priests marched around Jericho seven times on the seventh day; Jesus said that we are to forgive seventy times seven; the author of the book of Revelation is told to write to the seven churches, after which he has visions of seven seals, seven trumpets, seven angels, seven plagues and seven bowls.

The first list contained seven virtues, comprising the four cardinal virtues of prudence, justice, temperance and fortitude (from Greek philosophy) and the three theological virtues of faith, hope and love (from 1 Cor. 13:13). The second list contained seven deadly sins. Though the Bible does not limit the number of sins to seven, it does speak of their *deadliness,* as in Paul's letter to the Romans: "The wages of sin is death" (6:23).

The seven sins were originally called "cardinal" sins (like the cardinal virtues) or "capital" sins, meaning they were the cause or source of other sins. For instance, avarice or greed is a cardinal or capital sin because it leads to lying, cheating and stealing to achieve its ends. The following list of sins or vices—which kill us "spiritually" and weaken and destroy our faith—comes from Pope Gregory the Great in the late sixth century.

PRIDE

Pride is the first sin because it is the "root" or core sin, which issues forth in actual sins. C. S. Lewis said that pride is "the one vice of which no man in the world is free; which everyone in the world loathes when he sees it in someone else; and of which hardly any people, except Christians, ever imagine they are guilty of themselves" (*Mere Christianity*).

Pride is self-love. It is going our own way and doing our own thing, as Adam and Eve did in eating from the forbidden tree. It is "*my* will be done," not "*thy* will be done." If we are able to recognize that our prideful nature is destroying our spirit, the way back is to practice pride's *opposite* virtue, that of "humility," which many believe is the prime or principal virtue. What is *humility*? In his book *The Purpose-Driven Life*, Rick Warren says, "Humility is not thinking less of yourself; it is thinking of yourself less." Once we recognize the need for humility and for God in our lives, the work of the Spirit can begin.

ENVY

The second sin is envy, which often leads to the hatred of others, and sometimes even to the hatred of God. Envy is rarely confessed because it is so futile: envying something in another person—such as his or her intelligence or good looks or athletic or artistic abilities—does nothing to produce those qualities in ourselves. The result of envy is a poisoning of the soul and bitterness, loneliness and isolation. How does one overcome envy? As with pride, by practicing its opposite virtue, which is contentedness. When we realize that God loves us for who we are, and we love him and others in return, our inner life in Christ will begin to grow.

ANGER

The third sin is anger. Anger per se is not sinful. Jesus is recorded as being angry, as when he drove the moneychangers out of the temple (Mark

11:15–17). Anger becomes sinful when it is willfully and wrongfully directed or projected onto someone else in the form of hurtful speech or acts. How should we deal with anger? One way is to allow it to come out into the open with a pastor, family member or close friend so that it can be released.

SLOTH

The fourth sin is sloth or apathy—the sin of laziness, indolence and neglect, the sin of not seeking God or caring about one's neighbors—which robs us of the opportunity for spiritual growth. One way to overcome sloth and apathy is to be born "anew" in Christ.

AVARICE

The fifth sin is avarice and greed—the manipulation of people and circumstances to acquire possessions and power, which become "gods" in which we place our hope and trust. Avarice often creates the desire for more and more until, finally, one is caught. Unfortunately, it often seems that things must come to such a place before there can be a new beginning.

GLUTTONY

The sixth sin is gluttony, likely the most prevalent of the seven deadly sins among Christians in those areas of the world where the emphasis is on satisfying one's appetites, which for all too many become addictions. How do we overcome self-indulgent gluttony? By disciplining the physical or carnal side of our nature—perhaps by fasting, mentioned above, to which Jesus calls us in the Sermon on the Mount—feeding not our appetites but our soul.

LUST

The last sin is that of lust—the desire to gratify the flesh—which expresses itself in fornication, adultery, pornography and other sexual sins. Some think that lust should be higher on the list because of our unhealthy fascination with sex and its glorification and exploitation by the entertainment industry. How can we conquer the sin of lust? By practicing the cardinal virtue of temperance (the control of circumstances and thoughts that give rise to lustful desires) and by understanding that God's will is for us to be "pure in heart" (Matt. 5:8).

To grow in Christ, we need to be in prayer and study each day, we need to find avenues of service to others, and we need to avoid self-pride and conceit, envy and jealousy, anger and aggression, sloth and indifference, avarice and greed, and gluttony and lust.

THE MESSAGE OF EVANGELISM: JESUS CHRIST

As Christians, we need to grow in faith through prayer and study, and we need to share our faith through the witness of our lips and our lives. *What* do we share, and *how* do we share? The comments below address the first question: the content of our witness, which is Jesus Christ. The next section addresses the second question: how to share our faith with others.

"WHO DO PEOPLE SAY THAT I AM?"

As Christians, our witness is to share the good news, which means sharing Jesus Christ. We will not here repeat the details of Jesus' life, which are set out in chapters 3 and 4. Rather, we want to answer the question that Jesus posed to his disciples: "Who do people say that I am?" (Mark 8:27). This is the central question, even today.

In his book *Jesus Through the Centuries,* noted Yale historian Jaroslav Pelikan offers a series of eighteen portraits of Jesus as seen in the works of writers and artists down through the centuries. Some of Pelikan's portraits are of Jesus as a Jewish Rabbi, the Light of the Gentiles, the King of Kings, the Cosmic Christ, a Monk, the Universal Man, the Prince of Peace, a Teacher, a Poet and a Liberator. One conclusion from Pelikan's book is that each age has had a different understanding of Jesus.

What about our age? How are we to answer those who ask, Who is Jesus? Cynics, skeptics and believers have different answers. Either he was an *imposter,* or a *legend* in the minds and memories of his followers, or the resurrected, living, reigning *Lord* of the universe.

Imposter. Cynics say that Jesus was an imposter; that is, he claimed to be someone (the Son of God) whom he was not. But we do not find a deceitful person on the pages of the New Testament. Rather, we find someone who is loving, compassionate and forgiving. Even Josephus, the first-century Jewish historian, spoke of Jesus as a "wise man" and a "good man." If Jesus was an imposter, why did he refuse the Jews when they wanted to make him king (John 6:15)? And if he had been an imposter, would he have given his life for something he knew to be untrue?

Legend. Some skeptics say that Jesus was only a legend; that is, a man about whom his followers developed a legend after his death. But the first gospel (Mark) appeared just forty years after Jesus' death, and the other three followed shortly thereafter. If the things written about Jesus had been untrue, they would have been discredited, as would be the case, for instance, if someone today were to write untruths about the presidency of John F. Kennedy: too many people are alive today who were alive in the 1960s to allow such stories to ever get off the ground.

Lord and Savior. The last option is that Jesus is who he claimed to be, the one whom the New Testament said that he was, namely, the incarnate, living Son of the Creator of the universe; "True God from true God" (Nicene Creed); "the Lord of lords and King of kings" (Rev. 17:14); the one who is coming again to raise up all who have believed.

JESUS' RESURRECTION

We can say many things about Jesus, but at the end of the day it is always about the Resurrection: Was Jesus raised from the dead? This is the bedrock or cornerstone of Christianity. If Jesus was raised, our faith rests on a firm foundation, and all who believe and confess Jesus can be confident of their resurrection. If he was not raised, then, as Paul wrote to the Corinthians, "We are of all people most to be pitied" (1 Cor. 15:19). The case for Jesus' resurrection has been set forth elsewhere. Three arguments commonly advanced for Jesus' resurrection are as follows.

The Empty Tomb. According to most scholars, Jesus died on April 7 in the year 30. On May 27—fifty days later—his disciples began to preach that he had risen from the dead. If the Jews had wished to dispute this, they would have needed only to go to the family tomb of Joseph of Arimathea and produce Jesus' corpse. There is no record of anyone coming forward to say that the body was still in the tomb or that it had been stolen, either of which would have ended everything. Further, if Jesus had not been raised, there would have been no Gospels: Why? Because a dead, still-in-the-grave savior would not have been "good news."

The Disciples. The Gospels report that Jesus' disciples fled when he was arrested. They were afraid that the fate that had befallen their leader would also be theirs. But on the first Pentecost after Jesus' death, they were in the marketplace boldly proclaiming that Jesus had been raised from the dead (Acts 2). What gave them this newfound courage? They had experienced the risen Christ: he appeared to them after his crucifixion and ate with them (John 21:12–13) and spoke with them (Acts 1:3) before ascending to heaven. And he promised that they would be filled with the Holy Spirit (Acts 1:8), who came upon them ten days later on Pentecost.

The Martyrs. The word *martyr* comes from a Greek word meaning "witness." Christians who confessed and witnessed to their faith in Jesus were often persecuted; some were even rounded up and killed, many suffering cruel, gruesome deaths. What gave them the strength to endure rather than renounce—in the face of sure and certain persecution—their faith that Jesus had been raised? The strong, sure, believable oral and written testimony of those who had seen the risen Christ.

Could the worldwide church of Jesus Christ, the largest religion in the world, have developed, grown and sustained itself for twenty centuries if Jesus had remained in the grave? If he had not appeared to his disciples to confirm his resurrection? If the Holy Spirit had not come upon the church after he ascended? (John 16:7). If his only legacy was that he was a good person and a great moral teacher?

THE ESSENCE OF CHRISTIANITY

The center or *essence* of Christianity—the essence of our witness—is Jesus Christ. Some think that the essence of Christianity is assenting to certain beliefs, like the Apostles' and Nicene Creeds. Others think that it is being upright in character and conduct and following the Golden Rule. Still others think that it is being baptized and reading the Bible and attending church services. These are very important, but they are not the *essence* of Christianity. The essence is Jesus Christ.

Being a Christian means having a *personal* relationship with Jesus, as one would have with a good friend; it means believing and *trusting* that Jesus' saving death will make us righteous in the sight and presence of God; it means making Jesus *Lord* over every aspect of our public and private lives.

THE MECHANICS OF EVANGELISM: SHARING THE GOOD NEWS

In his letter to the Romans, Paul writes, "Everyone who calls on the name of the Lord shall be saved. But how are they to call on one in whom they have not believed? And how are they to believe in one of whom they have never heard? . . . How beautiful are the feet of those who bring good news!" (Rom. 10:13–15). In this section we will look at some suggestions for *bringing* the Good News and some things to avoid in doing so.

EVANGELISM: JESUS' CALL TO SHARE THE GOOD NEWS

Christians engage in evangelism for two reasons. First, Jesus' final charge or commission to his followers—the Great Commission—was that they do so, which makes it a charge to us as well. Second, we have something important and precious to say to the world, something the world needs to hear and know, something that will cure the world's pain and sin: the good news of Jesus Christ.

To be an effective cure for humankind's ills, the "antidote"—the good news—must be proclaimed and shared with those in need. In 1950 there was an outbreak of polio in the United States. In 1952 Dr. Jonas Salk invented a vaccine to prevent polio, and there was a widespread campaign of inoculation. Today polio has been eradicated in the United States and in most other countries in the world. But this would not have happened if the vaccine had remained in Dr. Salk's laboratory where it was discovered. It had to be distributed to those in need to be effective. The same is true of the gospel. It has lifesaving power, but it must get to the point of need to be effective. "How beautiful are the feet of those who bring good news!"

SUGGESTIONS FOR SHARING THE GOOD NEWS

It is often said that God has a *plan* for our lives. It might be more accurate to say that God has a *purpose* for our lives—to know Jesus Christ and to make him known to others. The following are some suggestions for making him "known" to others.

First, begin where the other person is rather than where you are, and ask about his or her religious beliefs. This often leads to their asking *What do you believe?* which opens the door for you to share your faith and beliefs and the distinctiveness of Christianity.

Second, focus on the central message, which is having a personal relationship with God through Jesus Christ. Do not get sidetracked trying to explain the mysteries of the faith, such as the Trinity (apologetics comes *after* evangelism, not before); or trying to explain divisions in the church or the lifestyles of particular Christians (our trust is in Jesus, not in fallen humanity and institutions); or trying to explain why there is evil and suffering in the world (much of which comes from humankind's own sin). Keep to your beliefs and faith and what they mean to you and for your life—that Christ has given you something to live *for* (his promises) and something to live *by* (his teachings). This is what searchers want to hear and know.

Third, avoid using Christian talk or lingo like the Bible being "the inspired Word of God" and being saved "by the cross (or blood) of Christ" and being "justified by faith" and being "born again."

Fourth, temper the exclusive claims of Christianity so that open discussion can take place, and be careful not to judge or condemn another person's beliefs.

Fifth, avoid arguments about Jesus being superior to Muhammad, Buddha and the founders of other religions. Arguing is a losing strategy: either you win the argument and lose the discussion, or your argument is not convincing and you lose both the argument and the discussion.

Last, remember our role as witnesses is to be *presenters*, not persuaders. We are to present the gospel as lovingly as we can, and then allow the inner witness of the Holy Spirit to take over.

PASCAL'S "WAGER": BETTING ON GOD

Blaise Pascal was a mathematician who, at age nineteen, invented the first workable calculating machine to help his father, a tax collector, prepare his daily reports; a physicist who invented Pascal's Law, which underlies the basic principles of hydraulics; and the inventor of the barometer, the first public trolley car and (some say) the first wristwatch. Pascal was born in Claremont, France, in 1623; he died at the young age of thirty-nine. At the end of his life, Pascal began writing out his thoughts on religion, which were published after his death as *Pensées* (French for "Thoughts"), which has become a Christian classic.

Peter Kreeft, the Roman Catholic writer and apologist, in his book *Christianity for Modern Pagans* (based on Pascal's *Pensées*), says that Pascal's "wager"—perhaps the best-known section in *Pensées*—is an attempt to show "that it is eminently reasonable for anyone to 'bet' on God, to hope that God is, to invest his life in God."

The wager, Kreeft says, "is not just about there being some sort of God, but the God of Christianity, the God who promises salvation. . . . In other words, [it is about] Christ, the man who claimed to be God and said that if and only if we believe in him will we be saved."

Pascal's argument is that we all make a wager or bet on God, whether we know it or not. If we bet on God and there is a God, we *win* everything; if we bet on God and there is no God, we lose *nothing*, for there is nothing to lose; if we bet against God and there is a God, we *lose everything*.

Betting on God is a good place to start a conversation because it focuses on three questions that people have been asking since the dawn of history.

Who am I? Answer: A child of God, made in his image and likeness and invited into his forever family.

What is the purpose of life? Answer: To enter into a saving relationship with God through his Son, Jesus Christ, and to show love, kindness and mercy to others.

Is there another life beyond this life? Answer: Yes, for those who "bet" on God and follow Jesus as their Lord and Savior. In the end, the wager comes down to believing and confessing Jesus. To quote from the refrain of the hymn "My Hope Is Built on Nothing Less": "On Christ the solid rock I stand; all other ground is sinking sand, all other ground is sinking sand."

CHAPTER 10

LIVING CHRISTIANLY

In Christ for my guardianship today.

Christ beside me, Christ within me.

Christ behind me, Christ before me.

Christ beneath me, Christ above me.

Christ to the right of me, Christ to the left of me.

Christ in lying down, Christ in sitting, Christ in rising up.

Christ in quiet, Christ in danger.

Christ in the heart of every person who may think of me.

Christ in the mouth of everyone who may speak to me.

Christ in every eye which may look upon me.

Christ in every ear which may hear me.

SAINT PATRICK
Patron Saint of Ireland

BIBLICAL GUIDELINES FOR LIVING THE CHRISTIAN FAITH

In the last chapter we looked at three challenges to the Christian faith. Actually, there is another challenge that is harder to answer than the other three: the failure of Christians to reflect the faith they profess in their every-day lives. Christian theologian and writer Os Guinness said, "The problem with most Christians is not that they aren't *where* they should be; the problem is that they're not *what* they should be right where they are."

In this chapter we will focus on living the Christian life, which is not *believing* certain things, like the Virgin Birth, or *doing* certain things, like attending church, but *being* Christ in and for the world. We will look at the Ten Commandments—what they meant in ancient Israel and what they mean today—the Sermon on the Mount, and the parables of the Good Samaritan, the Rich Fool and the Rich Man and Lazarus. We will end the chapter and the book by looking at three people who gave their lives "for Jesus' sake": Dietrich Bonhoeffer, Martin Luther King Jr. and Mother Teresa.

HOW TO THINK AS A CHRISTIAN

Thinking as a Christian—the first step in *living* the Christian life—has two aspects: first, understanding that Christianity is a biblical worldview and second, understanding that we live in a culture that is religiously pluralistic and very secular.

THE CHRISTIAN WORLDVIEW

A *worldview* is a particular way of looking at the world—a set of assumptions or beliefs about the origin and makeup of the world, about how human beings function and operate in the world, and about what happens, if anything, when life in this world comes to an end. Most Christians do not think in worldview terms or realize that there are worldviews other than the Christian worldview.

The Christian worldview is called *Theism*. It believes that there is a supreme God, not many "gods," as in Hinduism and other Eastern religions;

and that God created the universe and life on planet Earth, as opposed to everything coming into being as a result of blind chance, as in naturalism, or evolving from simple to complex life forms, as in Darwinism.

Theism also believes that God is separate and distinct from creation, rather than being "in" or a part of creation, as in pantheism; that God revealed his will and his purposes to prophets and apostles, which are recorded in the Old and New Testaments; that it is possible for fallen, finite human beings to have a personal relationship with God through Jesus Christ; and that there is a further, fuller life beyond this life, in contrast to those who believe that this life is all there is or who believe in reincarnation.

OTHER WORLDVIEWS

There are several major worldviews that are antithetical to the Christian worldview. Some of these are as follows:

Naturalism holds that observable nature is all there is, that the universe is a closed system and that there is no evidence to support "intelligent design," which rules out the possibility of a supernatural being who is behind or gave birth to the universe. Included in this view is secular humanism, the view that humankind is the measure of all things.

Polytheism believes that there are many gods (Hinduism has thousands of gods), none of whom is "personal," so it is not possible to have a relationship with God.

Pantheism, which includes the New Age Movement, believes that God is in everything (humans, animals, vegetation), or that everything is God ("monism"), rather than in a single, sovereign, transcendent God.

Hedonism is the atheistic pursuit of pleasure (hedonists are interested in life *before* death, not after death).

Other worldviews include Nihilism, the rejection of religious and moral values; certain forms of Existentialism, the belief that there is no ultimate purpose or meaning to existence; and two touched on earlier in the book, Deism, which has largely died out, and Animism, the worldview of many primitive societies.

There can be only one *true* worldview regarding such matters as God, creation and death. For instance:

God: Either there is no God, which is the position of naturalists and atheists; or God is an impersonal soul or force, which is the view of most Eastern religions; or God is a "person" with whom we can have a relationship.

Creation: Either the universe is *eternal* (it always was as it now is); or the universe came into being as the result of a *chance* explosion (an unexplained Big Bang); or God *created* "the heavens and the earth."

Death: Either this life is all there is; or we are reincarnated into lower and higher forms of life; or we live beyond the grave.

In each of the above examples, the three different worldviews are *mutually exclusive;* that is, only one of them can be true.

THE CASE FOR THE CHRISTIAN WORLDVIEW

One reason for believing the Christian worldview is that it is the most complete and comprehensive of the worldviews. Another reason is that it "squares" with the world around us—the intelligent design of the universe, the various forms and species of life, and the uniqueness of the human species (intelligence, creativity, conscience, worship). The Christian worldview is based on the following premises:

- First, the prophetic and apostolic witness to the biblical story—God calling Abraham to be the "father" of his people, saving the Israelites in Egypt, entering into covenants, calling prophets to speak his Word, preserving a remnant to continue on his purposes, coming among us in the person of Jesus of Nazareth, calling Paul on the road to Damascus, sending his Spirit upon the church—all of which occurred on the plane of history.

- Second, the historicity of the Resurrection, the touchstone of the Christian faith, which has been set forth several times in this book.

- Third, the historical reliability of the New Testament writings—their proximity to the events reported, the extensive underlying manuscript evidence (chapter 1), and the high regard in which this evidence is held by the scholarly community.

- Fourth, the witness of Christians down through the ages to the transforming power of the good news of Jesus in their lives and in the lives of others.

The Christian worldview is that Jesus Christ is the risen, living Son of the God of the universe. He died once that we might not die twice (at the end of our earthly lives and on Judgment Day); he accepts all who repent and come to him in faith (Acts 2:38); and he promises eternal life to all who believe in him (John 6:40).

THE PROBLEM OF DUALISM

Christians face the dilemma of wanting to accept scientific ways of looking at the world, while at the same time remaining true to the Bible's teachings. And so we divide our lives into secular and sacred, into things religious and nonreligious, into Sunday morning and the rest of the week. According to Brian Walsh and Richard Middleton (*The Transforming Vision*), we are giving in to the secular trinity of *science* and scientific methods of reasoning; *technology* and the use of machines to master and control our lives and the environment (we have become a machine-driven culture); and *capitalism* and the drive for ever-increasing growth, profits and wealth.

Some years ago the American theologian Francis Schaeffer said that the church is slowly accommodating itself to the norms and values of the world—becoming more concerned with being "politically correct" (the neutral middle road) than with the commandments and teachings of the Bible—and soon will have nothing precious or important to say to the world.

How can we overcome this? By understanding that there is a unique, all-embracing Christian worldview; by developing our Christian minds through prayer and study; and by asking "What Would Jesus Do?" if he were confronted with decisions we face in our vocations, in our marriages and parenting, in our use of the environment, in our leisure activities, and in responding to the needs of the marginalized in society.

THE TEN COMMANDMENTS: RULES FOR CHRISTIAN LIVING

Israel was called to be God's "light to the nations" (Isa. 42:6), something that would draw people to God. How was Israel to be such a people? By observing the commandments God gave to Moses on Mount Sinai. These commandments or utterances are contained in the books of Exodus (20:3–17) and Deuteronomy (5:7–21) and are affirmed by Jesus in his dialogue with the rich young man (Mark 10:19) and by the apostle Paul in his letter to the Romans (13:9).

Many people see the Ten Commandments as a series of narrow *shall nots* rather than as an expansion of the Old Testament commands to love God and to love others. Pastor James Moore, in his book on Christian living (*When All Else Fails . . . Read the Instructions*), says, "The Ten Commandments tell us how things work, how life holds together, how God meant things to be. Anyone who is awake enough to 'smell the coffee' can easily see that life is better when we love God and other people . . . when we respect our parents and tell the truth . . . when we are honest, faithful, kind and generous in all of our relationships."

THE TEN COMMANDMENTS: THEN AND NOW

The Ten Commandments are divided into two halves: four commandments having to do with our vertical relationship with God and six commandments having to do with our horizontal relationship with others. Roman Catholics and Lutherans follow Augustine's numbering and combine the first two commandments into one (no other gods and graven images) and divide the tenth commandment into two (coveting a neighbor's possessions and coveting a neighbor's spouse). The following are brief comments on each of the commandments.

1. No Other Gods. "You shall have no other gods before me." The word *gods* refers to the fact that there were many "gods" in the ancient world. But for Israel there was only one God—the "wholly other" God who called Abraham, who led the Israelites out of Egypt, who covenanted with Israel at Mount Sinai, who spoke through prophets. Israel was to love this God and no other.

Today we do not think of the world as being inhabited by many gods, but we do *worship* other "gods"—reputation, success, wealth, possessions, power, the pursuit of pleasure. After filming *The Ten Commandments,* Cecil B. DeMille was asked which commandment he thought people broke most often. He said, "The first one. It is the one Israel broke first, and the one we still break most." We are commanded to love God with our whole heart, soul, mind and strength (Mark 12:30), which means giving God and his purposes first priority in our lives.

2. Idols and Images. "You shall not make for yourself an idol. . . . You shall not bow down to them or worship them." God told Moses, "I AM WHO I AM" (Ex. 3:14). God spoke but was not seen. For this reason, no graven (sculptured, carved or chiseled) image could possibly have been accurate or adequate.

The Jews followed this commandment so faithfully that archaeologists have found no Jewish images or idols of God in postexilic Israel. And when the Romans entered Palestine in 63 B.C., they were surprised to learn that the Israelites, who were so fiercely monotheistic, had no image or idol of the God they worshiped, in contrast to the Roman army, which carried flags and standards with the emperor's image wherever it went.

Today some claim that paintings, statues and icons of Jesus are "images." They are symbolic representations of God's personification of himself in the human Jesus, not *images of God.* However, we do have idols, many of which we worship and "idolize"—rock musicians, movie and television stars, fashion models, professional athletes—until they burn out or fade away. We are not to worship created beings, either ourselves or others. We are to worship God and *only* God.

3. Name. "You shall not make wrongful use of the name of the Lord your God." The term *God* does not denote the "name" of God but the essence of God. The distinct and special name by which God made himself known (YHWH or Yahweh) was seldom uttered. The only exception was on the Day of Atonement when the high priest went into the Holy of Holies and called upon God to forgive Israel all its sins.

God's name was so sacred that in the Hebrew Scriptures God is usually referred to as Elohim ("God") or Adonai ("Lord"), or an apostrophe (') is placed in the text in lieu of the word *God.* In this commandment, Israel is ordered not to take the name of God "in vain" (from the Latin *vanus,* meaning "to empty"), which means to diminish God's name or to depreciate his name or to use it irreverently.

Today this commandment has come to refer, principally, to the use of language that profanes something that is holy and makes it common, as when we take God's name in vain in speech, jokes, writings and graffiti. To avoid profaning God's name, we substitute other words, such as *jeez* (Jesus), *cripes* (Christ) and *gosh* and *golly* (God), euphemisms that are now a part of our everyday vocabulary.

We are to take God's name in *earnest,* not in vain, as Jesus teaches us in the Lord's Prayer ("hallowed be thy name"). When we use profane language, or laugh at others who do, or invoke God's name in promises ("So help me, God") and in marriage vows and then break our promise, we take God's name "in vain."

4. *Sabbath.* "Remember the sabbath day, and keep it holy.... [On] the seventh day ... you shall not do any work." God rested on the seventh day so that he could enjoy his creation; Israel rested on the seventh day so that she could enjoy God.

There is a story of a conversation between God and Israel. God said, "If you obey my commandments, I will give you a great gift." Israel asked, "What is this gift?" God answered, "The world to come." Israel asked, "What will the world to come be like?" God answered, "It will be like one long, continuous, everlasting Sabbath."

Today the Christian Sunday is different from the Jewish Sabbath, that is, the two commemorate different events. The Sabbath, the seventh day of the week, remembers the day God rested after making the heavens and the earth. Sunday, the first day of the week (at least in the United States), remembers the day on which Christ rose from the dead; it is the day that we celebrate Christ's resurrection.

Rules regarding the Sabbath were very strict in Jesus' day, as were rules about Sunday in early periods of American history when "blue laws" (printed on blue paper) prohibited commercial activities on Sunday. The pendulum has now swung to the opposite extreme: Sunday has moved from being a holy day to a holiday (ironically, *holiday* is a shortened form of *holy day*)—a day for shopping, entertainment, sports and the like. We *honor* the fourth commandment by spending time in prayer and study (Sunday "quiet time"), by worshiping with other believers, and by doing acts of love for shut-ins, the sick and others who need a "God-touch" in their lives.

5. *Father and Mother.* "Honor your father and your mother, so that your days may be long," the only commandment that comes to us with a *promise.* The subject of the first four commandments is God; the subject of the remaining six commandments is our relationship with others—our parents, our spouse and our neighbors. The first of these—and the only commandment without a "shall not"—has to do with our father and mother, whom we are called to honor for taking care of us when we were not able to do so ourselves, for the sacrifices they made for us, and for loving us.

Today we have a diminished view or vision of the family, and also of the elderly (we admire youth and youthfulness, not old age). We need to remember, and care for if possible, those who have no family—those for whom we can *become* family—inviting them into our homes and showing them the kind of hospitality Jesus referred to when he said, "I was a stranger and you welcomed me" (Matt. 25:35).

Commandments five through ten are being interpreted more widely today than was the case in the past. For example, with regard to the fifth commandment, children are to be obedient, support and show respect for their parents, and parents are to care for, develop and encourage their children, which Paul sets out in his letters to the Colossians (3:20–21) and the Ephesians (6:1–4).

Furthermore, some interpret the term *honoring* to include more than one's immediate family. British scholar John R. W. Stott believes that it includes all who are in authority over us, including the state, our employers and both teachers and pastors (*Christian Basics*). We will look at other expansions of the commandments in the paragraphs that follow.

6. Murder. "You shall not murder." This commandment is a prohibition against the unauthorized, intentional, blood-revenge killing of a fellow Israelite. This commandment did not prohibit the killing of enemies in battle, as did the armies of Joshua, Saul and David, capital punishment (Israel's jurisprudence was "an eye for an eye"), killing in self-defense, or the slaughter of animals for sacrifices in the temple.

Today the sixth commandment has to do with the sanctity of life. It has been widened by some to include any form of killing and furnishes the biblical basis for those who oppose capital punishment, war (even "just war"), suicide, euthanasia ("mercy killings") and recruitment by the government into the armed services.

The sixth commandment also underlies arguments regarding abortion, which was legalized by the U.S. Supreme Court in 1972 (Roe v. Wade).

Does life begin at conception? Or during pregnancy? Or at birth? Pro-life activists believe that aborting an embryo—a human being in the making—is killing one made in the "image and likeness" of God. The gift of life is a precious, inexpressible gift, and purposely ending one's own life or another person's life is an offense to God.

7. Adultery. "You shall not commit adultery." This commandment protects the institution of marriage, though polygamy (having multiple wives) was an accepted practice in ancient Israel, as was the fathering of children through maidservants.

Today, in our monogamous (one spouse) society, the thrust of this commandment is against the infidelity of married persons, whom God joins together to "become one flesh" (Gen. 2:24; Mark 10:6–9).

The violation of this commandment has contributed to the breakdown of the family unit and, many believe, is responsible for the decline in sexual morality—the exploitation of sex in movies, novels, television and advertising; the legalization of pornography; the proliferation of abortion clinics; sexual activity among young people (half of the babies born in many United States cities today are being delivered by unwed teenage mothers); and sexual harassment. Sex is one of God's wonderful gifts, but it must be enjoyed monogamously and within marriage, not promiscuously or irresponsibly.

8. Steal. "You shall not steal." This commandment prohibited the stealing of another Israelite's property, particularly the property of those who were poor and powerless.

Today the eighth commandment has to do with honesty and with the theft of property and property rights. In its broadest form, the commandment condemns the misappropriation of property and funds, the bribery of government and corporate officials, the manipulation of the economic system for personal gain, and the falsification of reports and records. We need to live more simply so that we are not driven to dishonesty and manipulation to satisfy our spiraling desires for more and more.

9. False Witness. "You shall not bear false witness against your neighbor." In ancient times, false witness against another was a serious offense, because the accused was "guilty until proven innocent," the opposite of our jurisprudence. In capital crimes, the one bringing the charge had to throw the first stone. If the evidence against the accused was shown to be false, the one who brought the charge was stoned in his or her place.

Today the thrust of the ninth commandment has to do with "truthfulness." It has been enlarged to include perjury, slander, libel and gossip—in fact, the protection of another's reputation against any form of false witness, even remaining silent when the truth is known. We need to tell "the whole truth and nothing but the truth," and also stand up for the truth.

10. Covet. "You shall not covet." The final commandment is a prohibition against desiring and lusting after things that do not belong to us, which often creates insatiable demands for these things, as in the stories of David coveting Bathsheba (2 Sam. 11) and King Ahab coveting Naboth's vineyard (1 Kings 21).

Today coveting is one of the most prevalent and destructive sins, and one of the Seven Deadly Sins, that of envy. We covet status and success, cars and other possessions, health and youthfulness, and pleasure without limits. The way to control our coveting—our desire for "forbidden fruit"—is to practice its opposite, which is contentedness.

THE TEN COMMANDMENTS TODAY

Are the Ten Commandments applicable today, or are they old, out-of-date, antiquated rules for another society and another time? According to a 1990s *Barna Report,* 64 percent of Americans "strongly agree" and another 15 percent "somewhat agree" that the Ten Commandments are "relevant for people living today." Television journalist Ted Koppel, in his address to the graduating class at Duke University in May 1987, said that Moses came down from Mount Sinai with Ten *Commandments,* not Ten *Suggestions.* "The sheer beauty of the Commandments," Koppel said, "is that they codify in a handful of words acceptable human behavior, not just for then or now, but for all time."

THE SERMON ON THE MOUNT: THE CHRISTIAN MANIFESTO

There are two so-called sermons in the Gospels: the *Sermon on the Mount* in Matthew 5:1–7:29 ("He went up the mountain," 5:1) and the *Sermon on the Plain* in Luke 6:17–49 ("He came down with them and stood on a level place," 6:17). Of the two sermons, Matthew's is longer, more concentrated and, in the history and life of the church, the more important. Some have called it the Constitution of Christianity.

As mentioned in chapter 4, the principal teaching of the early church was how to *enter* the kingdom and how to *live* in the kingdom. The clearest and fullest teaching about how to "live" in the kingdom is the Sermon on the Mount. The sermon begins with Jesus going up on a "mountain." In the Bible, *mountains* are places of special revelation, some examples being Mount Moriah, Mount Sinai, Mount Carmel and the Mount of Transfiguration. Precisely on what mount or mountain Jesus may have delivered the sermon is not known. In fact, as was indicated in chapter 4, it is possible that what Matthew offers as a single, self-contained sermon originally comprised discourses that Jesus delivered on different occasions. The reasons for this view are the complexity of the sermon and the different placement of its various components by Luke in his gospel.

THE BEATITUDES (MATTHEW 5:3—12)

The Sermon on the Mount is addressed to the Christian community, not to the world at large. The sermon begins with a series of eight beatitudes—eight spiritual qualities that should be reflected in the lives of Christians, similar to Paul's nine fruits of the Spirit in Galatians 5.

The word *beatitude* means "blessed," not "happy," as in some translations (those who mourn and are persecuted are not "happy"). Being *blessed* means that we have found God's favor in this life—Blessed *are* those who are mournful, meek, merciful and pure, and the assurance of God's special favor in the next life—for they *will* be comforted, inherit the earth, receive mercy and see God. The following are brief comments on each of the eight Beatitudes.

1. Poor in Spirit. "Blessed are the poor in spirit, for theirs is the kingdom of heaven." The first beatitude reminds us of our helplessness to save ourselves. It calls us to put our whole trust and hope in God—or on God—which means betting or wagering everything on the grace and mercy of God. "Simon Peter answered him, 'Lord, to whom can we go? You [alone] have the words of eternal life' " (John 6:68).

2. Mourn. "Blessed are those who mourn, for they will be comforted."

This beatitude calls us to be compassionate, to grieve over the cruelty and pains of the world, to be moved by the helplessness and sufferings of others and to offer them comfort rather than passing by, as the Good Samaritan did when he took pity on a man who was robbed and beaten on the road to Jericho, bandaging his wounds and taking him to the inn and paying for his care (Luke 10:33–34).

3. Meek. "Blessed are the meek, for they will inherit the earth." This beatitude calls us to be gentle and even-tempered, to care deeply for and about others, to be humble and thoughtful, like the father who humbled himself before his wasteful younger son and his angry older son in the parable of the Prodigal Son (Luke 15:20–24).

4. Righteousness. "Blessed are those who hunger and thirst for righteousness, for they will be filled." This beatitude calls us to hunger to be "right" with God, to thirst after his will and his desires, to be morally upright and acceptable in his sight. God said to the Israelites, "I take no delight in your solemn assemblies . . . your burnt offerings . . . the noise of your songs. . . . Let justice roll down like waters, and righteousness like an ever-flowing stream" (Amos 5:21–24).

5. Mercy. "Blessed are the merciful, for they will receive mercy." This beatitude calls us not to repay evil with evil but with love, to show kindness and mercy to all, even the unworthy, to be willing to forgive and forget our grievances. "Then Jesus said, 'Father, forgive them; for they do not know what they are doing' " (Luke 23:34).

6. Pure. "Blessed are the pure in heart, for they will see [be near to] God." This beatitude calls us to pray for an inner purity of heart, to have motives that are genuine and sincere, to think about and serve others rather than ourselves. David said, after his adultery, "Create in me a clean heart, O God, and put a new and right spirit within me" (Psalm 51).

7. Peacemakers. "Blessed are the peacemakers, for they will be called children of God." This beatitude calls us to strive for peace and for right relationships and to be peace*makers* between those who are at enmity with one another, asking as did Saint Francis of Assisi, "Lord, make me an instrument of your peace."

8. Persecuted. "Blessed are those who are persecuted for righteousness' sake, for theirs is the kingdom of heaven." This beatitude calls us to be willing to suffer for the kingdom, to speak out against social and political injustice, to defend Christ's name before others. Jesus said to his disciples, "You will be hated by all because of my name. But [those who endure] to the end will be saved" (Mark 13:13).

JESUS' OTHER SERMONIC TEACHINGS

Many see the Beatitudes as a preamble to the Sermon on the Mount. Some important teachings in the rest of the sermon are set out below.

Salt and Light (Matt. 5:13–16). Jesus called his disciples to be "the salt of the earth" and "the light of the world." As salt and light, we are to be holy, pure and distinctive (as is salt), and to be an illuminating witness (a light) to God's presence, so that others will come to know him. If we are neither salt nor light—if we are indistinguishable from non-Christians—how will others be drawn to consider the claims of Christ? As is often said, Christians are called to be *in* the world but not *of* the world.

The Law and the Prophets (5:17–20). Jesus said that he did not come to abolish the law and the prophets—that is, the Jewish Scriptures—but to fulfill them or bring them to completion. One reason we need to read the Old Testament is to know what Jesus came to "fulfill." To the Jew, the law was the terminal revelation of God, and to fulfill the law (the 248 do's and the 365 do not's) was all that was required. Jesus said that we need to do more than merely observe and keep God's law; we need to *share* God's love with those around us, as the Good Samaritan did in the parable that bears his name.

The Six Antitheses (5:21–48). An *antithesis* is a contrast of opposites. There are six so-called "antitheses" in the Sermon on the Mount, statements in which Jesus says, "You have heard that it was said ... But I say to you ..." In these antitheses, Jesus is not setting forth a new law but explaining the true meaning or intent of the Scriptures.

The first four antitheses have to do with deep-seated *anger,* which can lead to murder (see 1 John 3:15); with *lust,* which often leads to sexual sin (Jesus says, hyperbolically, "If your right eye causes you to sin, tear it out and throw it away"); with *divorce,* which Jesus outlaws except for marital unfaithfulness (see also Matt. 19:9); and with *oaths,* which should not be required of Christians except in courts of law (see James 5:12).

In the fifth antithesis, Jesus rejects the ancient law of *lex talionis*—"an eye for an eye"—and demands the reverse: turning the other cheek when someone strikes you with the back of the hand (insults you), giving the outer cloak (the more expensive garment) and going the extra mile (Roman soldiers could require civilians to carry their belongings a distance of one mile).

In the sixth antithesis, Jesus tells his listeners, "Love your enemies and pray for those who persecute you," his most unique teaching. The world's rule is "one good turn deserves another." Jesus says that even bad turns are to be repaid with good. How difficult this teaching is, but how essential if Christians are to make a difference in the world.

The Lord's Prayer (6:9–13). Of all Jesus' teachings in the Sermon on the Mount, the Lord's Prayer—sometimes called the "Our Father"—is the best known. The Lord's Prayer is used by most Christian churches in corporate worship. Comments on the Lord's Prayer were included in the section on prayer in chapter 9.

Two Masters (6:24). Jesus told his listeners, "No one can serve two masters. . . . You cannot serve God and wealth." Jesus is not condemning wealth; he is talking about the pursuit and use of wealth. First, the love of money must not come before our love for God and others. Second, we must use our money and resources responsibly, not storing them up like the farmer in the parable of the Rich Fool (Luke 12:13–21), but remembering Jesus' admonition that from those "to whom much has been given [and entrusted], much will be required" (Luke 12:48).

Seek First (6:25–34). Jesus tells us to "strive first for the kingdom of God and his righteousness" and our needs will be taken care of. This does not mean that God will grant every prayer petition—as mentioned in chapter 9, sometimes God's answer is no—or that life will be free of difficulty and pain. It means that once we put our trust in and are obedient to the One who is the Creator and Sustainer of life, everything else falls into place.

The Golden Rule (7:12). The great Rabbi Hillel (first century B.C.) said, "What is hateful to yourself, do to no other. That is the whole of the law; the rest is commentary." Jesus turned this teaching from a negative to a positive, saying, "In everything, *do* to others as you would have them do to you."

The Two Ways (7:13–27). Jesus ends his Sermon on the Mount by telling his listeners of the two ways or outcomes or destinations. There are two kinds of *gates*: one that is wide and one that is narrow; the gate of eternal life is narrow and "there are few who find it." There are two kinds of *trees*: one that bears good fruit and one that bears bad fruit; trees that do not bear good fruit are to be "cut down and thrown into the fire." There are two kinds of *house builders*: those who build upon rock (on Jesus' words) and those who build upon sand; those who hear and do Jesus' words are like the wise man who built his house upon rock, for "the floods came, and the winds blew . . . but it did not fall."

Who are Jesus' true disciples? Not those who say, "Lord, Lord," but those who do "the will of my Father in heaven." To the others, Jesus said he will say, "I never knew you; go away from me" (7:21–23).

THE SERMON ON THE MOUNT TODAY

How can we live out the Sermon on the Mount? One way is by keeping our focus on the "preacher" of the sermon, namely, Jesus. Charles Blondin, the French tightrope walker, crossed over Niagara Falls several times in the summer of 1859. When he was asked how he did it, Blondin said, "I keep my eyes on an object on the far side of the falls and never look away." How can we live the Sermon on the Mount? By keeping our eyes on Jesus. If we do this, we will be salt and light in the world, which is the best *sermon* that we can offer.

THE PARABLE OF THE GOOD SAMARITAN

Rabbis taught in parables, and the Old Testament contains parables such as the one Nathan told to David about the poor man with the one ewe lamb, referring to David's taking of Bathsheba (2 Sam. 12). According to the German scholar Joachim Jeremias, all of Jesus' parables are unique. When we read or hear Jesus' parables, we are listening to *Jesu ipsissima verba*, that is, "Jesus' very words." In the parables, Jeremias says, we encounter Jesus "face to face."

The following sections contain three parables of Jesus. The parable of the Good Samaritan is considered by many to be Jesus' most memorable parable. It is a teaching about how to *be* Jesus in the world. The parables of the Rich Fool and the Rich Man and Lazarus are concerned with wealth and possessions.

The parable of the Good Samaritan appears only in Luke's gospel (10:25–37). We refer to the Samaritan as *good,* but he is not called "good" in the parable. This is a later interpretation, one that has made its way into everyday usage, even into the media with reports such as, "Today a Good Samaritan rescued . . ."

The parable of the Good Samaritan appears at the beginning of the travel narrative in Luke's gospel when Jesus "set his face to go to Jerusalem" (Luke 9:51). Jesus seems to be speaking to a crowd because the questioner "stood up." The questioner is called a "lawyer," probably meaning that he was an expert in the law. The lawyer's question was, "What must I do to inherit eternal life?" Jesus replied, "What is written in the law?" The questioner answered, "Love the Lord your God . . . and your neighbor as yourself." Jesus said, "You have given the right answer." But the questioner went on, "Who is my neighbor?"—that is, to whom must I *be* a neighbor?

THE PARABLE

The parable of the Good Samaritan has four characters, as follows:

- A *man* who, while traveling from Jerusalem to Jericho—a narrow, rocky, dangerous road of some twenty miles—"fell into the hands of robbers, who stripped him, beat him and went away, leaving him half dead."
- A *priest,* and later a *Levite* (a priestly assistant), who, coming upon the man, "passed by on the other side."
- A *Samaritan* who, upon seeing the man, "was moved with pity" and cared for him. The special nuance given the parable is that the man who showed pity was a Samaritan, a member of a despised race of hybrid Jews who had intermarried with Assyrians and lived in Samaria, located between Judea and Galilee. Samaritans and Jews became archenemies following the Jews' return from exile in Babylon in the 500s B.C. and had nothing to do with one another (see John 4:9). It is said that the Jews hated the Samaritans more than they hated the Romans.

The man struck down on the road to Jericho was not dead, but must have appeared so, and the priest and the Levite could not be certain without examining him. If he was dead and they touched him, they would have been defiled for seven days (Num. 19:11).

THE MEANING OF THE PARABLE

The questioner (the lawyer) answered his own question about eternal life—love God (Deut. 6:5) and love one's neighbor (Lev. 19:18). He understood what it meant to love God. He did not understand what it meant to love a *neighbor*—especially an "unclean neighbor" who had fallen on the road to Jericho.

The key to the parable of the Good Samaritan is mercy and compassion. The priest and the Levite were more interested in keeping the law than in showing mercy, more interested in loving the law than in showing love to one in need.

The Good Samaritan was and is the perfect model or example of loving one's neighbor. He did something that was not expected, he did it spontaneously, and he did more than the minimum—he not only treated the man's wounds, he transported him to the inn and paid for his care, and he agreed to pay more if more was needed. What does it mean to love one's "neighbor"? It means to love *without limits* anyone who is in need.

A MODERN ADAPTATION

We sometimes think that the parables have little to say to us "moderns": the road to Jericho? a priest and a Levite? a Samaritan? What do these have to do with twenty-first-century America? In *The Cotton Patch Version of Luke and Acts,* Clarence Jordan, a Southern Baptist minister, reset the parable of the Good Samaritan in the racially tense South in the 1950s.

A man was going from Atlanta to Albany [Georgia] and some gangsters held him up. When they had robbed him of his wallet and brand-new suit, they beat him up and drove off in his car, leaving him unconscious on the shoulder of the highway.

Now it just so happened that a white preacher was going down the same highway. When he saw the fellow he stepped on the gas and went scooting by.

Shortly afterward a white gospel song leader came down the road, and when he saw what had happened he too stepped on the gas and went scooting by.

Then a black man traveling that way came upon the fellow and what he saw moved him to tears. He stopped and bound up his wounds as best he could, drew some water from his water jug to wipe away the blood, and laid the man on the back seat of his car. He drove on into Albany and took him to the hospital and said to the nurse, "You all take care of this white man I found on the highway. Here's the only two dollars I got, but you keep account of what he owes you, and if he can't pay it, I'll settle up with you when I make a pay day."

The parable of the Good Samaritan presents a problem: Are we to care for everyone who crosses our path? If not, where do we draw the line? The command to love one's neighbor is a universal command, not a narrow one, not one limited to those who are easy or convenient to love. Today, in Israel, it might mean an Israelite showing love to a Palestinian or vice versa; in the United States it might mean showing love to an immigrant from the Middle East or someone with HIV or someone suspected of a crime or someone who is homeless or unemployed. Are *these*—or are these *not*—"the least of these who are members of my [Jesus'] family" (Matt. 25:40)?

PARABLES OF WEALTH AND POSSESSIONS

The parables of the Rich Farmer or Fool (Luke 12:13–21) and the Rich Man and Lazarus (Luke 16:19–31) deal with wealth and possessions, themes that are important to Luke. These parables are two more that are found only in Luke's gospel.

THE RICH FARMER OR FOOL

The setting of the parable of the Rich Fool is similar to many others: someone asks Jesus a question, in this case to settle a dispute the questioner is having with his brother over his inheritance. Jesus refuses to intervene in what is a private matter, but uses the occasion to tell a parable having to do with wealth and the use of one's possessions.

In the parable, the rich man's concern is only for himself: "What should I do, for I have no place to store my crops." The rich man is called a *fool* because he put his security in his possessions. When we leave this life, the only thing we take with us is ourselves; everything else we leave behind.

The teaching of the parable is that our life will be measured by our relationship with God, not our money, possessions, and investment portfolios. In fact, Jesus said, "It is easier for a camel to go through the eye of a needle than for someone who is rich [and selfish] to enter the kingdom of God" (Luke 18:25). Faith in the one whom God sent—Jesus Christ—is the only security ("riches") we need to store up.

The farmer in the parable, in his greed, hoards his harvest. He does not see that his good fortune—the blessing he has received—should be shared with those in need.

When John Wesley was on the faculty at Oxford University, he earned 30 pounds a year. He lived on 28 pounds and gave 2 pounds to the poor. When his income reached 120 pounds a year, he still lived on 28 pounds, which enabled him to give 92 pounds to the poor.

A few years ago an American businessman sold his company for several million dollars. A friend of his knew that he tithed to support various Christian ministries. Knowing how much money the man was now worth, he asked, "Do you still intend to tithe?" The businessman replied, to his friend's surprise, "Yes, but to myself. I can live on 10 percent."

THE RICH MAN AND LAZARUS

The parable of the Rich Man and the crippled beggar at his gate, Lazarus, is another Lukan parable on wealth, and on the responsibility of those blessed with wealth to care for others. It is the only parable in which a character in the story has a name, in this case Lazarus, who is not to be confused with the Lazarus in John's gospel.

In the parable, the rich man, sometimes referred to as *Dives* (not a name but a Latin term from the *Vulgate* meaning "rich man"), "feasted sumptuously every day." A poor man named Lazarus, who was covered with sores, lay at the rich man's gate hoping for a few crumbs from his table "to satisfy his hunger."

The poor man died and was carried away by angels. The rich man died and went to Hades (the "netherland" between heaven and hell, and in the parable a place of torment). The surprise twist is that the unclean poor man, whose sores were licked by dogs, went to heaven, while the rich man did not. Why? Because the rich man ignored the beggar at his gate, and in so doing ignored God as well.

The apostle John echoes Luke's teaching about the necessity of loving those in need, saying, "How does God's love abide in anyone who has the world's goods and sees a brother or sister in need and yet refuses to help?" (1 John 3:17). One day, like the rich man, we will be called to account for the gifts and blessings we have received.

Pastor Bruce Larson, in his commentary on Luke, says that Albert Schweitzer was convicted by the parable of the Rich Man and Lazarus. Schweitzer "believed Africa was the poor man at the gate of Europe. He left the academic world, where he had received several Ph.D.'s, and went to care for his poor brothers and sisters 'at the gate' in Lambaréné [present-day Gabon in west central Africa]." Each of us, like the rich man, has someone in need at *our* gate.

"HOW THEN SHOULD WE LIVE?"

The year 1989 saw the publication of Stephen Covey's national bestseller, *The Seven Habits of Highly Effective People,* the word "habit" coming from Aristotle: "We are what we repeatedly do. Excellence is not an act but a habit." How are we to live as Christians? Or to quote the title of Francis Schaeffer's popular book, *How Should We Then Live?* One way would be to develop "Habits of Highly Godly People" from the Bible's teachings on Christian virtue, character and behavior. Some sources might be as follows:

- The six "second tablet" *commandments* in the Decalogue (five through ten): honoring one's parents and others, defending the sanctity of life, fidelity and faithfulness in marriage, honest dealings with others, truthfulness in all things, and contentedness (Ex. 20:12–17).
- Peter's seven *characteristics* of Christian faith: goodness ("faith in action") knowledge of the truth, self-control, perseverance and endurance, godliness in thought and deed, warmhearted affection toward

others and agape love (2 Peter 1:5–7).

- Matthew's eight *Beatitudes* or "blesseds" in the Sermon on the Mount: being God-centered rather than self-centered, having and showing compassion, being gentle and humble, seeking after righteousness, being merciful and forgiving, having pure and honest thoughts and motives, being a peacemaker, and standing up for what is right and just (Matt. 5:3–10).

- Paul's nine manifestations of *the fruit of the Spirit* in his letter to the Galatians: love for others, inner peace, outer joy, patience in difficult circumstances, kindness in dealing with others, generosity in all things, faithfulness in relationships, gentleness and sensitivity, and self-control of thoughts, words and deeds (Gal. 5:22–23).

- Paul's ten *virtues* in his letter to the Colossians: compassion, kindness, humility, meekness, patience, forbearance, forgiveness, love, peace and thankfulness (Col. 3:12–15).

From the above and other texts in the Bible—Jesus' "antitheses" in the Sermon on the Mount (Matt. 5:21–48), Paul's teachings on Christian behavior in Romans (12:9–21), Paul's attributes of love in First Corinthians (13:4–8), and the exhortations in Hebrews (13:1–5)—we can develop personal, tailor-made "Habits of Highly Godly People" to guide us in living "Christianly" in the world.

THREE WHO LIVED "FOR JESUS' SAKE"

One way that Christians have grown in their faith is by reading about and studying the writings of great "heroes" of the faith. The following are three twentieth-century Christians who put their faith on the line "for Jesus' sake."

DIETRICH BONHOEFFER (1906–1945)

Are there still *martyrs*? Many believe that Dietrich Bonhoeffer, who was executed in 1945, is a modern-day martyr. Bonhoeffer was born in Breslau, Germany (now Wroclaw, Poland), but grew up in Berlin, where his father, a noted physician, was head of the department of psychiatry at the University of Berlin. He studied theology at Tübingen and Berlin and was student chaplain and lecturer at the University of Berlin when Hitler came to power in January 1933.

Bonhoeffer went to London in the fall of 1933 to serve two German-speaking congregations. He returned to Germany in 1935 to run a small theological seminary for the Confessing Church (the non-state church that "confessed" Jesus rather than Hitler), which the Nazis closed in 1937. Bonhoeffer was forbidden to lecture or preach in Berlin, and later to write for publication. In 1939 he was offered a teaching position at Union Seminary in New York, where he had been a Sloane Fellow in 1930. Soon after arriving, he left the safety and security of the United States to return to Germany to work for the underground church and for the Resistance movement.

In April 1943, Bonhoeffer was imprisoned for smuggling fourteen Jews into Switzerland. While in prison he was implicated in the July 1944 plot on Hitler's life. In April 1945, just days before the end of the war, he was executed by hanging at Flossenbürg, Germany. Bonhoeffer's last recorded words were, "This is the end. For me, the beginning of life."

Bonhoeffer's best-known prewar book is *The Cost of Discipleship,* a commentary on the Sermon on the Mount, in which he wrote, "The essence of grace, we suppose, is that the account has been paid in advance, and because it has been paid, it can be had for nothing." Bonhoeffer called this "cheap grace"—grace without repentance, grace without discipleship (following Jesus), grace without the Cross.

Bonhoeffer was critical of the German church for not raising its voice against Hitler when he began abolishing human rights, unilaterally went to war against Poland in 1939, and began his "Final Solution" to eliminate the Jews. In one of his more famous quotes, Bonhoeffer said, "The church is the church only when it exists for others."

Bonhoeffer is best remembered for his *Letters and Papers from Prison,* which were smuggled out of prison by a guard he befriended, and for his willingness to stand against the demonic forces of Nazism. He has had a tremendous influence on postwar theology, challenging Christians to put God at the *center* of their lives rather that seeing him only in the "gaps" or restricting him to the "boundaries" of their lives.

MARTIN LUTHER KING JR. (1929–1968)

Martin Luther King Jr. was the incarnation of Jesus' message of social justice. His public career spanned only twelve years (1956–1968), but he did much to transform the South, as well as the United States in general.

King was born in Atlanta, the son of a Baptist minister. He graduated from Morehouse College (Atlanta, Georgia) and Crozier Theological Seminary (Chester, Pennsylvania) and earned a doctorate in theology from Boston University. King received several offers to teach in the North, but accepted a call to become pastor of Dexter Avenue Baptist Church in Montgomery, Alabama.

King led the Civil Rights movement in the South, a nonviolent protest against segregation, discrimination and brutality, saying, "We have for too long been trampled under by the iron feet of oppression." In 1955 and 1956, King led the successful Montgomery bus boycott, which broke the "Jim Crow" laws, the South's apartheid system that legalized the separation of whites and blacks.

King's leadership of the black struggle for civil rights led to the passage of the Civil Rights Bill in 1964, the same year that he was awarded the Nobel Peace Prize. King was assassinated in April 1968 in Memphis, Tennessee.

King's most remembered writing is his *Letter From a Birmingham Jail,* in which he wrote, "Injustice anywhere threatens justice everywhere." His most celebrated speech was "I Have a Dream," delivered at a civil rights gathering in Washington, D.C., in August 1963, in which he said,

> I have a dream: That one day this nation will rise up and live out the true meaning of its creed that all men are created equal . . . [that there will be] freedom and justice . . . [that] my four little children will not be judged by the color of their skin but by the content of their character. . . .

In 1983 the birthday of Martin Luther King Jr. was made a national holiday (celebrated on the third Monday in January), an honor previously accorded only to George Washington and Abraham Lincoln.

MOTHER TERESA (1910—1997)

The story of Mother Teresa is one of loving the unlovable. Teresa was born Agnes Gonxha Bojaxhiu, of Albanian parents, in Skopje, Yugoslavia, the youngest of three surviving children. She was greatly influenced by her mother, a devout and strong-willed woman.

When Agnes was eighteen she joined the Sisters of Loreto, an Irish order of missionaries and educators, founded in the seventeenth century. In 1929, at age nineteen, she went to Darjeeling, India, where she taught history and geography. She made her first vows in 1931, taking the name Teresa, honoring both saints of the same name, Teresa of Avila (Spain) and Therese of Lisieux (France).

In 1946 Teresa felt a call to leave her order to serve God "among the poorest of the poor," setting aside the habit she had worn as a Loreto sister in favor of a plain white, blue-trimmed Indian woman's sari. In 1950 she founded the Congregation of the Missionaries of Charity to work with lepers, the dismembered and the abandoned in Calcutta. The congregation was recognized by Rome in 1965; today it is worldwide, witnessing to the good news of Jesus among the diseased and the destitute.

Mother (for Mother Superior of her order) Teresa said, "I see Christ in everyone, even the filthiest person lying in the gutter." Speaking in and to the West, she frequently spoke out against abortion, saying, "How can a civilization descend any lower than to allow a mother to kill her own child?"

In 1979, when she received the Nobel Peace Prize, Mother Teresa prayed the prayer of Saint Francis: "Lord, make me a channel of your peace." In the words of the British journalist and author Malcolm Muggeridge, Mother Teresa is truly "Something Beautiful for God," the title of a book he wrote about her in 1971. Teresa died in 1997. She was beatified in 2003.

WORLD RELIGIONS AND BELIEF SYSTEMS: 1900–2000–2050

The following is a comparison of Christianity with other world religions in terms of numbers, percentages and growth. The data was derived from the *World Christian Encyclopedia* (second edition, 2001), compiled by church demographers David Barrett, George Kurian and Todd Johnson. The *WCE* is the most complete and authoritative source of statistical information on religions and belief systems available. The numbers are in millions.

World and United States: 1900 and 2000

	1900	World: 2000 Millions	World: 2000 Percent of total	USA: 2000 Millions	USA: 2000 Percent of total
Christians					
Catholics	266	1,057	17%	58	21%
Protestants[1]	142	833	14	156	56
Orthodox	116	215	3	6	2
Unaffiliated[2]	37	111	2	44	16
Adjustment[3]	(3)	(216)	(3)	(28)	(10)
	558	2,000	33%	236	85%
Non-Christians					
Muslims	200	1,188	20%	4	1%
Hindus	203	811	13	1	—
Buddhists	127	360	6	2	—
All Other[4]	532	1,696	28	35	13
	1,062	4,055	67	42	15
Total	1,620	6,055	100%	278	100%

See next page for footnotes.

Growth Rates: 1900–2000–2050

	1900–2000			2000–2050	
	1900	2000	Growth	2050 Est.	Growth
Christians					
Catholics	266	1,057	297%	1,565	48%
Protestants[1]	142	833	487	1,463	76
Orthodox	116	215	85	267	24
Unaffiliated[2]	37	111	200	125	12
Adjustment[3]	(3)	(216)	—	(370)	—
	558	2,000	258%	3,050	53%
Non-Christians					
Muslims	200	1,188	494%	2,229	88%
Hindus	203	811	299	1,175	45
Buddhists	127	360	183	424	18
All Other[4]	532	1,696	219	2,031	20
	1,062	4,055	282	5,859	44
Total	1,620	6,055	274%	8,909	47%

[1]Mainline denominations, independent churches, Bible churches and what *WCE* calls "marginal Christians" (Mormons, Jehovah's Witnesses, Christian Scientists, Moonies, Unitarians and others).

[2]Professing Christians who are not affiliated with a church.

[3]Adjustment for persons baptized in two or more denominations or churches; persons included on church rosters in different dioceses, parishes and states; and persons on church membership rolls who have repudiated their membership.

[4]"All Other" includes secularists, materialists, agnostics and others who profess no interest in religion; adherents of Chinese folk religions such as Confucianism; those who venerate ancestors, local divinities and deified heroes; polytheists, animists and shamanists; atheists; and Sikhs, Jews, Taoists, Jains, Baha'is and others, net of adjustment for double counting those who practice more than one religion.

The World of the Old and New Testaments

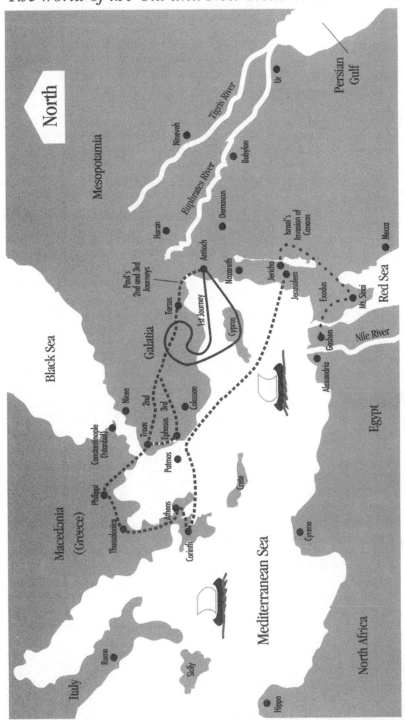

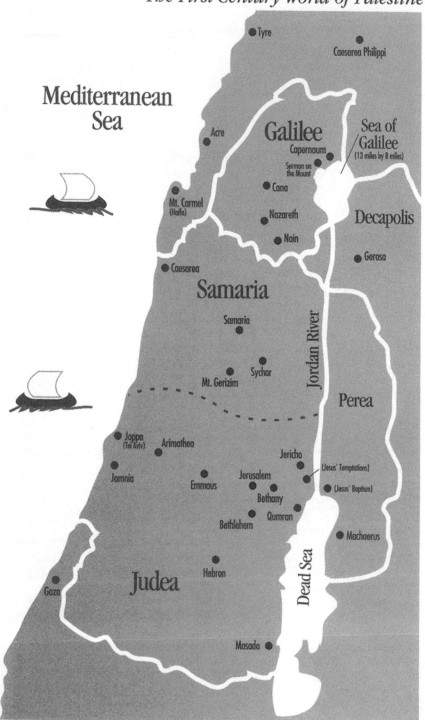

The First-Century World of Palestine

Tyre

Caesarea Philippi

Mediterranean Sea

Acre

Galilee

Capernaum

Sea of Galilee
(13 miles by 8 miles)

Sermon on the Mount

Cana

Mt. Carmel
(Haifa)

Nazareth

Decapolis

Nain

Gerasa

Caesarea

Samaria

Samaria

Sychar

Mt. Gerizim

Jordan River

Perea

Joppa
(Tel Aviv)

Arimathea

Jericho

(Jesus' Temptations)

Jamnia

Emmaus

Jerusalem

(Jesus' Baptism)

Bethany

Bethlehem

Qumran

Machaerus

Hebron

Dead Sea

Gaza

Judea

Masada

INDEX

Circumcision, 40, 65, 131, 203

Claudius, Emperor (10 B.C.-A.D.54), 66, 134

Clement of Alexandria (150–215), 115

Clement of Rome (c. 100), 135, 149

Clement VII, Pope (c. 1475–1534), 165

Cleopatra (69–30 B.C.), 65

Clergy/clergy titles, 188, 204–205

Codex Sinaiticus, 19, 23, 25, 100

Codex Vaticanus, 19, 100

Colossae/Colossians, letter of, 139

Columbus, Christopher (1451–1506), 168–169, 171–172, 181

Confession, 202

Confirmation, 202

Confucius/Confucianism (551–479 B.C.), 173, 221

Congress (United States), 177

Constantine the Great, (280–337), 61, 77, 86, 90, 126, 144, 148, 150, 168, 181

Constantinople, city/Council of, 148, 150, 152, 154–155, 193

Constitution (United States), 177

Corinth/Corinthians (letter of), 136–138, 195–196

Cornelius, 21, 125

Covenant, 12, 19, 21–22, 34, 40–41, 43–44, 54

Covey, Stephen R. (b. 1932), 291

Cranmer, Thomas (1489–1556), 164–165, 182

Creation, stories/doctrine of, 36, 188–190

Crusades (the), 155–156

Cullmann, Oscar (1902–1999), 99

Culpepper, R. Alan (b. 1946), 115

Cults, 232–242

Curate, 205

Cyprian (200–258), 149

Cyprus, 126, 128

Cyrus, 49

Damascus, 126–127, 131, 138, 196

Daniel, 18, 51

Darrow, Clarence (1857–1938), 179–180

Darwin, Charles/Darwinism (1809–

1882), 182, 190, 273

Dates (in Christian history), 181–182

David, King, 21–22, 39, 41, 47–48, 55–56. 69, 74, 89, 105–106, 146, 283

Day of Atonement (see *Yom Kippur*)

Day of Reckoning, 228

Deacon, 205

Dead Sea (the), 67–68, 71

Dead Sea Scrolls (the), 25, 71, 182

Declaration of Independence, 176

Deism, 188

DeMille, Cecil B. (1881–1959), 276

Demons/Evil spirits, 211

Denney, James (1856–1917), 108

Denominations, 203–204

Deuterocanonical, 17

Deuteronomy, book of, 35, 46

Diaspora/Dispersion (the), 49, 73, 127, 145, 234

Diatessaron, 95

Dionysius, 76

Disciples, 77, 80–82

Dispensationalism, 144

Dodd, C. H. (1884–1973), 21

Dome of the Rock, 48

Dominic, St. (1170–1221), 157

Dominican Order (the), 156–157, 159, 169, 172

Domitian, Emperor (51–96), 143

Donatists (the)/Donatus, 151–152

Drane, John W. (b. 1946), 51, 260

Dualism, 275

Easter, 61, 87, 206–207

Eastern Orthodox Church, 154–155, 204

Ecclesiastes, 55

Eckankar, 242

Eddy, Mary Baker (1821–1910), 238–239

Edict of Milan, 150

Edict of Toleration, 144

Edwards, Jonathan (1703–1758), 176, 182

Egypt/Egyptian, 44–45, 56, 64, 66, 131, 157

Eightfold Path (Noble), 219–220

ABOUT THE AUTHOR

John Schwarz has academic degrees in business management and law and has spent his working life in the corporate business world. He also has a degree from Regent College, an international school of theology in Vancouver, British Columbia. Schwarz took early retirement and went to Africa, where he taught business classes in a Christian college, taught the Bible in an indigenous church and started a primary school in a large slum. Schwarz was raised an Episcopalian. As an adult, he and his wife and children were active members of a Congregational church; while in seminary, he and his wife attended a Plymouth Brethren chapel; when they lived in Nairobi, they worshiped in an indigenous Baptist church; today they are members of an inner-city Methodist church in Minneapolis in the summer and a suburban Presbyterian church in Scottsdale in the winter.